What Makes an Assembly?
Stories, Experiments, and Inquiries

What Makes an Assembly?

Stories, Experiments, and Inquiries

Edited by Anne Davidian
& Laurent Jeanpierre

Evens Foundation & Sternberg Press

Contents

II.

III.

IV.

Anne Davidian
& Laurent Jeanpierre

What Makes

an Assembly?

Popular assembly, M-15 Movement, Segovia, Spain, May 2011

For more than ten years, we have been witnessing the rise of political assemblies in social movements. This wave began during the revolts in the Arab world in 2011 and swelled during the movements of the squares, before spreading from this epicenter to many countries in the Northern Hemisphere, including the United States, Spain, and France. The development of the alterglobalist movements since the late 1990s has led to the generalization of assembly practices—even if, of course, these ways of doing politics are not new in the long history of protests. Secret societies, conspiracies, private meetings, and public deliberations of all kinds have always been part of the history of disputes and power relations. But over the course of the past decade, assemblies, often associated with occupations, have again acquired a public and open character. The idea that there is, as one student slogan in France has asserted, "no movement without a general assembly" has taken hold internationally.[1] At once a symptom of the distrust of traditional forms

1. Julie Le Mazier, *"Pas de mouvement sans AG": les conditions d'appropriation de l'assemblée générale dans les mobilisations étudiantes en France (2006–2010). Contribution à l'étude des répertoires contestataires* (PhD thesis, Paris 1 Panthéon-Sorbonne University, 2015).

First session of the Citizens' Convention for Climate, Paris, France, October 2019

of authority and representation—in parliaments, parties, unions, associations—and a reflection of demands for radical and direct democracy, the relative proliferation of protest assemblies illustrates a growing and profound desire to change the ways in which democracy is practiced and political subjects are shaped.

In parallel to this recent trend of a revival of assemblies within social movements, other citizen collectives have been created by the public authorities in order to combat extreme social polarization and to respond to the lack of confidence in existing political institutions. Developed in 1989 in Porto Alegre, Brazil, participatory budgets have become one of the most common of these citizen mechanisms. For some time, new participatory structures (for instance citizens' assemblies) have been added to those set up decades ago, encouraging deliberation on complex or controversial issues across science, technology, and the environment. The scales and fields of social life concerned with these democratic innovations are as diverse as the objects of public policies, even if the economic sector and the corporate world still shrink from engaging with these internal democratic processes. These technologies of government can also be combined with other procedures, such as the drawing of lots or the bringing together of experts and citizens—the number and type of these new assemblies has become so prolific that it would be impossible to draw up a comprehensive inventory.

A whole industry has developed worldwide, making citizens' assemblies a considerable body of particular and specialized knowledge. Initially regarded by the authorities to be instruments liable for restoring legitimacy and consent, they have served on the one hand to divert or neutralize other forms of political participation, and on the other, to revive and renew contestation.

But a careful chronological examination should lead one to question the independence of these two historical trends.[2] The markets of participatory and deliberative democracy would not have developed without the demand for direct democracy expressed in the worker and student movements in several countries from 1968 onwards. Their formatted instruments were then integrated into the ordinary arsenal of governments seeking to legitimize their actions through the citizens. Likewise, we must ask ourselves whether the wave of protest assemblies today should not be interpreted as an indirect and global response to the development and routinization—which is often nothing more than a depoliticization—of participatory structures. Which is to say that there is already an interpenetration, a dialogue, an entire historical dialectic between instituted assemblies and instituting assemblies, between assemblies "from above" and assemblies "from below." No one can yet tell whether this movement will constitute, in the long term, a factor of democratic deepening, or whether it will contribute to reproducing the political structure of power relations. The fact remains that the citizens' assembly is not simply a resurgent civic body, at a time when all representative bodies are going through a particularly obvious crisis, but is the locus of a theoretical and practical battle seeking to alter its political function. The case of the G1000 in Brussels, arguably the largest citizens' assembly ever convened in Europe, is a

2. Julie Le Mazier, "Assemblées générales étudiantes et démocratie participative: un air de famille ?", *Participations* 10, no. 3 (2014): 61–83; and Cécile Blatrix, *La "démocratie participative," de Mai 68 aux mobilisations anti-TGV. Processus de consolidation d'institutions sociales émergentes* (PhD thesis, Paris 1 Panthéon-Sorbonne University, 2015).

Germanic Thing, in Emanuel Müller-Baden, *Bibliothek des allgemeinen und praktischen Wissen* (Berlin: Deutsches Verlagshaus Bong, 1904)

recent example of this ambiguity. Inevitably, our book is set within this field of forces. It casts light on artistic and political experiments that are ongoing. It brings together knowledge that suggests new ways of seeing assembly practices in order to better grasp their potentialities.

From Procedural Ideal to Formal Realism

The reason for such an approach is simple: much of the intellectual attention focused on existing assemblies consists of determining their ideal procedures, such as a rational discussion, for a pure and perfect democracy. This recalls the pure and perfect competition imagined by neoclassical economists when they defined the market on the basis of a shared imaginary ideal, rather than on observing the realities of its form and functions. As the very opposite of these theoretical democratic utopias, empirical studies of assemblies have often measured the gap between the observed reality of concrete debates and the norms of ideal deliberation. This confrontation between ideals and realities tends to relaunch a new, identical cycle of research, one that feeds greater demands for effective assemblies. Thus, the greater part of the scholarly discourse on assemblies, which is deeply linked to the new forms of governing of democracy, has become autonomous. Idealist philosophical anthropology, which postulates a rational humanity whose main content resides essentially in communicative action, has resulted in an approach to assemblies following purely procedural terms. This approach is one of the main reasons this discourse has turned in on itself and become increasingly technicized. The notion of "form," to which we will return below, makes it possible to avoid the effects of this intellectualist bias by shifting attention from the modus operandi of assemblies to a deeper consideration of how they are made, substituting a *formal realism* for the abstract formalism of pure theorists of pure democracy.

Anthropologist and philosopher Bruno Latour and artist and media theorist Peter Weibel had already called for a similar form of new, even unprecedented, political realism in their vast exhibition-inquiry *Making Things Public* (2005) at ZKM in Karlsruhe. They emphasized that *Realpolitik*, like political theory, would remain unreal as long as they did not take into account the vast sum of everyday or exceptional problems around which humans enter into controversy—that is, the very things that make up social life, the whole range of objects and non-humans, with all the debates they entail.[3] Latour and Weibel wondered what an "object-oriented democracy" might consist of. They decided to call this democracy *Dingpolitik*, recalling that the word "ding," like "thing," originally designated an archaic type of assembly, traces of which are still present in some current names for parliaments in some Nordic and English-speaking countries.[4] This new framing led to supplementing exclusively procedural approaches to politics with a reasoned inventory and description of the extraordinary diversity of forms of representation and assembly, well beyond the political sphere itself, in science, technology, the arts, the media, the economy, and religion. The price to be paid for such an extension of the political gaze was, paradoxically,

3. Bruno Latour and Peter Weibel, eds., *Making Things Public: Atmospheres of Democracy* (Cambridge, MA: MIT Press, 2005).
4. Bruno Latour, "From Realpolitik to Dingpolitik or How to Make Things Public," in Latour and Weibel, 4–31.

the losing sight of—or rather the drowning out of—political assemblies, whilst emphatically insisting on the ubiquitous, rudimentary character of their architectures and formats. Similarly, the material elements (the architectures, designs, technologies, facilities, logistics) of assemblies that are not related to the act of political representation were left out of the analysis. We believe the complex, nuanced analyses of these elements woven throughout the texts gathered here to be essential in advancing the discourse.

The Savagery of the Democratic Assembly

Historians and anthropologists of democratic practices have long-since adopted this bias we share, in favor of attending to material reality in the study of political assemblies. Against a tenacious academic vulgate, they have stressed, as did David Graeber in a powerful essay, that neither democracy nor egalitarian assemblies are Western inventions, any more than their origins can be located in ancient Greece.[5] Behind their irreducible phenomenal diversity, assemblies are in fact a widespread, if not universal, form of collective life. They appear at the foundations of many cultures, and assemblies of deities are a constant in mythologies. Several specialists even see in the latter projections of political forms that already existed in ancient history, as for example in Mesopotamia.[6] Despite the transhistorical and transcultural recurrence of the assembly motif, the variety of forms and functions dominates in space and time. The real history of assemblies is above all a discontinuous history that has been masked by the apparent permanence of the urban forms, places, or spaces where they have taken place and are held. To compare assemblies is always to take the

5. "There Never Was a West: Or, Democracy Emerges from the Space in Between," in David Graeber, *Possibilities: Essays on Hierarchy, Rebellion, and Desire* (Edinburgh: AK Press, 2007), 329–74.
6. Corinne Bonnet, "Divine Assembly," *Encyclopedia of the Bible and its Reception*, vol. 6, eds. Dale C. Allison, Hans-Josef Klauck, and Volker Leppin (Berlin: De Gruyter, 2013), 965–66.

risk, as Marcel Détienne has pointed out, of "comparing incomparables."[7]

Amidst this profusion, we have centered our attention, though not exclusively, on democratic assemblies with an egalitarian and inclusive vocation, but have done so by combining them (contrary to what theorists of democracy generally do) in broader ensembles of types of gatherings and deliberations. This is the case, for example, of street parliaments in several African countries today, which cannot be understood without being linked to other agoras: electoral rallies, union assemblies, village assemblies, seminars,

7. Marcel Detienne, ed., *Le Genre humain*, no. 40–41, "Qui veut prendre la parole?" (Paris: Seuil, 2003); and Marcel Detienne, *Comparing the Incomparable* (Stanford: Stanford University Press, 2008).

Gram Sabha (village assembly), Mendha-Lekha, India, 2014
After decades of struggle for self-rule, the villagers declared their private land and the surrounding forest as commons, instituting the village assembly as the legal owner and manager of community resources, recognized by the Indian state.

Bruno Serralongue, *Assemblée générale des salariés en grève, New Fabris, Châtellerault, jeudi 23 juillet 2009* (General assembly of striking workers at the New Fabris factory, Châtellerault, Tuesday, July 23, 2009), 2009, *New Fabris* series, ilfochrome print on aluminum, 127.5 × 158.5 cm

and participatory events organized by NGOs, and religious sermons [Richard Banégas, Florence Brisset-Foucault, Armando Cutolo]. Far more than the national parliament, the assembly of equals has been the essential institution of democratic progress for many years. In fact, the entire political history of modes of government would benefit from being reread from this perspective. In Europe, the medieval and modern periods, with their rural and village assemblies and the invention of communal assemblies, appear as decisive driving forces. The emergence of communal institutions in the Middle Ages was accompanied by a proliferation of deliberative spaces and their forms [Patrick Boucheron]. The latter are part of the very fabric of growing cities (as in the Guarani tribes of Brazil, where there is also a whole topography of meeting places according to their purposes and the occasions). The "age of revolutions" might indeed prove to be less revolutionary than it seems, insofar as it led to the imposition of the oligarchic principle of parliamentary representation (or bureaucratic representation, in the later case of the Russian and Chinese revolutions) and to the marginalization or even condemnation of the multitude of local assemblies. Is this why freedom of assembly became a fundamental constitutional right in several countries between the late-eighteenth and early-twentieth centuries, indeed a central condition of all democratic politics? Because it remains irreducible to any stabilized institutionalization, because it manifests itself in the fabric of situations of revolt and popular upheaval as an irruption that is above all unpredictable, the assembly is the embodiment *par excellence* of the "savage" character with which Claude Lefort defined the difference between democracy and any other type of political regime and organization.[8]

What Is a Form?

And yet it is most likely around the institution of parliament that the question of the assembly forms was first problematized most explicitly. Traces of this can be found in the introduction written by Swiss pastor Étienne Dumont to the French edition of Jeremy Bentham's *Essay on Political Tactics* (1791).[9] The English philosopher had written this text in reaction to the convocation of the Estates General during the French Revolution. As an observer of British parliamentary life, he intended to provide a few rules for the proper functioning of an institution that had not been convened for

8. See Claude Lefort, *Democracy and Political Theory* (Minneapolis: University of Minnesota Press, 1988); and "Politics and Human Rights" in *The Political Forms of Modern Society: Bureaucracy, Democracy, Totalitarianism*, ed. John B. Thompson (Cambridge: MIT Press, 1986), 239–72. The insistence on this savage nature of the conception of democracy by Claude Lefort recurs in the rereading proposed by Miguel Abensour, "'Savage Democracy' and 'Principle of Anarchy'" trans. Max Blechman, *Philosophy and Social Criticism* 28, no. 6 (November 2002 [1994]): 703–26.
9. Jeremy Bentham, "An Essay on Political Tactics" in *The Collected Works of Jeremy Bentham: Political Tactics*, eds. Michael James, Cyprian Blamires, and Catherine Pease-Watkin (Oxford: Clarendon Press, 1999).

175 years so that it would avoid what were, in his view, the two most common fates of any assembly, whether parliamentary or not: tyranny and anarchy. An assembly without rules, or without form, he suggested, was doomed not to remain democratic for long. Although it remains little-known, Bentham's text serves as a radical antidote to any idealization of the assembly for its own sake. In his 1843 introduction to the work of the English philosopher, Dumont writes:

> "We have not sufficiently understood what influence the mode adopted for the operations of an assembly should have on these very operations. It has been said that these are forms, and for superficial minds, this word form immediately lowers the dignity of the object. [...] If we could trace exactly the history of several political bodies, we would see that such and such a one has been preserved, such and such another has been destroyed by the mere difference in their mode of deliberation and action."[10]

Even if Dumont tends to reduce what he himself calls the "forms" of the body politic to its procedures, his reading of Bentham raises new questions about the concrete effects of the *formal* differences between the various kinds of assemblies.

The examination of history shows that this concern is in fact older, and is as much aesthetic and architectural as it is philosophical and legal. In a pioneering study, French political scientist Jean-Philippe Heurtin has outlined the different positions of the French revolutionaries of 1789 when faced with the choice of the most appropriate architectural form for a parliamentary assembly.[11] To understand the nature of these debates, it was necessary to move away from a purely formal determinism that never gets very far, except to express its surprise that the face-to-face layout facilitated

10. Étienne Dumont, "Discours préliminaire de l'éditeur," in *The Collected Works of Jeremy Bentham*, 6. Our translation.
11. Jean-Philippe Heurtin, *L'Espace public parlementaire : essai sur les raisons du législateur* (Paris: PUF, 1999).

The Sámi Parliament of Norway, Karasjok, Norway

discussion and grouping into distinct political camps, or that the form of the amphitheater did indeed encourage longer speeches before a more passive audience. An architecture, Heurtin suggested, is always something more than a purely material device: it is a "moral form," an intrigue, a contract between objects and subjects, an image of the political bond as well as an economy of the senses at stake as judgments and decisions are formed. It is not a static given that represents mechanically, through the layout of spaces, a vision of the world or a political order and that would fix practices.

In this analytical framework, the decision during the French Revolution to choose the hemicycle, rather than the circle, appears to be tied to the mechanism of parliamentary representation of the will of the people and to the aesthetics of the modern theater stage, which separates the actors from the spectators. A look at Europe in the nineteenth century—especially its revolutionary moments, as in 1848 with the worker-poet Constant Hilbey in Paris—shows that the place of the public in parliamentary assemblies was

Bruno Serralongue, *Assemblée des résidents du foyer pour travailleurs immigrés ADEF au cours de laquelle Boubacar Diallo fait le point sur la lutte menée contre leur expulsion pour permettre la construction du village des athlètes des Jeux Olympiques de Paris 2024, Saint-Ouen, 16 février 2020* (Assembly at the ADEF residence for migrant workers with Boubacar Diallo discussing the inhabitants' fight against eviction, in advance of the construction of the athlete's village of Paris 2024 Olympic Games, Saint-Ouen, February 16, 2020), 2020, inkjet print on Baryta paper mounted on Dibond, 127 × 156 cm

constantly being debated [Laurent Jeanpierre]. Of course, the typology of the assembly forms and the many places intended for meetings goes far beyond the simple circular or semicircular figures that are curiously dominant in the architectures of parliaments [Markus Miessen, Charlotte Malterre-Barthes].[12] The case of the Dewaniya in Kuwait is one example. An in-depth study of the morphology of spaces dedicated to gatherings and deliberation could open up a whole new range of possibilities for the confrontation of points of view. This is all the more true given that the forms and places for gathering are potentially infinite: here it can

12. For a broader architectural and typological analysis on parliaments, see XML, *Parliament* (Amsterdam: Idea Books, 2016).

be a hammam, a dining table, a café, a kitchen, the backstage area of a theater; elsewhere it can be a place of prayer, or in certain circumstances it can be the street or the square.

The "assembly" form has not only been deployed in the social world and its public spaces. It is also increasingly being staged within theaters; spaces within which assemblies could on the one hand risk losing their political content, but which are also vitally experimental sites where political theatricality can be analyzed and deconstructed with unusual freedom to explore new possibilities. [Frédérique Aït-Touati and Florian Malzacher in conversation with Piersandra di Matteo]. The experiments of the Théâtre of Négociations were carried out in Nanterre by Frédérique Aït Touati and Bruno Latour, on the model of and in parallel with the COP 21 discussions. They once again stressed the importance of architecture in assembly practices: thus, according to the protagonists, furniture (designed by raumlabor) that encouraged mobility made it possible to avoid the fixation of opposing camps and to maximize the search for alliances that changed according to the issues being addressed.

But if the assembly can be regarded as a form, it is not in the ideal and restricted sense demanded by the aesthetic view on artworks. On the contrary, "form" here is understood in a concrete and expanded sense, as in the expression "form of life," or when, inspired by the title of a famous work by Émile Durkheim, one suggests that the assembly is an "elementary form" of political life. A whole theoretical tradition has made "form"—rather than the individual or society—the primary element of the human and social sciences, in psychology and sociology in particular. In the following pages, other notions with the same descriptive and analytical properties are sometimes proposed in order to compare assemblies and their ways of being, their possibilities and impossibilities. This is true of the idea of "assemblage," which enables the investigation to go beyond the visible material or procedural elements that constitute the assembly, and has the advantage of warding off its static representations [Hans Asenbaum]. For an assembly is always more than the assembly.

Assembly Elements and Scripts

This is what a materialist and feminist perspective on the life of parliaments has long-since illuminated—a perspective that highlights a forgotten infrastructure, whether that of the laundresses or bailiffs. An assembly can only function on a daily and long-term basis thanks to a variety of agents and of actions that are largely invisible and underground [Delphine Gardey]. A political culture valorizing above all the fact of coming together should necessarily take care of its sites of assembly as well as of all those who populate them. Assembly debates also involve protagonists who are not members of the assembly—human, non-human, other-than-human, individual or collective agents—and who are literally transported into or, rather, "ventriloquized" in the public arena [François Cooren]. Similarly, in Africa the palaver can only be held in the presence of spectral or even invisible entities, especially ancestors [Jean Godefroy Bidima]. Insofar as it is democratic, the assembly as gathering, instituted by the public authorities or emerging from social movements, gives those who are usually not heard the opportunity to speak. It transforms who they are and shifts their identifications.

And if democracy, in its essence, is based on a principle of *ensauvagement*, the assembly cannot be reduced to its design alone. The latter remains necessary because it participates in the political reflexivity seeking to advance democracy. But any assembly process is by nature open and incomplete. Other dramaturgies can be added to or hybridized with its own, like the ordeals that accompany certain palavers, or moments of riots, or even trials. And so it is because the assembly can also be seen as a form—rather than as an institution like any other—that it can be experienced, as Judith Butler has pointed out, as a performance or, in another lexicon, as an experiment: neither a naked expression of spontaneity, nor the simple result of an organization, but the ongoing effort to shape, or take shaping (Lefort speaks of the "gift of form"[13]), destined first and foremost to make possible its own overflowing, its crisis, its *deformation.* The modular architecture of Andreas Angelidakis—as seen in Paul B. Preciado's "Parliament of Bodies," whose sessions took place in a former detention center in Athens, the headquarters of the military police designed for torture under the Regime of the Colonels—strikingly illustrates this possibility. The artist sums up the spirit of the work as follows: "Each demo is demolished to make way for the next demos." Isn't this same tension between the fixed rules of the game and the game itself to be found in the performing arts, and could this not make theater or dance a cardinal allegory of any assembly?

It follows from this inherently unstable state of assemblies that the group they embody never exists in advance of their forming. The political subject of the assembly is itself a product of the performance of the assembly, as is shown by the close observation of street demonstrations [Stacey Liou]. The relative contingency of political subjectivation by the assembly does not mean that the possibilities are limitless—for these political gestures to be intelligible, they must still be inspired at least in part by inherited scripts—in other words, they must respect a certain formalism.

It is because such a script does not yet exist for certain new types of meetings or of being-together that it is difficult to say, for example, whether online discussion forums actually function as fully democratic assemblies [Tallulah Frappier]. The same is true of remote assemblies brought into being through video conferencing software, especially since the global pandemic of 2020. Careful examination of this recent period in terms of forms of gathering would perhaps allow us to qualify the idea that it has first and

13. "no economic or technical determinations, and no dimensions of social space exist until they have been given form. Giving them a form implies both giving them meaning (*mise en sens*) and staging them (*mise en scène*)." Claude Lefort, *Democracy and Political Theory* (Minneapolis: University of Minnesota Press, 1988), 11–12.

foremost contributed to drastically slowing down a previously rising wave of protest mobilizations on a global scale: other (admittedly ephemeral) groupings have been created and, with them, a different political spatiality—one that is no doubt often virtual, but which, under certain conditions, could be expressed outside of digital networks.

Assessing a Decade

It is on the basis of this formal approach—which is yet to be systematized—that we also wished to offer an initial, partial, but also selective assessment of the last historical wave of protest assemblies in recent years. Several elements have been identified across these texts, enabling us to question them: their boundaries; their rules and codes; their use of public or occupied spaces; their scale, which largely determines the vertical or horizontal character of their oratory model; their material equipment, such as desks, screens, boards, and symbols, etc. Looking at gatherings and assemblies from the perspective of artistic practice, such as choreography, also enables us to pay particular attention to elements that are too often neglected by theoretical or empirical approaches within traditional social sciences. What do the bodies of the assembly do and say? How are they arranged? How do they meet and relate to each other? How do their gestures interact? With what kinds of objects, clothing, or decoration do the bodies present themselves [Alana Gerecke, Laura Levin]?

Tensions or variations appear in the light of the most recent experiences. Do the individuals present in the assembly speak for themselves? Do they speak for an imaginary collective or for a real one? It is never easy to decide. Does the form an assembly assumes reflect the processes that it may give rise to—does it later reflect its results? Here too, conceptions diverge [Pascale Dufour]. Many of today's direct democracy activists would like to divest assembly practices of instrumental rationality. Others, however, denounce the empty formalism of general and abstract deliberations, the

Bruno Serralongue, La Realidad, Chiapas, Mexico, 1996

fetishism of the assembly. An important distinction must also be made between ephemeral assemblies and lasting "deliberative bodies"; between spaces of expression and spaces of decision, which compel participants; between consensus-based decisions and those based on a qualified majority [Philippe Urfalino]. The study of street parliaments in Africa, contemporaneous with the "Third Wave" of democratization on the continent, reminds us that the street is not only a place for protest movements stemming from civil society: it is also invested by the State and by the bureaucracies that can make use of it. There is no *a priori* guarantee that a citizens' assembly, even one that is democratic in its methods, is autonomous or emancipatory.

Although each national case is different, the knowledges and the circulation of models from one political space to another is now increasingly intense and rapid. This is reflected in the unexpected French social movement known as the "Yellow Vests," some of whose actors sought to establish a national network of local assemblies. This was to be a form that would link several other direct democratic arenas, a flexible structure that could promote deliberation and education, without eschewing the possibility of the need for direct, and indeed sometimes violent action. In their efforts to establish a federation of assemblies from a small town in eastern France, they drew their inspiration from almost every continent: from Rojava and its democratic confederalism inspired by the North American anarchist theorist Murray Bookchin, from the Oaxaca Commune in Mexico, to the Zapatistas and Catalan and Spanish municipalism. It is also this same question of the interweaving of living forms of assemblies that we find in other national experiences such as the one that took place in Chile after the 2019 uprising or, at the same time, among the Sudanese Resistance Committees that played a crucial role in the overthrow of the ruling government.

For a quarter of a century, the example of the Zapatistas in Chiapas has occupied a central position in this constellation of new assembly experiences—whose function is not only to protest unlivable conditions, but to anticipate and deliver an entirely different political organization of society. This case shows once again the limits of Western-centric conceptions of democracy and assemblies. For the Indians of Chiapas, democracy is not a matter of separating or controlling powers but a method by which to seek the good life. Consequently, among the Zapatistas and those inspired by them, there is no fetishing of decision-making and efficiency: the assembly is first and foremost a threshold, an escape, a rear base in the face of other, more heteronomous collective spaces. It is also a place for questioning and collective learning. Careful examination of the Zapatista political assembly shows that there is no single, definitive form of political assembly, but rather a network of deliberative spaces with diverse contours and configurations, as is ultimately the case in many societies. In Chiapas, all of these spaces tend to be linked to concrete tasks, collective projects, and educational matters. They also tend to respond to the group's need to subsist [Manuel Callahan].

For one thing is certain: even when it proves to be an effective tool of politicization, assembly for the sake of assembly is probably not much better than art for art's sake. To be relevant, it must be connected to life. The political rise of assemblies of all kinds over the past fifty years, whether from above or from below, has resulted in a slow process of rationalization, of professionalization, in other words, of *formalization* of the rules of speaking and deliberation. This has gradually given rise to its counterpart: the desire to escape the instrumental rationality of the ever-growing number of experts in participatory, deliberative, or direct democracy, whether professionals or activists; and the desire to rediscover the substantive motivations for gathering, and to immerse these motivations in the in the concrete reality of life.

This is what several of the architectural proposals commissioned for this book express, in their own way, as do the experiments with existing creations they shed light on. Does Markus Miessen not suggest a form of assembly that is integrated into everyday life, the opposite of an identified, self-referential political object? It is a platform, an ordinary infrastructure of social existence, whose quality will first be tested in relation to its proximity. A similar concern permeates Aleksandra Wasilkowska's *Parliament of Bazaaristan*, which aims to combat political separation, to re-embed the assembly among market stalls, and to inscribe it in the vocabulary of mobile and transitory architectures. Equally polymorphic and versatile is the assembly structure designed by architect Andrés Jaque in a former slaughterhouse in Madrid. Now that it has been converted, inhabitants are free to define the uses to which it is put. Other designers of new assemblies, like raumlabor, go so far as to challenge the idea that the deliberative arena can have a given political functionality and make this critique the very condition for the survival of an authentic politics. The assembly is then anything but an immutable space: it is a multipurpose place and even a place of loss, of disorientation, open to many uses.

The Fridskul Common Library, documenta 15, Kassel, Germany, 2022
A collective project, the Common Library was assembled after one year of holding monthly *majelises* (a loose translation for "assembly" in Arabic), which were organized by the eleven collectives governing and inhabiting the "Fridskul," (or Fridericianum as School), the main venue of documenta 15. Spatial design by El Warcha, Sourabh Phadke, Iswanto Hartono, Niki Dimopoulou, with the help of Mona Schmidt, Steffen Och, Jona Wentzler, and Lukas Laudage.

The Assembly as a Form of Life?

More radically still, it may be a question of turning assemblies and meetings into a form of life: this is the task that certain societies, groups, and alternative political theories have set themselves. As the testimonies collected here remind us, the practice of the assembly among the sixteen Indigenous peoples of the Brazilian region of Xingu, who draw on an ancestral and yet ever-renewed tradition, is closely connected to the defense of their own territory [Ana Terra Yawalapiti and Sandra Benites, in conversation with Pablo Lafuente]. The power of this social form is such that it is not impossible to get different peoples with different languages but shared interests to speak together and reach a common position in the face of the Brazilian State's political power. Is this not a source of inspiration for larger but no less multicultural assemblies, such as those of international or regional organizations? Indigenous practices also show the strong intertwining of deliberation and activity: discussions take place, among women especially, at the same time as work. Among the Guarani, the notion of assembly is so broad that it seems to encompass any form of collective meeting. Confrontation and conflict receive less attention than education and transmission in an attempt to consider, or better still, to incorporate, the lifestyles of all participants. According to the Indigenous leaders, this dialogue is very different to that established with non-Indigenous citizens, if only because it requires a particular ability to listen, whereby the whole body is engaged.

And so, what if our forms of assembly define, better than any other criterion, our forms of life? And what if the ways of assembling allowed us to gradually transform our ways of living [Ayreen Anastas & Rene Gabri]? Artists and activists conceive gathering times and spaces as a wide-ranging and ongoing preparation for rituals of assembly inscribed in the political sphere whilst being disseminated in several points of everyday life. On the basis of this junction, existence can be seen as the more or less attentive care given to the multiple forms and places of assembly. For every gathering implies the possibility of assembly. And every assembly must also be interpreted in terms of the promise of autonomy it represents for those taking part in it. Hence the possibility that assemblies come and go, that they live and die—that those that remain ephemeral are, for some, more valuable than those that last. Where does the power of the assembly lie? Is it in its presence, its action or, on the contrary, in its withdrawal, its dispersion? If democracy is indeed that unstable, savage regime, it is because at any moment a new assembly can emerge, one which was not foreseen in the existing system of assemblies and gatherings. It is because a group of bodies has withdrawn from the social body in order to reappear there in a new form. That is why the assembly is, for some, always already more than an organ of government, and will always bear the potential to be the anarchist practice of the non-governable [Catherine Malabou].

***

Let us now gather these fragments of observations on assemblies into a succession of theses and proposals to be extended and experimented with through inquiry, practice, or theory.

1) An analysis of the quality and especially of the power of assemblies cannot be reduced to a study of their procedures. It is necessary to consider their forms, how they are put together. How are assemblies made? What makes an assembly? This is the best indicator of what they can do.

2) Today the assembly is a place of intense and probably unprecedented political investment, both governmental and anti-governmental. Some are formed to curtail democracy, others to extend it. Other societies and other historical phases have already made this form of sociality the main vector of politics and, beyond that, of the organization of collective life. They can inspire the present.

3) Attention to the assembly forms is first and foremost attention to their historical, anthropological, and ordinary

diversity. For those who know how to observe in this way, daily life is saturated with potential gatherings and assemblies. Assemblies can emerge at any moment.

4) The "party-form" has been the main structure adopted by the political struggles of the last century, especially as the number of representative democracies increased. Will the "assembly-form" succeed the "party-form"? Will it complement or maintain it? This is one of the major political enigmas of the present age.

5) If the party-form has its "iron laws" (such as the leaning towards oligarchy revealed a century ago by Italian sociologist Robert Michels), things should be no different for the "assembly-form." In the modern era, Bentham was certainly one of the first to search for such laws when he asserted that assemblies that lacked sufficient form always collapse into tyranny or chaos.

6) A parliament is an assembly but an assembly is not a parliament, even if it is reinvented as a "parliament of things" or of humans and non-humans. The issue of an assembly is not only representation but also presence.

7) The form of the assembly exceeds the perimeter of the assembly. The number of its protagonists exceeds the number of its participants.

8) The form of the assembly maintains a dialectical relation with the practices of the assembly. Depending on the case, this relation leads to deformation, formalism, and formalization. More than others, an assembly with no direct link to daily life and subsistence runs the risk of remaining merely formal. There can be no living assembly without the habit of assembling. But for the assembly to become a part of life, it must be cared for.

9) The subject of the assembly is never fixed or given, because any assembly practice is also a performance. And this performance can always be wild, provided that we remember that everything that is wild is not always chaotic, but is first and foremost non-governable and non-assignable.

Anne Davidian
Laurent Jeanpierre

I.

Stacey Liou

Roiling River, Sea of Flags:

Popular Assembly and Performativity

1994. It's a Sunday morning in the middle of October, in the city of Los Angeles. Tens of thousands of people from across Southern California are congregated in the eastside neighborhood of Boyle Heights, which has historically been the heart of Chicano Los Angeles. They have assembled to challenge a statewide measure known as Proposition 187, which proposes to bar undocumented immigrants from accessing state-provided services such as healthcare and education. Marching the four miles down Cesar E. Chavez Avenue to City Hall, those gathered sing, chant slogans in English, Tagalog, Spanish, and other languages—*El pueblo unido jamás será vencido* (The people, united, will never be defeated) is one of these slogans—and wave Mexican and other countries' flags. The avenue is thick with bodies, and when it arrives downtown several hours later, the procession is estimated to number 100,000 participants—the largest demonstration in Los Angeles since the protests against the Vietnam War.

This massive demonstration generated intense controversy amongst public audiences. *Los Angeles Times*, in a front-page report on the march, described it as an "orderly, regimented crowd, [...] a roiling river of banners, flags and placards moving triumphantly down Cesar E. Chavez Avenue."[1] But numerous letters written to the paper's editor expressed concerns about the "sea of red, green and white Mexican flags" and the "flood" of immigrants it represented.[2] The assembly was also controversial amongst anti-Prop. 187 activists themselves, some of whom were concerned that "a sea of brown faces marching through downtown Los Angeles would only antagonize many voters come election day in November."[3]

"Roiling river," "sea" of flags and faces, "*el pueblo unido.*" Consider these alongside other ordinary terms for popular assembly—terms such as crowds, mobs, masses, multitude.

1. Patrick J. McDonnell and Robert J. Lopez, "L.A. March Against Prop. 187 Draws 70,000," *Los Angeles Times*, October 17, 1994, A1.
2. "March Against Proposition 187," *Los Angeles Times*, October 25, 1994.
3. McDonnell and Lopez.

All images: Mario Fernando Vazquez, Anti-"Proposition 187" march on Cesar E. Chavez Avenue, Los Angeles, United States, October 1994

Notice the de-individuating effect of this language. Instead of orienting us toward the individuals participating in protests, demonstrations, riots, and so on, the everyday language we use to describe assemblies directs our attention to the group assembled. We characterize public gatherings not as individuals standing alongside one another but as collectivities in themselves. After all, when we see people gathered in a plaza or a square, we don't ask "why is this person holding a Mexican flag standing here?" Rather, we register the collective body, asking "what do they want?" or "what are they doing?" We assume a "they" with an pre-articulated want—a unified subject with a unified intention.

This ordinary focus on collectivity is a puzzling one, for there is no natural "they," no pre-given group known as "*the* anti-Prop. 187 people," much less a group mind with a conscious goal that drives the assembling. The individuals in this October march, for instance, have gathered for a variety of reasons—to oppose Prop. 187; because their friends and families are participating; or because they've long wanted to see civil rights activist and labor organizer Dolores Huerta, who will give a speech in front of City Hall—and some of

these individual reasons may indeed conflict with others. Similarly, we would be hard-pressed to say that there is an essential and cohesive "they" that precedes or follows the march—for these people, gathered in this form, on this Sunday, have never before assembled and will never again assemble in exactly this manner. Nevertheless, in the assembly, we register a collectivity; our puzzle persists.

Perhaps this collective—the "they" marching down Cesar E. Chavez Avenue, the "sea" of faces and flags in front of City Hall—is created in the material act of gathering. Perhaps assembling many individual participants together creates a collective subject that did not exist before the moment of assembly. I am proposing here that popular assemblies are performative.

But what is it, to call an assembly performative? I don't mean that assemblies are performances, tactical actions directed toward specific audiences—though, of course, they also can be. This sense of the performative would be akin to Erving Goffman's dramaturgical characterization of self-presentation in social action, and it would suggest a masterful collective subject which precedes the collective act of assembly and directs that assembly's social appearance. Political activists, organizations, and collectives do plan protests, marches, and rallies, but it would be a mistake to understand assemblies as performative in only this sense. To do so presupposes as a given—and thus as not subject to politics—the coherence of a "they" and, moreover, assumes this subject has sovereign control over the assembly and its public reception.

By "performative," however, neither do I mean to contrast this assembly with some ideal of the "genuine" or "authentic." This meaning of performative signifies the appearance of political commitment without working to create material change in service of such commitments. To call an assembly performative, in this sense, would be to accuse it of being politically hollow, or at best of being politically naive and sterile—a claim that could be argued for some assemblies, such as those staged by authoritarian regimes, though certainly not for all of them.

No, in calling popular assemblies performative, I return us to an understanding of the performative that Judith Butler has developed in regard to gender identity. To recall, the argument here is that there is no essential gender identity, only the illusion of one that is produced by gendered acts repeated over time. In Butler's Nietzschean words, there is no doer behind the deed, no gendered subject that preexists and originates gendered acts: the deed is everything.[4] Such acts create the appearance of a stable and meaningful gender by citing pre-existing norms about gendered acts, roles, and practices, which is to say that such norms regulate and produce what can appear as a socially meaningful gender in the first place. "Performative" in this sense, however, does not mean that one can wake up one morning and choose to appear a different gender. Thinking in terms of a subject who chooses a gender misdirects us, for there is no doer behind the deed.

4. Judith Butler, *Gender Trouble* (London: Routledge, 1999), 25.

What can such a theory of gender performativity mean for popular assembly? I have been suggesting that there is no subject behind the act of assembly, no doer that precedes the act. Instead, this collective subject—the “we” or “they,” the “roiling river,” the “sea” of faces and flags—is produced through the acts that are later attributed to it.[5] Because each assembly occurs at a particular time, in a particular place, with a particular group of people, within a particular historical context—and therefore can never be replicated exactly—each assembly creates a singular collectivity anew.

Yet, tempering this radical novelty is the fact that such gatherings become socially meaningful only insofar as they sufficiently reference preexisting norms about what “counts” as a meaningful popular assembly. To illustrate: in our current political culture, we generally consider protests to be gatherings that challenge some current or proposed state of affairs; they involve more than just one or two people, acting or speaking together, perhaps holding banners and

5. Judith Butler, *Notes Toward a Performative Theory of Assembly* (Cambridge, MA: Harvard University Press, 2015).

UE
UNITED ELECTRICAL RADIO & MACHINE WORKERS OF AMERICA
NO
ON PROPOSITION
187
LOS ANGELES COUNTY ORGANIZING COMMITTEE TO DEFEAT PROPOSITION 187
VOTE FOR JUSTICE
DEFEND THE RIGHTS OF IMMIGRANT WOMEN AND MEN AND THEIR FAMILIES

RACIST FASCIST
THUGS
187
NO
187
187 NO
NO
187
EEDS NATIONAL HEALTH CARE
ERICA NEEDS UNIONS
LAN DE SALUD
NO TE DEJES
INMIGRANTE
DEFIENDETE
RADIO & MACHINE WORKERS
UE
OF AMERICA
OCAL
421

signs; occur at a physical site both public and relevant to the issue at hand; and are (or should be) non-violent, and so on. These are ordinary criteria for popular assembly that posit and regulate what it means to be a protest. Such norms are historically specific and are conceived differently depending on who is assembling, as changed expectations regarding non-violence over the course of the twentieth century illustrate.

Such a framework of governing norms is evident in the march against Prop. 187, which created a new collective subject in part by citing preexisting norms about what counts as a march, snaking as an orderly unit down Cesar E. Chavez Avenue and amassing before City Hall—and, of course, obtaining a permit to assemble, which cannot be understated as a requirement of political legibility. The choice to rally through a major thoroughfare named after a labor leader associated with Latino civil rights further underscored the sense of unified purpose and so the social meaning attributed to the event. My point here is that a popular assembly creates the appearance of a meaningful collectivity insofar as it can be situated in relation to past assemblies,

past strategies, past tactics—whether or not those gathered themselves make such connections.

More specifically, these productive norms operate across many different axes. They concern the spatial distribution of bodies and the role of material objects in assembly, its emotional or affective dimensions, as well as the central importance of unity and intention in the making of the collective "they." Take, for instance, a group of people assembled digitally, perhaps in a discussion forum or on videoconference. This could be interpreted as some sort of assembly, some form of gathering, but it does not qualify as a popular assembly according to our conventional, which is to say, normative, understanding of it. In the latter, people are gathered physically, acting or moving together, holding signs but not balloons, not in someone's home but in a public place with some relation to the issue they are addressing. These are also norms that govern who belongs in public space. Racialized, gendered, or other bodies who are marginalized or excluded often invoke fear and anxiety in dominant publics, such that their gathering in public appears a- or anti-political, perhaps performative but in no politically legible sense. The fact that what happened in Stonewall in 1969, or Los Angeles in 1992, or Paris in 2005 were called "riots" or "émeutes," for instance—rather than the explicitly political "uprisings" or "*soulèvements*"—evidences on one level this political erasure, or at least delegitimation, of minoritized acts and claims.

These norms governing material embodiment and affective posture shape the collectivity that we see and expect from a popular assembly. However, this performative collectivity also demands a sense of unified intention. After all, without some sense that those assembled share a common purpose, the gathering appears random and coincidental (or, even impulsive and chaotic) rather than as being the deliberate and considered action of a political subject. Put differently, intention is also a norm of collectivity and thus of popular assembly.

Intention, however, returns us to the puzzle posed earlier: if there is no collective "they" that precedes the assembly, and no collective mind that directs the assembly, from whence this intention? My suggestion is that intention is both a preexisting norm of assembly, in the way I have been developing, as well as its performative effect. Let me illustrate this by reference to the 1994 march against Prop. 187, which also indicates the importance of performative acts sustained over place and time—the repetition that Butler makes central to the concept of gender performativity.

This major march held in October had in fact been planned for several months, and it was the result of several activist groups working and organizing together—not without internal disagreement about the strategic value of such a large demonstration. On this level of strategy and repertoire,[6] and by the observation that the march opposed Prop. 187, it could be said that there was a clear and unified intention behind the assembly; here, intention functions as a preexisting norm of assembly. Organizing and planning are, of course, important factors in ascertaining the march's intention, but they are not decisive; unplanned gatherings, too, create the appearance of purposeful collective, and even planned ones can fail to do so. And, again, not all people participated in this (or any) march for the same reasons, nor did they share a singular understanding of the assembly's social and political importance—which is to say that the activist coalitions who planned and organized the march did not and could not determine the gathering's public appearance as a collectivity. But consider this organizing alongside the material and affective characteristics of the assembly: audiences, including participants themselves, interpret the spatial arrangement, material embodiment, physical location, flags and banners, organization, and other such qualities together and see them as emanating from a united collective. Intention here is produced in the

6. Charles Tilly, *Contentious Performances* (Cambridge: Cambridge University Press, 2008).

act of gathering, and it is something that audiences attribute to those gathered rather than anything essential in the act itself, or in its diverse participants. It is for these reasons I write that intention is a condition of collectivity, and simultaneously also its performative effect.

Consider also, in the case of the anti-Prop. 187 march, the fact that several such assemblies occurred across California throughout 1994. Especially in the lead-up to November's election day, the state saw dozens of rallies, demonstrations, and other gatherings to oppose the bill, in cities liberal and conservative, in schools and city plazas alike. Many of these protests and walk-outs were not organized or even endorsed by the formal anti-Prop. 187 campaigns, and they of course varied as to participants involved, location, timing, tactics, and many other factors. Nevertheless, when considered together and especially because they occurred over a short period of time, they fashioned what appeared to be an intentional collective subject—*the* anti-Prop. 187 coalition, or even *the* immigrant rights activists—from what might otherwise have been a series of unrelated events. In other words, many gatherings that occur over time and which are interpreted similarly help sediment the sense of an active collectivity. Sustained by repetition, the performative force of a popular assembly has a deeply temporal character.

Though this October march against Prop. 187 conformed in many ways to reigning norms about popular assembly—from the material form of the gathering, to its festive emotions, to the intentional collective and constellation of similar gatherings—the march disrupted others at the same time. Most notably, the gathering challenged expectations about which bodies belong in public space. Here, it was not universal, raceless (i.e., white) citizens moving along Cesar E. Chavez Avenue, but instead many who were racialized and seen as non-citizens, foreigners. After all, anti-Prop. 187 activists would only have worried about a "sea of Mexican flags and brown faces" in these terms if there was a presumption that those flags and those faces shouldn't be there in the first place. In these conditions, rallying in the heart of Los Angeles was a performative claim, a declaration that "we" too are members of the public and are also entitled to public care.

The success of this claim, however, resulted from a delicate balance between citing and subverting preexisting norms, which suggests that the performative force of popular assemblies relies in part on a certain conservativism. Those assemblies that reference such norms more legibly create the appearance of a coherent collective subject, but doing so further entrenches these normative expectations. Public gatherings that stray too far from them fail to consolidate any sense of intentioned collectivity and appear as no more than a disorganized, random, and confusing accident of a gathering. Popular assemblies can, in this sense, reinforce the status quo. But because normative regimes can never regulate all popular assemblies completely, because they posit normative ideals that are impossible to actualize, such regimes also—paradoxically—leave room for unexpected forms of assembly and sociality to surface.

Some Co-Instigators of the Yellow Vests' Assembly of Assemblies

An Autonomous Power

in the Making

On November 17, 2018, France experienced a political earthquake. Across the country, nearly 300,000 people blocked major roads, occupied roundabouts, and put themselves in physical danger in order to disrupt the course of the economy. Unified in their anger, with each wearing a "yellow vest" typically worn by roadway security, they both protested against the hike in carbon tax and diminished purchasing power, and expressed their exasperation with a contemptuous and aloof political elite.

Self-organizing their activity through calls on social media, and acting independently from either existing unions or networks of militants, the Yellow Vests instigated a significant break from the history of "social movements" in France. Comprised largely of "primo-protesters," their identities and ethos diverged from those of the militant groups that preceded them, identifying more closely with the French Revolution of 1789 than with the events of May 1968. Throughout the winter of 2018–19 they implemented an agenda consisting of weekly mobilizations, numbered like the acts of a play, and created their own spaces of protest: hundreds of roundabouts across France were occupied by tents and fire pits, with French flags flying high above. Through carnivalesque reappropriation, these "non-places," usually serving to transport people and merchandise, were transformed into spaces of living solidarity and self-organization—starting points for actions that eventually lead to the obstruction of economic flows.[1]

Though the first day of protests was deemed "peaceful," the demonstrations quickly became violent in their encounters with police repression. "Act III," on December 1, 2018, was a moment of rare insurrectional intensity: riots down the road from the Élysée presidential palace in Paris; the prefecture of Puy-en-Velay partially burned down; highway toll booths set on fire in Narbonne. Paris was ablaze

1. Quentin Ravelli, "Les Huits fonctions du rond-point," *AOC* [Analyse Opinion Critique], February 3, 2020, https://hal.archives-ouvertes.fr/hal-03101127/document.

ASSE
aison du peuple

SERIGRAPHIE
CANTINES
CHAPITEAU
TOILETTES
PEUPLE DEBOUT
RONd-POINT
HELLO GJ
DE FRANCE
113 bd

as demonstrators sang the *Marseillaise*. Police forces were overwhelmed and the government in a panic.

A Government in Search of Intermediaries

Legal and police repression was then unleashed upon demonstrators, with a severity unseen since the 2005 French suburban riots and the demonstrations of May 1968. Ten deaths were pronounced over the course of the movement, including one death directly at the hands of the police. Twenty-five demonstrators had eyes torn out, five demonstrators had their hands torn off, and hundreds more were injured. But the government and its media outlets sought other means to deescalate the tensions. Through offering to speak with a "delegation of spokespeople" from within the Yellow Vest movement, they sought to coax forth legitimate "representatives" with whom to negotiate, and to give the impression of the possibility of fruitful discussion, aligned with outdated methods for negotiating with unions inherited from the Fordist compromise. This tactic also sought to spark divisions within the movement itself, between its insurrectional fringes and its other more moderate factions—those willing to "play the game" of establishing a dialogue with the government.

The question of representation sparked a heated debate among the Yellow Vests. Who then, from within this multi-faceted "anti-movement" held the legitimacy to field discussion and negotiation with the government, and under which circumstances? Though decentralized, flexible, and often based on "chaos organized in clusters of roundabouts,"[2] the movement was not without leadership. Figures emerged at the national level, and were often administrators of enormous Facebook groups acting as the movement's independent media groups—key leaders Éric Drouet, Maxime Nicolle, and Priscilla Ludovsky were later

Previous pages: The Yellow Vests' "People's House," Saint-Nazaire, France, April 7, 2019

2. Quentin Ravelli, "Un chaos organisé. La grappe de ronds-points comme structure politique souple," *Condition humaine / Conditions politiques* 1, no. 1 (2020), http://revues.mshparisnord.fr/chcp/index.php?id=141.

joined by Jérôme Rodriguez and François Boulo. These leaders indicated a new form of representation, presenting themselves as "relays," rather than as "spokespeople." Their legitimacy, which held firm throughout the movement, derived from a kind of plebiscitary democratic control in real time, comprised of the numerous live broadcasts organized on their Facebook pages, the frequent polls made available to their followers, and their actual presence in the streets. Opportunistic politicians of the more traditional kind, "national figures" promoted by mainstream media, were strongly rejected by the movement. Its leaders also emerged at the regional level, provoking a scurry amongst intelligence services to better map and target them with various forms of judicial repression.

The Proposal of the "Assembly of Assemblies"

It was from within this ebullient context that the core groups of Yellow Vests, based in the cities of Commercy and Saint-Nazaire, proposed to organize the "Assembly of Assemblies" (*l'Assemblée des assemblées*, or AdA): a national democratic meeting of local groups of Yellow Vests that has now been held six times since January 2019. Central to the meeting's original agenda was strategizing how best to undercut the traps laid by the government, and how to open up new alternatives to organizing purely through social media, which was seen as too vertical, and insufficiently secure. How, without falling into bureaucracy, could the group strategically organize both beyond a local scale, and beyond the moments of collective incandescence and "experiential politics," such as occupations, blockades, demonstrations, and different forms of mutual assistance and living together?[3] This was our question.

3. Michalis Lianos, "Une politique expérientielle: les Gilets jaunes en tant que peuple," *lundimatin*, no. 170, December, 2018, https://lundi.am/Une-politique-experientielle-Les-gilets-jaunes-en-tant-que-peuple.

Commercy is a sub-prefecture of 5,800 inhabitants in the Meuse, Lorraine, a city that has been historically dependent on the military economy of the region. Saint-Nazaire is an industrial port city of 70,000 in the Loire-Atlantique with a significant history of struggles for workers' rights and ecological issues. At the start of the movement, both cities were the sites of combative, self-organized, and locally based initiatives instigated by the Yellow Vests. A building formerly used by the sub-prefecture was occupied and transformed into a "People's House" in Saint-Nazaire, while in Commercy, a shack was set up in the city center. On November 20, 2018, the "Yellow Vests of the port area of Saint-Nazaire" published, at nightfall and from their blockade picket line, a video call that went viral.

"Our objective," they declared, "is [...] to give the power of decision-making, as soon as possible, back to the people, by the people, for the people. [...] We will not wait anymore for solutions to come from above." They then called for "all the cities of France to organize, on November 24, at the same time, an assembly at the location where executive power [was] exercised."

The proposition immediately resonated in Commercy. After the first day of blockades, the megaphone provided by a local initiator of the first preparatory meetings malfunctioned. The need for a daily practice of collective and egalitarian discussion addressing practical issues was suddenly made clear. The nature of this daily practice was not initially aligned with "popular assembly"—its formalism and adherence to protocol was minimal. But this practice—followed daily at the start of the movement, then two to three times a week when the movement stagnated—served as a starting point for the elaboration of "the call from the Yellow Vests of Commercy to set up popular assemblies," that had also been launched by video broadcast at the end of November 2018.

This call, initially shared by networks of militants, then within certain groups of Yellow Vests, categorically refused any form of vertical structuring: "No selling out! Long live direct democracy! We want no 'representatives' who would end up talking for us!" The Commercy call strengthened the affirmation of self-organization put forth by the Yellow Vests of Saint-Nazaire, and encouraged "the creation throughout France of popular committees that function like regular general assemblies. [...] If there must be delegates, it is at the level of each local Yellow Vest people's committee [...] With binding, revocable, and rotating mandates." Soon after, in December 2018, a second communiqué called for an "assembly of assemblies," "with delegates from throughout France to mutualize the list of demands, [to] debate, all together, over the next steps of our movement, and to decide on a collective, authentically democratic mode of organization for the Yellow Vests." Relative success was guaranteed. Some groups of Yellow Vests, such as those in Montreuil, even made videos in response. In roughly two weeks almost 70 groups signed up, and 400 people soon gathered in a small reception hall near Commercy.

Setting up the First Assembly of Assemblies (Commercy, January 26–27, 2019)

The meeting was meticulously planned. A ten-page guide was sent ahead of time: it specified the program, and provided a central outline each group could use to collect their demands and contributions to discussion topics.[4] Preparatory documents were sent a few days before the meeting in order for demands and grievances to be compiled.[5] This process aimed to build confidence among participants, but above all, to avoid the pitfalls of bureaucracy and political manipulation. A few of us from within the Yellow Vests of Commercy were able to use our experience with different previous struggles

4. "Précisions pour la préparation de la coordination nationale démocratique des Gilets jaunes à Commercy les 26 et 27 janvier 2019," https://we.riseup.net/assets/525896/397298527-Guide-de-l-Assemblee-des-Assemblees-des-Gilets-Jaunes-de-Commercy.pdf.
5. "Synthèse des revendications," https://fr.scribd.com/document/398246816/Synthese-Des-Revendications-Des-Groupes-Locaux-AdA-GJ-Commercy-26-27-Janvier-2019); and "Compilation des propositions stratégiques," https://fr.scribd.com/document/398216732/AdA-Commercy-26-27-Janvier-2019-Compilation-Des-Propositions-Strategiques.

Plenary session of the second Yellow Vests' Assembly of Assemblies, Saint-Nazaire, France, April 6, 2019

as a compass, and to clarify our focus on the potential pitfalls we were keen to avoid: some of us had participated in the assemblies of the public squares occupied during Nuit debout in 2016, which had left us frustrated by the ineffective banter taking place and the never-ending discussions on procedure, to which we preferred direct action. While we were convinced of the need for a space dedicated to face-to-face national planning, we wanted to prevent the AdA from creating a trend of assemblies, which might contribute to thickening the bureaucracy of the movement, to marginalizing our direct actions, and to the favoring of creating spaces dedicated to mere deliberation.

Following the dissemination of the first "Commercy call," some of us wondered if it was wise to bring to the forefront the concept of "popular assemblies," which was largely unfamiliar to most "primo-protesters." But after the systematic evacuation of all roundabouts by the government in January 2019, what other "basic unit" could we refer to? The term "local group" seemed too generic. Although the term "popular assembly" to a certain extent risked opening the

A workshop at the second Yellow Vests' Assembly of Assemblies, Saint-Nazaire, France, April 6, 2019

door to "assemblyism" or to other militant over-encoding, it was reminiscent of a practice with a very long and significant history, and its functions could always be adapted. Our imaginary of popular assemblies had been fed by many different inspirations; particularly Murray Bookchin, the democratic confederalism of Rojava, the strategy of democratic autonomy in Turkish Kurdistan, the Commune of Oaxaca in Mexico, the Zapatist experience in Chiapas, the assemblies of sections of *sans-culottes* during the French Revolution, and the Commune of Paris—as well as Spanish and Catalan municipalism, and even the experience of the "Republic of Saillans" in France. Not to mention the experiments in self-governance and "assemblies of uses" within the French *Zones à défendre* (zones to defend, or ZADs), in which the political sphere was an inherent aspect of living together. These examples were inspirations, but were by no means unquestioned models or received ideas we sought to apply to the movement—they were prompts to be analyzed, critiqued, or refined.

We therefore attempted to create a framework based on exchange, one which would enable us to avoid fetishizing the assembly and to approach it instead as a strategic tool, anchored in common practices. A few ground rules were clearly established: first that two people were mandated by each local group, one woman and one man, second that the many observers present could not intervene during the plenary session but could do so during the workshops, and third that interventions were limited in time during plenary sessions and workshops. To get around the delicate issue of demands (which we felt were likely to lead to abstract debates ending in stalemate), voting was limited in most cases to "votes of confidence" on the compilations of contributions from local groups, put together by the secretariat, and was conducted with colored cards.

The discussions that followed were largely concerned with tactical and strategic issues: which actions should be taken to maintain bargaining power? Beyond roundabouts, how should we organize at a local scale? How can we strengthen our solidarity and protect ourselves from government attacks (including the police, judicial systems, and the media)? Should we present a Yellow Vest list for the elections? How could we organize, at all levels, in the most democratic of ways? Sundays were dedicated to the discussion of these issues in small groups, followed by the return to plenary meetings without voting—two days of debate which, for the sake of transparency and to avoid any accusation of political recovery, were broadcast live, in accordance with the standards of the movement.

The issue of the role of decision-making and voting was a particularly sensitive point. Was the AdA, which brought together delegates from local groups, to be purely deliberative? Could it propose orientations? Did it have decision-making power on motions or actions? The delegates' mandates had not been precisely defined in the guide sent ahead of time, but were left to the appreciation of the local groups in order to preserve direct democracy. It was a matter of allowing Yellow Vest members unfamiliar with the formalism of assemblies to take responsibility for defining these mandates in their own ways. It was also a matter of avoiding a "binding mandate" that might be too restrictive, due to time-consuming back and forth: in the context of an urgent mobilization, the delegates gathering at the AdA had to be able to exercise their ability to make proposals with a certain pragmatism. It was therefore suggested within the agenda that "a final declaration and video statement of the assemblies/groups present would be released," despite the fact that the delegates had not necessarily debated over this possibility within the local groups. At the end of the first day, after an hour of intense debate over what mandates could or could not pass, the proposal was validated by the large majority of the 150 delegates present at Commercy, in an electric atmosphere. This moment of "institutive power" was to become decisive for the future dynamic of the AdAs. This was made possible largely due to the personal qualities of the teams of facilitators who possessed strong emotional intelligence that allowed them to remain calm and optimistic, as well as excellent listening skills and the ability to faithfully reformulate what was said, and who could offer up solutions to further debate in case of stalemate without forcing anyone.

Within this trust-conducive framework, the delegates in attendance interpreted their mandates to be "semi-binding." It appeared to be important for the AdA to be more than the mere deliberative sum of the local groups. It also had to serve as a platform for proposals, and even for coordination, should the need arise. During such an important political moment—when the government was attempting to trap the movement through the evacuation of roundabouts, pressure on electoral lists, efforts to decrease affluence at demonstrations, and the organization of the Great National Debate[6]—the choice of radical democracy could in no way

6. National dialogue launched by the President of the French republic from January 15 to March 15, 2019, in the context of the Yellow Vest movement with the basic principle of gathering opinions from the population on different objects of public policy: ecological transition, taxes, democracy, citizenship, public services.

ILS NE SONT
GRANDS
QUE
REPUBLIQUE
MARCHE

FORCE
ET
HONNEU
BLEUS
ET

prevent the seventy delegates in attendance from proposing their own collective initiative, which would then be submitted for approval or rejection by the local groups.

Amidst the euphoria of the moment, "the call for an Assembly of Assemblies" was video recorded. Adopting a tone more closely associated with social movements—but not without discussion, so as to attenuate some of the vocabulary associated with the far left—the AdA put forth the basic demands compiled by local groups, and called for a "massive renewable strike," for the formation of "committees at places of work and study." The call specified that in the face of attempts by the government to stigmatize the movement, the Yellow Vests were in no way "racist, sexist or homophobic." This was then sent to the local groups for the obtention of signatures, of which almost sixty were amassed.

The Second Assembly of Assemblies (Saint-Nazaire, April 5–7, 2019)

After this initial moment, largely perceived by the delegates present to have been a success, the Saint-Nazaire group welcomed the second AdA at their famous People's House. Between tents stationed outside the building, self-managed cafeterias, and the many traces of five months of occupation, the participants were welcomed into the heart of the local group's shared living space. It had been chosen specifically for its strong collective dynamic and its anti-formalist, action-oriented practices of assembly, and for the fact that the AdA was held within one of the worlds that had co-founded it was seen as a good way to avoid its bureaucratization. The tacit confidence and trust between the Saint-Nazaire group and the Commercy group further facilitated the transmission of this shared sensitivity. The meeting also successfully expanded the movement, with approximately 236 groups and 700 people present—some requests to participate were even refused, such as those of Yellow Vests members who were close to certain national figures, on

Previous page: Plenary session of the second Yellow Vests' Assembly of Assemblies, Saint-Nazaire, France, April 6, 2019

the basis that their organization by co-op was not inclusive enough, or linked to a specific roundabout or local group.

One of the key focuses of the AdA in Saint-Nazaire was to determine the limits, initially sketched out in Commercy, of the "platform for the sharing of experiences and proposals" that might accompany the strategic evolution of the movement at the moment in which it faced decline, in spring 2019. A highly decentralized framework was proposed, with a view to facilitating the suggestions and needs of local groups (collected ahead of time, or on the spot) and enabling meetings to be held on specific subjects, such as: "How to open our spaces and the People's Houses? How, in addition to the Yellow Vest's popular assemblies, to create communal assemblies? How can we better organize against repression?" The plenary session was dedicated to hearing the groups' proposals and to the re-establishment of the working commissions. These commissions were productive, and four specific calls that emerged out of the working groups were put forth for validation by the 235 local groups: the call to organize a "huge national act 27" on May 18, 2019, for the amnesty of imprisoned Yellow Vests; a demand to "let us regain decision-making power, let there be citizens' assemblies"; a "call for ecological convergence"; and a "call to organize a mobilization on the occasion of the European elections and for convergence in Belgium."

It is significant that it was AdA's more "centralist" output that would be the first to falter. The structuring commissions—on internal communication tools and on the drafting of the AdA's declaration of self-definition—would eventually stagnate. Yet again, a plan for a "final call" was put forth, and was this time adopted, after much persuasion and tough debate over terms considered too anti-capitalist, as were numerous attempts to maneuver the editorial secretariat. It would nonetheless clarify the direction taken in Commercy.

"We recognize that the Assembly of Assemblies can hear proposals from local assemblies and declare orientations, just as the first Assembly of Assemblies in Commercy did. These orientations are then systematically submitted to the local groups. The Assembly of Assemblies defends its independence with respect to political parties and unions, and recognizes no self-proclaimed leader."

This second experience demonstrates the contrast between, on the one hand, the powerful collective intelligence coming out of the working groups and the fluidity that allowed for these frameworks of discussion, and on the other hand, the heaviness and tension inherent in the potential occupation of power that could be felt during the plenary assembly. Contrary to the euphoria of the initial moment of "institutive power" within Commercy, the hesitant approval of this "final call" was experienced by some members of the organizing groups as an example of the bureaucratic and political excess that was to be avoided in the future. The first collective call by the AdA of Commercy was surely necessary in order to lay out a basic common ground, but the calls that followed were destined to play out the old bureaucratic reflexes within a movement that had absolutely no need for them.

***

The AdAs that would follow did not however allow for the bureaucratic excess to be countered—due to the movement's decline, to the ladder effect complicating interpersonal confidence, and to the difficulty transmitting non-formalist sensitivity among the organizing groups. Despite the lessons learned and the advice shared by the group liaising between Commercy and Saint-Nazaire, the AdA in Montceau-les-Mines in June 2019—though much more "representative" of the diversity of the Yellow Vests—was bogged down once again by attempts to agree upon the expected "final call"—a decision which couldn't even be produced, much to the detriment of specific proposals and concrete takeaways coming out of the working groups, as had been the case in Saint-Nazaire.

In addition to the threat of bureaucratization, another important limit was the lack of concrete effect in terms of field action. The "direct action" wing that had organized the concrete aspects of the demonstrations and blockades across France was not the dominant group at the AdA. Furthermore, despite both the strength of certain calls and their validation by most of the local groups, the calls were often insufficiently relayed. The AdA's social media outlets—with their total 5,000 or so members—hardly formed a counterweight to the "national figures," some of whom counted more than 250,000 followers (such as *La France en colère!* or: Angry France!). These figures and their teams of moderators shrugged off the AdA, ignored it, or spread condescending rumors regarding its activities. None relayed the calls.

The AdA's internal communication tools also remained rather rudimentary. There were plans to launch a digital platform, which would have enabled local groups and individuals to communicate securely, for proposals to be fine-tuned, and for quicker back and forth communications between local groups and the rotating secretariat. But it never really took shape. Yet again, the AdA was outpaced by another Yellow Vest "figure," François Boulo, who proposed the platform *La Ligne Jaune* (The Yellow Line) which certainly allowed for a greater fluidity in communication and the exchange of information, but which remained almost entirely disconnected from the material space of this national meeting.

This contextualized overview is necessarily partial, in both senses of the term. The proposal of the AdA, no matter what we may think of its bureaucratic turn, continues to exist today at a low intensity; just as the Yellow Vests continue to demonstrate, publicly or less visibly, all over the country. Furthermore, it is perhaps best to see the AdA as an imperfect but concrete contribution to the long-term process of reconfiguring responses to the historical "issue of organization" regarding "impure" popular uprisings—thus breaking with frameworks stemming from workers' movements, Leninist avant-gardism, and social democracy. In the face of counter-insurrectional forces and the authoritarian turn taken by neoliberal systems, this essential question should be raised internationally, be it with respect to the "Resistance committees" spear-heading the self-organized Sudanese revolution in 2019, or to the ephemeral *Coordinadora de los Assembleas Territoriales* during the popular uprising in Chili in the fall of 2019.

Pascale Dufour

Campaigning in Assemblies:

Five Difficulties to Overcome

The assembly form, which gathers people in a given space to discuss, debate, and to possibly form decisions about common issues, long preceded the nocturnal events held at Place de la République in Paris in 2016, known as the Nuit debout movement; indeed it even precedes what some have called over the past decade the *mouvement des places*. In his book *La Peur du peuple. Agoraphobie et agoraphilie Politique* (The fear of the people: agoraphobia and political agoraphilia), Quebec political scientist Francis Dupuis-Déri evokes gatherings ranging "from the assemblies of the Mohawk tribes in North America to the assemblies of contemporary Occupy-the-Square movements via the councils of Imperial China, the movement of communes in medieval Europe, the deliberative village assemblies in Africa and India, labor and trade-union democracy, the affinity-based practices of feminist and anarchist groups since the 1970s, the direct democracy of the alterglobalist movement and neighbourhood assemblies in South America."[1] Of course, these diverse political forms differ from one another in their specific characteristics, tones, ambiences—constituted as they each are by the historical background and the political contexts within which they are embedded. Nevertheless, if we take an aerial view of their activity for a moment, it is possible to see them as a particular repertoire of political action taken with a view to enabling a community to govern itself.

We propose to address here five issues that are intrinsic to the practices of the popular assembly. They indicate potential limitations to the possibilities of the form, regardless of the political contexts in which it is deployed, but they also clarify the offer political assemblies can present, of concrete opportunities for collective decision-making, without relying on the mediation of representatives.

1. Francis Dupuis-Déri, *La Peur du peuple. Agoraphobie et agoraphilie politique* (Montreal: Lux Éditeur, 2017).

The "Popular Assembly" Form: What Are Its Boundaries?

The first issue facing participants in popular assemblies is that of boundaries. Who is part of the assembly? Who has the right to speak? In its ideal-typical form, the primary principle of assemblies is to provide the opportunity to speak to anyone present who wishes to do so. But it is very rare for this principle to be respected in practice. Indeed, gaps, at times unbridgeable, exist between those qualifying as members of the assembly (or as citizens), and those who are not considered to be members. These exclusions are sometimes linked to specific legislation (for example, not considering women to be politically mature), but they can also either relate to social status, or be the result of power relations between participants—both of which will lead to the *de facto* exclusion of certain individuals. In this case, exclusion is not defined *a priori* but is in fact the result of a process. Here, the question of exclusion from the assembly is more insidious. Should newcomers be given the same opportunities as long-standing participants, when decisions have been made at previous assemblies, by a differently composed group? How can we prevent one or more people from monopolizing the floor or exerting excessive power during the debates as a result of their mastery of the codes shaping and governing the assembly form, their involvement in its organization, or the ease with which they express themselves orally? And what about people who commit a "transgression" in the very way in which they speak? This question may seem trivial, but it is essential as it underpins the foundations for the implicit or explicit rules determining how an assembly will be run, and who will be able to fully and meaningfully participate.

Campaigning in Assemblies: Learning How the Assembly Functions

At first sight, one might think that popular assemblies are spontaneous creations whose internal functioning is a product of chance more than anything else. Given how they unfold, can assemblies be understood as akin to a free-for-all, or perhaps a joyful chaos? Most of the forms of political assembly mentioned above tend to be governed by very strict codes that perpetuate their structure, allowing certain steps to unfold that are relatively predictable, even if the initiative of the assembly responds to a more spontaneous form of collective self-organization. What then are the common rules of contemporary assemblies?

In the majority of the most recent cases (the Occupy movement, the Indignados, Nuit debout and the neighborhood popular assemblies), the rules of deliberation and decision-making are based on either consensus or on the majority (with each participant allocated one vote), but with no designated leader. Several rules also govern the act of speaking: priority is given to people who have not yet spoken; there is parity in speaking turns so as to encourage the participation of women, who in certain instances have been less frequently socialized in this type of public exercise; speeches are timed; it is possible to express oneself in one's mother tongue with a translation given through an interpreter, etc. The deliberative process itself is thus subject to public discussion, and it is the assembly that decides, if necessary, the subsequent functioning of committees and subcommittees. Ideally, several assembly sessions can be organized to build up a consensus (if that is indeed a core objective). Many of these rules and norms are adopted in an attempt to counteract inequalities among participants and to allow everyone to learn the procedures governing the political exercise, all the while counteracting, insofar as possible, the effects of over-specialisation in a task. Carminda MacLaurin has shown clearly how the "media" committee during the Occupy Montreal event (October 15 to November 25, 2011) gradually came to detach itself from the life of the other Occupy groups simply because it responded to requests from external parties, wrote press releases, and functioned in increasing isolation, without always reporting to the general assembly of the square.[2] The vast majority of these procedures, tips, and tricks were developed beforehand in libertarian and anarchist circles.

Registration in the Public Space: Conflict of Uses

When people gather in the public space, conflicts of use often arise. Indeed, before people decide to gather, other individuals may already have habits in relation to this place and these practices can be turned upside down by the occupation and the holding of assemblies. During the Occupy Montreal event, for example, people occupying and camping in "Place du Peuple" or People's Square (officially named Victoria Square) were competing with another occupation of that space by homeless people (as well as people in suits carrying briefcases crossing the square to get to their offices, as People's Square is located in Montreal's business district—a choice of location which was of course no accident). Although a certain solidarity with the homeless held form at the start of the occupation, including sharing food, clothes and sleeping space, as time passed the internal management of this dynamic drew a lot of energy from the Occupy Montreal activists, who were not trained to intervene in relation to the homeless. Should they have called on the police to intervene and deal with people in crisis or showing troublesome behavior in relation to the collective? Should the focus have been on internal management only, at the risk of insensitivity, a gradual process of long-term exclusion and possible clashes between the different uses of the space? Amongst many others, this issue was particularly

2. Carminda MacLaurin, *Espaces transnationaux de mobilisation post-2011: propositions pour une analyse complexe* (PhD diss. in applied human sciences, Université de Montréal, 2020).

acute in the Montreal case, owing to the fact that the occupation lasted several weeks; whereas in Spain, for example, the ongoing occupation of Puerta del Sol in Madrid lasted only a few days—during which the activists returned regularly, even weekly at first, but did not remain there permanently, a decision which diminished and reframed the risks of potential conflicts of use. It should also be mentioned that most occupations and popular assemblies involve a large deployment of police forces. These forces do not always necessarily intervene violently—here the question of political context is central—but their objective is clearly to put an end to the occupation (whether of the public space or the factory).

The Individual vs. the Collective

One of the central issues related to the assembly form is knowing who speaks for whom. A priori, in a popular assembly or citizens' assembly, individuals speak on their own behalf, not on behalf of collectives. Thus, during the neighborhood popular assemblies that spread throughout Montreal (as well as throughout other cities in Quebec) during the student movement in the spring of 2012, all neighborhood residents were invited to participate, regardless of their political allegiance and/or membership of one or more pre-existing collectives. Naturally, in practice it is often difficult to separate the role of person X, as a leader of a group or member of a political party, from his or her function as a citizen of the neighborhood speaking in his or her own name. This person cannot help but be shaped by all the complexities of his or her various involvements: they are at once a member of the party, group or collective, but also a parent, a resident, a worker. This indeterminacy of the person's "primary" identity arouses suspicion that often weighs on public figures (even local ones) as to the supposed autonomy of their commitment. For instance, during the first assemblies organized by the borough of Plateau Mont-Royal in Montreal on the subject of the neighborhood's participatory budget, it was not difficult to identify among the participants the spokespersons of community groups or trade unions. Were they defending the actions and agenda of "their" organization in the neighborhood (e.g. greening) or were they "simple" citizens who based their comments on expertise developed outside the assembly? Should this voice, which has sometimes been labeled "biased" because it is committed and not politically neutral, have the same legitimacy within the assembly as another citizen voice that does not have these external resources to advance its reflection? Is this a legitimate concern?

At the World Social Forum, and in some local Social Forums, on the last day of the meeting an assembly of social movements was usually organized, which brought together representatives of the various groups and collectives that made up the Forum within the same space, and grouped them by "sector" (e.g. the international women's movement via the World March of Women, the environment with Friends of the Earth, debt cancellation with the international organization ATTAC, and the experiences of peasants such as Via Campesina). This assembly of discrete social movements borrowed from the "popular assembly" form while assuming the privileged status of groups and collectives in the decision-making process. The main groups were invited to meet in an "assembly," in order to discuss the progress made during their meetings, to share their objectives, and occasionally to draw up a common declaration in their name (rather than in the name of the World Social Forum). This assembly did not have the "force of law" in the sense that the participants did not make decisions that would later be formally or legally binding. In other words, it was not a decision-making body of the Forum, nor a central organ of anything necessarily long-term, but it could serve as a place of convergence for the struggles between the different participants. It was there that the global actions for peace were decided in 2001 during the World Social Forum in Porto Alegre. The year 2003 was then the scene of global mobilizations against the war in Iraq. From its earliest days the Forum has been marked by a tension between organized civil society (the groups) and the "ordinary citizens" who are mobilized, but are not formal members of an organization. As was exacerbated in the case of the World Social Forums, this tension is also present in popular assemblies, where it is frequently impossible to bring out the possible collective of the participants, i.e. via their membership or affiliation to a group.

The Process vs the Result

But what is the point of an assembly? Many commentators point to the difficulty (and slow pace) of the decision-making process, which does not allow for quick action and does not seem to be able to achieve specific objectives.

This tension between process (learning democracy, learning to speak, learning to find a consensus, learning the codes of public deliberation, learning from the collective and its diversities) and result (making a decision, taking action following the meeting, meeting the expectations of journalists regarding these results, setting goals and objectives) thus also raises the question of the sustainability of these experiences.

Anarchists and libertarians have an answer to this criticism: there is a level of formalization that is necessary for the assembly to be able to function and to last, and there are other norms and rules that make it possible to avoid the main shortcomings mentioned above concerning inequalities between the members of an assembly, the monopolizing of power by a few, or the possibility of ending up only with like-minded people (and thus with people who are generally in agreement with each other). Several of these modalities work well and have in fact been exported from the militant environments in which they were created, as mentioned above (even into the classroom, within feminist teaching, for example): the gendered management of speaking turns and the number of interventions; the policy of rotating certain tasks so that everyone can take part in each of them; and avoiding giving an individual undue power over the collective. This being said, the management of differences between participants is in fact always more complex than can ever be fully anticipated—there is no miracle formula for reaching a consensus unless, at the very least, a certain political culture is shared between the members of the assembly. Conflict resolution is never a given. An issue, a conflict, a common situation to be self-governed is no doubt necessary for the involvements of both sides to remain actively engaged and for compromises to be formulated.

Popular assemblies are part of political life and are here to stay. In the current global climate and within the cases elaborated here, they provide people with the opportunity to assume power over the decisions that affect them and to learn, in concrete and pragmatic terms, what democratic life means. While they are sometimes denigrated because they take place outside and beyond institutionalized (and therefore less controllable) spaces, they have the distinct advantage of meaningfully embodying politics: that is, they are not only concrete experiences for the people who experience politics, but are literally alive in the bodies of the participants. Assemblies are not static events, but processes that transform over time. Normatively, through the horizontality of their functioning and the safeguards adopted to ensure a form of political equality of participation, they bear the potential to produce the best.

Philippe Urfalino

Deliberative Bodies

In conversation
with Laurent Jeanpierre

and
Petitionary
Assemblies

L*aurent* J*eanpierre*: Your latest book, *Décider ensemble. La Fabrique de l'obligation collective* (Deciding Together: The Making of Collective Obligation), is about what you call "deliberative bodies," more precisely about how they should be considered from the viewpoint of social ontology and the ways in which they decide and enforce their decisions.[1] In your investigation that is at once empirical and conceptual, you examine a wide variety of assemblies. The Athenian assembly on the fate of the inhabitants of Mytilene evoked by Thucydides, the village assemblies of Khuriet in Sudan, those of the Ochollo in Ethiopia, and the village assemblies in contemporary Kabylia appear alongside the United Nations Security Council, the Board of Regents of the University of California, Constitutional Courts, drug evaluation committees, book clubs, and even the citizen assemblies of the social movements of this past decade. A central argument of your book is to see these arrangements not as deliberative arenas or social technologies of coordination, but as places capable of producing a "collective obligation." Whereas the scientific literature has in recent decades emphasized the debate and discussion in assembly, you focus your attention on the moment of the decision, on the decision-making rules and on the ways in which these rules are implemented. You claim that one of the characteristic features of "deliberative bodies" is that they remain "the same despite changes to their components." Such a criterion seems to place the popular assemblies of social movements—which by their very nature are ephemeral—on the fringes of your enquiry. They often lack clear objectives as well as the material and social infrastructure (statutes, funds, premises) that are essential to "deliberative bodies." In other words, there are assemblies and

1. Philippe Urfalino, *Décider ensemble. La Fabrique de l'obligation collective* (Paris: Seuil, 2021).

assemblies... How then can we define and characterize these other assemblies, which are less instituted than the collective entities you have studied? Are some of the conclusions you drew from your study of the latter transposable to citizen assemblies?

Philippe Urfalino: Among the main theses of my book, there are two assertions that enable us to reflect, by means of a comparison, on the nature of the assemblies of protest movements. The first is that decision-making in general and collective decision-making in particular is a normative phenomenon, and not only a phenomenon involving the coordination or aggregation of preferences: the collective decision produces a collective obligation to implement the decision. The second assertion is that the collective decision is the decision of a *particular* collective. This collective is a collective entity. The existence of a collective entity presupposes, on the one hand, that its members assign it the ends to achieve with regard to its environment and, on the other hand, that the members themselves see their plurality as a totality with regard to this environment. It is the emergence and existence of these collectives that make it possible to distinguish collective decision-making from other collective choice phenomena, such as fair sharing, or collective bargaining. It is important to understand that it is this idea of totality that makes possible phenomena related to representation: this person, or that sub-group, is allowed to speak for the whole group.

I became interested in assemblyist movements such as M15, Occupy Wall Street, and Nuit debout primarily because many observers thought they were using a method of collective decision-making that I have studied in detail and which is most often misleadingly referred to as "consensus decision-making." In fact, it was more a question of voting by a very high qualified majority, of the order of 90%. The attention that was legitimately paid to the use of this decision-making rule may have suggested that these assemblies showed us original ways of taking collective decisions. This interpretation was supported by the claim of these movements that they were showing what "real" democracy should be, which was readily equated with a way of ensuring that collective decisions are determined in an egalitarian and inclusive manner. But what ultimately seems interesting to me is that these assemblies do not really make decisions. They are mainly expressive. Firstly, they do not generate any obligation, including for those who participate in the assemblies.[2] Secondly, unlike real deliberative bodies, the assemblies on the squares did not form a collective entity, a totality distinguishable from its environment and whose parts could be considered.

These movements are torn between two conceptions of themselves. On the one hand, they tend to present themselves as the manifestation of a political body, the "real" political body undermined by a minority: "We are the 99%." This image is reinforced by the desire to exemplify "real" democracy through the functioning of assemblies, allowing each and every individual to speak, rejecting majority rule and any form of representation. As such, as a political body and model of democracy, they aspire to be a totality. This was reflected in the desire, apparent in the early days of these movements, to welcome all opinions, including right-wing ones. This idea was consistent with the respect for pluralism associated with democracy and with the proceduralism of assemblies identified with modes of operation and not with partly predefined political options. But, on the other hand, they are social movements and, as such, they express the point of view of part of public opinion, part of the political body of the societies where they have taken place. Like

2. The point is well made by Benjamin Sourice, *La Démocratie des places. Des Indignados à Nuit debout, vers un nouvel horizon politique* (Paris: Éditions Charles Leopold Meyer, 2017), 117.

any social movement engaged in a political struggle, they were led to reject from their ranks those whose opinions deviated from the main themes of the protest. There was indeed a great diversity of positions, ideologies, and conceptions of what the movement should be and become, but the assemblies could not bring together the diversity of opinions that animate a political body and that confront each other in a democracy. This tension lends these movements a hybrid nature. It is also found within the assemblies themselves: they were supposed to exemplify democracy while being unanimist, which is rather contradictory. To summarize, and drawing on the English utilitarian philosopher Jeremy Bentham, I would say that the assemblies of the assemblyist movements are not deliberative bodies but petitionary assemblies. They don't so much make collective decisions as issue petitions of sorts.

Laurent Jeanpierre: You refer to Bentham and his conception of political bodies to explain the nature of majority rule. Can you explain why his thoughts on assemblies are so valuable?

Philippe Urfalino: In *Political Tactics,*[3] Bentham proposed a definition of political bodies that contradicts his astute observations on political assemblies, the model of which, for him, was the House of Commons. In doing so, he unwittingly drew attention to a conceptualization of the difference between two models of assembly: the deliberative body and the petition. A rigorous nominalist, Bentham wanted to ponder assemblies and political bodies while considering that the alleged existence of a community or a collective body was only imaginary: only individuals exist and so the identity of a group cannot be other than the acknowledgement of the similarity of opinion of the individuals who compose it. This leads him to

3. Jeremy Bentham, "An Essay on Political Tactics," in *The Collected Works of Jeremy Bentham: Political Tactics*, eds. Michael James, Cyprian Blamires, and Catherine Pease-Watkin (Oxford: Clarendon Press, 1999).

consider the petition as the model of the political body. What is a petition? It is a text, formulating a position or a political claim, associated with the list of names of those who agree to publicly support the opinion recorded in the text. The criterion of identity of a petition, that which makes it possible to distinguish one petition from another, is the text. The same signatories may appear under two different texts, which will result in two different petitions; on the other hand, the list of names associated with a text varies with the addition of new signatories over time, and yet it is still the same petition. Bentham was right, the petition does correspond to a nominalist conception of groups. However, his analysis of the mechanisms of an assembly runs counter to this nominalist conception. This becomes clear, for instance, when he considers the procedures necessary for its proper functioning. To combat absenteeism among parliamentarians, he proposes the establishment of a quorum and, to ensure that irreconcilable disagreements do not paralyze the assembly's decisions, he recommends the use of majority rule. Both procedures are advocated as simple formulas, but they involve a conception of the assembly that contradicts his nominalist vision: they presuppose that the group of deputies is no longer envisaged as an aggregate, but as a whole whose integrity is preserved by the definition of thresholds beyond which a party can legitimately deliberate (the quorum) and decide (the numerical majority) in the name of the whole group, and below which one is dealing with a faction that speaks and acts unduly in the name of the group. On the other hand, the list of petitioners is not a totality, but an aggregate, and the logic of the petition is unanimist in the sense that one cannot imagine a series of signatures being indexed to a text including two contradictory opinions, like two parties opposing each other in an assembly. The opposition of the two models, provided by Bentham's analysis, gives me a key to understanding the Nuit debout or Occupy assemblies: they were petitionary. This is why they aspired to say "we" without really being able to assume such an enunciation, as you noted in your article on Nuit debout.[4] Why is this? Because representation is not only rejected, but also impossible: an assembly, at any given moment, cannot speak for the movement. Its "decisions" are in fact "petitions" that only commit those present at the time.

L*aurent* J*eanpierre*: You distinguish two types of configuration of speech and listening in an assembly: the "oratory model," undemanding, asymmetrical by nature and agonistic, which dominates both the Athenian assembly and parliamentary arrangements, and the "discussion model," mobilizing, horizontal, and cooperative. The former is more stable than the latter, which you believe characterizes certain citizen and popular assemblies, particularly when they are small and manage to avoid the return of the oratory model. Can we develop this "discussion model" in direct democracy assemblies as in representative assemblies?

P*hilippe* U*rfalino*: The configurations of the debate are closely linked to two parameters: the size and the stakes of the collective decision-making. The discussion model where everyone can speak and listen in turn is only possible for a very small number of participants; once it exceeds ten or twenty people, some no longer speak and only listen. Furthermore, the discussion model supposes cooperation and fails to meet high stakes if they divide the group into opposing parties. Numbers and stakes explain why assemblies in so-called direct democratic regimes such as the Athenian ecclesia and representative assemblies are only familiar with the oratory model, in which

4. Laurent Jeanpierre, "Nuit Debout, la diagonale du 'nous,'" *Critique* 841–42 (June–July 2017): 484–97.

speakers confront each other in front of a public. However, smaller assemblies such as the Massachusetts Town Meetings can take a cooperative turn towards the discussion model, as Jane Mansbridge has shown.[5]

Laurent Jeanpierre: The purpose of *Political Tactics*, conceived by Bentham from May 1789 onwards to advise the representatives of the Estates General, is, he writes, "to prevent the difficulties, which must result from a large assembly of men being called to deliberate in common."[6] Taking this question further, you write that these difficulties can be of two general types: on the one hand, the possibility of disorder, in particular of violence, and on the other hand, the fact that some people may take advantage of this situation to direct the work of the assembly according to their own views, which may result in all sorts of fraud. That is why there can be no fully democratic assembly without a set of minimum rules. In other words, there can be no assembly without a forming process. Is it really the case, first of all, that the assembly necessarily degenerates into a violent mob? Is this not a form of Hobbesian prejudice? And how would you define what is to be understood by "form"? In your analysis of "deliberative bodies," you suggest that the formal aspects of assemblies are subordinate to their purposes.[7] It is true that the rituals, conventions, agendas, and design of assemblies vary greatly, depending on place, time, and arrangement, but in your view it is the intention to make a decision and the resulting collective obligation as well as the constraints it imposes that seem to govern the chosen forms. Is that how you see the forms and rules of the assembly, as primarily functional realities? What role can or should be given to materiality: the architecture, scenography, aesthetics, atmosphere

5. Jane J. Mansbridge, *Beyond Adversary Democracy* (Chicago: University of Chicago Press, 1983 [1980]).
6. Bentham, "Political Tactics," 15.
7. Urfalino, *Décider ensemble*, 140.

of the assembly? Do we even know how these elements contribute to the proper functioning of an assembly that is both deliberative and decision-making?

Philippe Urfalino: Bentham does not mention violence. Most often, disorder does not find its source in a deliberate act. It arises spontaneously out of the complexity of the tasks and the coordination necessary for the smooth running of the work of an assembly. He insists on a banal fact: the variable distribution of motivations and attention. The least motivated and the most inattentive enable the accumulation of delegations and small disorders, which in turn offer the most motivated the opportunity to put forward the options that are most in line with their interests or convictions.

The "forms," both the procedures and rules, are essential for the proper functioning of deliberative bodies because they can limit disorder and dysfunction and because they can preserve the standards of fairness that the assembly feels it must respect. On the other hand, ends are decisive for the definition of the assembly as a collective entity; they are the identity criteria of the assembly because they concern the articulation of the interior of the deliberative body with its exterior.

There is no doubt that the material elements you mention are likely to constrain, slow down or, on the contrary, facilitate, encourage or even inspire the participants in an assembly and, as such, are likely to affect its smooth running in one way or another. Here again, the conceivable recommendations will first have a negative purpose, as they consist mainly in avoiding nuisances, as Bentham stated. Bentham envisages three types of material devices in *Political Tactics*. The first concerns the architecture of the building hosting the assembly. The magnificence of the building seemed to him to be contrary to its purpose. On the other hand, it should make it easier for the speakers to listen, for the president of the session to see the whole assembly, and finally for the members to work and for the sessions to proceed quickly. To this end, he recommended a circular shape and amphitheater-like seating, as well as the elevated position of the president of the assembly. The second type of physical arrangement he mentions is the construction of a gallery visible to all and close to the seat of the president. This gallery would be the only place where representatives could speak. The obligation to go to this rostrum to address the assembly solemnizes the speeches and, as such, avoids insignificant or impulsive remarks while making sure that the conditions of their enunciation are the same for every speaker. Lastly, the third material device he recommends is a board, making the motion or part of a law under discussion visible and legible to everyone. Two mobile panels, on which sufficiently large letters would be hung, would present the text under discussion in full view of everyone. The purpose of this device is to concentrate attention—to avoid distraction and involuntary or unintentional errors so that there is no doubt about the exact content of the proposal under debate. The table of motions supplements the memory of the speakers and enables them to concentrate their efforts on the argument alone. Eventually, Bentham's reflection is grounded in this mere idea: collective decision-making and collective deliberation are not spontaneous or innate phenomena; their smooth running needs artificial devices, "tactics," as he called them—which means there must be a formal organization, a constitutional design.

G1000 Citizen Summit, Brussels, Belgium, November 2011

Ben Eersels

G1000: the Citizen Takeover

The G1000 was initiated by a group of citizens, frustrated with the lack of progress during the coalition negotiations that followed the Belgian federal elections of 2010. The organizers wanted to demonstrate that even though the electoral results in Belgium were very different across the several regions of the country, people with diverging backgrounds are still able to reach forms of consensus and compromise on important policy issues, if the right conditions for debate can be generated.

The broader Belgian population was invited to take part in the initial agenda-setting for the process. Using an online platform, the organizers generated ideas and propositions which were then clustered into twenty-five themes, and put to a vote. Three subjects were subsequently elected: immigration, social security, and wealth redistribution in times of crisis.

A large citizens' summit was then organized on November 11, 2011. Participants were drawn by lot (using gender, age, and region as stratification criteria), but 10% of the seats were reserved for citizens that were predicted to be the least likely to participate (such as homeless people, analphabets, et cetera). Each of the three subjects was introduced by two academic experts, and deliberations took place on bilingual (33) and unilingual (48) tables. The conclusions of each table were articulated into recommendations and then put to a vote. 32 participants were drawn by lot to further elaborate on these recommendations, and chose to focus on the question: "How can we deal with work and unemployment in our society?" Finally, these participants handed over the final recommendations of the assembly to the presidents of the Federal and Regional Belgian parliaments, exactly one year after the citizens' summit.

With more than 700 participants, the G1000 remains one of the biggest citizen assemblies that has ever been organized in Europe. The process generated enormous traction: 800 volunteers, 85 voluntary facilitators, 40 voluntary interpreters, and 3,040 funders made the event possible, with a budget of €450,000 raised by the organizers. A public manifesto, which announced the process in the spring of 2011, obtained more than 10,000 signatures.

The political impact of the policy recommendations, however, remained very limited. The presidents of all-Belgian parliaments accepted the recommendations, but provided no formal follow-up. As a consequence, the organizers learned to emphasize the importance of a very clear mandate and a hard governmental commitment to follow up on the proposals. The event nonetheless inspired numerous citizen initiatives and governments to organize similar one-shot events on a municipal scale (K35 in Kortrijk, or G100 in Leuven), and the methodology of deliberative democracy became well-known in Belgium.

In the longer term, the G1000 played an important role in encouraging MP's from the regional parliaments of Brussels and the German-speaking community to institutionalize citizen panels, by formally integrating them in their decision-making processes. The model that was developed for the latter region, the "Ostbelgien Model," in fact became the world's first permanent political structure composed of citizens drafted by lot. Officially known as the *Permanenter Bürgerdialog* (Permanent Citizens' Dialogue), the Ostbelgien Model consists of two types of institutions, with citizens drafted by lot. The permanent Citizens' Council sets the agenda of a "policy cycle" and can decide to initiate Citizens' Assemblies. Those assemblies then debate the subject that the Citizens' Council has decided upon. At the end of the deliberations, the recommendations are discussed in a joint committee between the members of the Citizens' Assembly, elected representatives, and the minister in charge. The latter two then need to indicate whether, and how, the recommendations will be implemented by parliamentary or governmental measures—with rejections requiring specific justification. The Citizens' Council is also mandated to observe the follow-up by the government and the parliament, and thus to "monitoring" the entire policy cycle.

Frédérique Aït-Touati
& Florian Malzacher

Theater as Pre-Enactment

In conversation
with Piersandra di Matteo

Piersandra Di Matteo: In recent years the performing arts field has distinguished itself as being uniquely positioned for instituting new ways of being together, for devising and articulating strategies of common struggle, and for generating critical investigations into the role of art institutions and the redistribution of power. With this framework in mind, I'd like to begin our conversation by returning to a particular historical event: the 1960 Greensboro Sit-in, North Carolina, in which four Black students staged a sit-in at the segregated local dime-store, F. W. Woolworth Company. From this initial group of four, ("The Greensboro Four"), the sit-in amassed over 1,000 further participants as each subsequent day came to pass, eventually spreading to nine other states throughout the South, across multiple shops and institutions. The event is considered to have been a catalyst for the subsequent sit-ins involving over 70,000 people, and preceded the Civil Rights Act of 1964, which mandated desegregation in public accommodations. It was also frequently described in media reportage at the time as a "spontaneous" event—whereas of course the demonstration was triggered by a specific contingency, a particular contextual moment. It was the culmination of the widespread discontent and discussion that preceded it—it was indeed a manifestation of the intelligence and strength of the multitude, coming together to make a common political gesture. I would like to begin by discussing the possibility of reconsidering this false opposition between spontaneity and organization, as a condition for gathering together and taking action in a common struggle.

Florian Malzacher: Events like the Greensboro Sit-in, the protests in 1968, or Occupy Wall Street in 2011 are usually linked to a specific momentum—to a certain collective mood. They are simultaneously both spontaneous and not spontaneous. There is a context, but the momentum cannot, or at least can very seldom,

Florian Malzacher, Jonas Staal, and Joanna Warsza, *Artist Organisations International*, HAU 1 Theater, Berlin, Germany, 2015

artist organisations
choose the form
of the organisation
artist organisations
choose the form
of the organisation
propose
political
by artists

be forced. The Austrian theorist Oliver Marchart stresses that a political moment cannot be exactly planned—it emerges. One can prepare for it—for example by pre-enacting it—but one cannot predict when and how it will happen. Occupy Wall Street is a good example; it's often subjected to a mythic narrative of spontaneous occupation, but many of those involved had of course been organizing for a long time. What was not, and could not be anticipated, was the momentum it gained, the political moment it formed. This tension and oscillation between spontaneity, momentum, preparation, and organization is very interesting, because it relates to the condition of performing arts, of theater—there can never be full control over what is going to happen.

Frédérique Aït-Touati: I agree. In fact, for me, the theatrical space is the means of resolving, or at least negotiating, this apparent contradiction between spontaneity and organization. Theater is one of the devices through which we can produce the conditions of possibility for an event. It is the location *par excellence* for spontaneous action, because it organizes, prepares, and enables an event whose outcome can never be wholly predicted. It is both the place and the means of an experiment, in the scientific sense of the term: the preparation and organization of the unforeseeable. It is from this perspective that I have been developing my stage experiments with Bruno Latour over the past ten years, be it with only one person on stage or with several hundred participants. Beyond this diversity of format, what these experiments have in common is that they explore the heuristic capacities of the stage, as a place for reconfiguring agencies and rearranging political forces. Creating the conditions of possibility for something spontaneous to emerge is a good way to describe the experiment we conducted with Bruno Latour in 2015, six months before the COP 21 and the Paris Agreement, under the name *Theater of Negotiations*. For six days, we brought together 200 students and artists from all over the world at the Amandiers theater in Nanterre, to perform an international climate conference that was both real and fictional. Real in the sense that it was about real issues, real crises, real data, and performed not by actors but by students with an interest in becoming real negotiators soon afterwards; and fictional, because we stipulated that they modify certain elements of the COP in order to open the negotiations to non-humans, thereby rethinking the traditional protocols. It was not a show or a play, in the classical sense of those words, as nothing was written in advance, and every spoken word was improvised on the spot (except for a few written speeches, as in the real COPs). But it was indeed a very contemporary use of performing arts, i.e. an attempt to explore the political and activist potentialities of theater, as Piersandra has also suggested: if we are to figure theater firstly as an environment for inventing new ways of being together and for testing new alliances, and secondly as a device for integrating fiction into processes of reconfiguration of political forces. While relying on the well-established codes and devices (perhaps we could even say rituals) of climate negotiations, the experiment profoundly modified their presuppositions and introduced, through fiction, a "parliament of things."

It is the modeling capacity of the theater that is mobilized here, its capacity to create an assembly and a world. The effect of the theatrical space on this kind of event should not be underestimated—it recalls, through its architectural device, political and scholarly gathering places (the political assembly, the university), but simultaneously opens, through the fictional charge it carries, a breach in the reality it represents.

Florian Malzacher: This raises an important question: what kind of assemblies can or should happen in the space of art, especially of theater? What does this context produce that is different from other sites? For me theater is first and foremost a space in which things are actual and symbolic, real and fictitious at once—and I believe it is this paradoxical situation that informs theater's unique potential within the relation between art and politics.

These situations are productive precisely because they generate a tension between the "real" and the imaginary, the "factual" and the speculative, as well as between activism (or politics in general) and art. In 2015, with the artist Jonas Staal and the curator Joanna Warsza we initiated a congress called *Artist Organisations International* at the HAU 1 theater in Berlin. Our guests came from very different places and practices—for instance artists from Rojava, the Artist Association of Azawad, the Concerned Artists of the Philippines, Tania Bruguera's Immigrant Movement International, Forensic Architecture, The Silent University or The Laboratory of Insurrectionary Imagination. At the core of this event was our observation that these artists increasingly seek to replace prevailing project-oriented concepts with a more sustainable model of organization. These "organizations" are not just a means to enable artistic work, they *are* the artistic work.

The venue of the former Hebbel-Theater (now HAU 1) has an old-fashioned proscenium stage (where we reversed the seating order, placing the audience on stage and the speakers on top of the auditorium) and a long artistic history, including directors such as Erwin Piscator. The congress was very crowded and intense, and there was quite an explosive energy from the very beginning—partly because there was a keen awareness amongst all participants of the need to ask: why is this assembly happening in a theater, and what does this mean regarding its political potential but also regarding authorship, decision making and so on? This tension is encapsulated in a phrase I hear quite often,

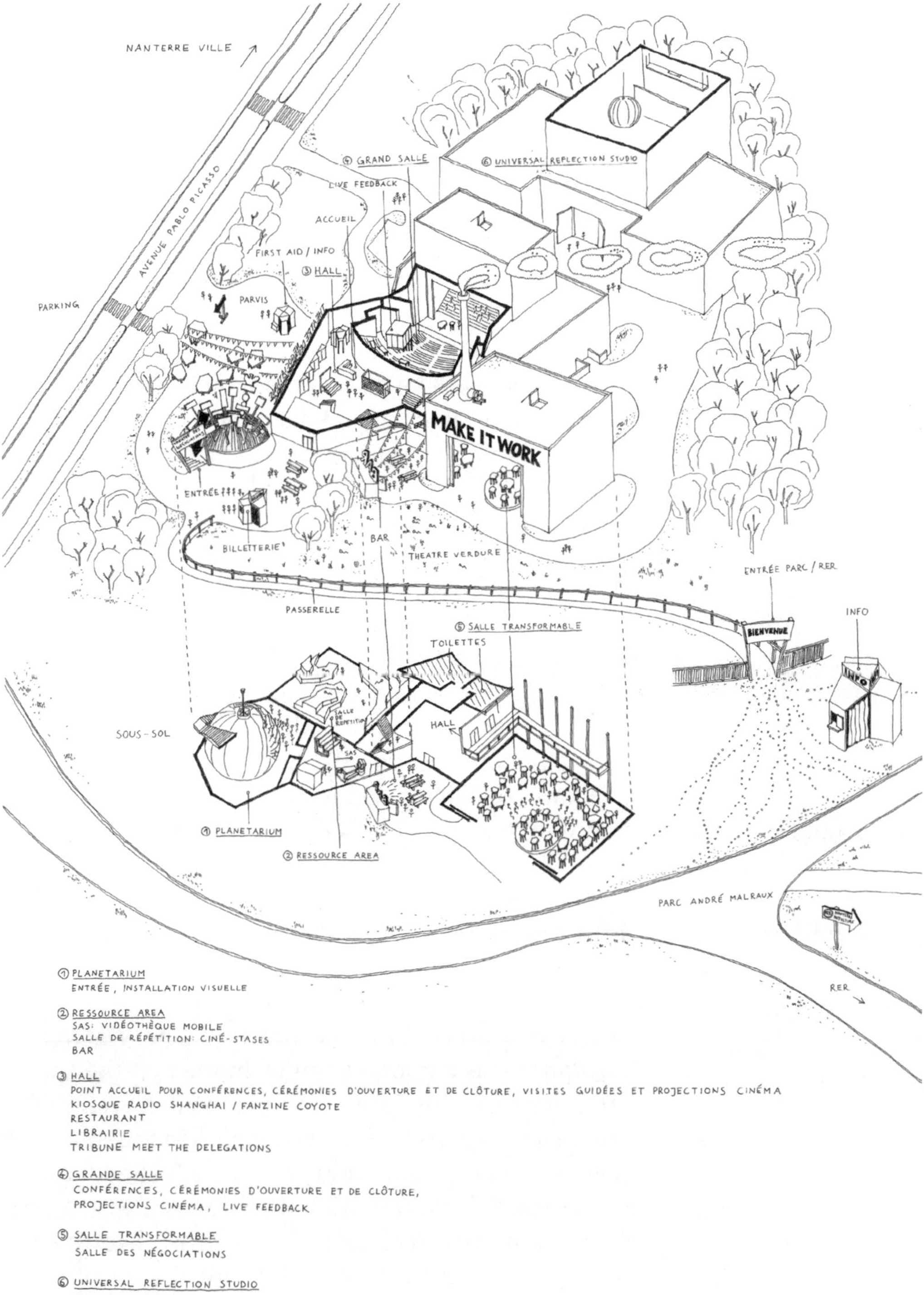

raumlabor, map of the *Theater of Negotiations*, 2015

which usually comes from dedicated activists: "Why are you making theater out of this?" Meaning: why do you push concrete political issues into the realm of fiction where they cannot have any impact? This conflict also came up in Milo Rau's "General Assembly" at Schaubühne in Berlin a few years later. There was a conflict about the indeed not unproblematic role of Milo Rau as a director and author of an assembly that was supposed to be a radical democratic event. At one point a delegate said: "For you it's theater, but for us it's our lives"—which brings the whole dilemma into sharp focus. However, while I understand this concern, I would argue that this binary is too reductive; assemblies in the sphere of theater are both real and speculative at the same time—and this has a strong political potential. It might actually be the most important thing theater can contribute to political struggles.

Piersandra Di Matteo: That's exactly the point. What we have experienced is the possibility for theater to create an environment in which a real assembly can take place—it presents an opportunity to address, consider, and articulate potential reinventions of society. This means conceiving of theater as a public sphere, a common space for discussing "performativity" as a type of political action that can generate new forms of participation. What are the possibilities in our field for rethinking the notion of participation in relation to live gatherings and ideas of assembly?

Frédérique Aït-Touati: The *Theater of Negotiations* is a good example, indeed, of the speculative dimension of the assembly in theater. I really like Florian's formulation that "assemblies in the sphere of theater are both real and speculative." The idea was to pre-enact this international conference with a very clear theoretical question: how can we use theater as a space for reflection and political experimentation? This brings us to the interlinking questions of action, participation, organization and the multitude you asked. In terms of participation, the way it actually engaged the participants was fascinating. There were two categories of participants: in the first category, the two hundred students, artists, architects we worked with and who undertook the project together, were absolutely transformed. They were transformed because they had to think together, they had to study the long history of climate negotiations, and then imagine and invent new rules of the game, apply them and make them stick for a week of continuous performance. What happens to assemblies when they take place in a theater? One possible criticism, as Florian reminded us, would be to say that assemblies lose their political significance when they take place in a fictional space. But one could also say the opposite—that it is precisely because in a theater the theatricality of politics, the theatricality of our world and of our relationships suddenly becomes visible, and obvious, that it can be a space of unfolding and showing in a much more lucid way how politics works.

The second type of participant was the "usual" audience of the Amandiers theater (invited, free of charge, to follow the negotiations). It seems to me that it was in the relationship between this "assembly" of fictional negotiators and the public that we partly failed. In fact, most of the participants could not identify with the activity: they were strangers to these technical negotiations, which took place in English and were conducted by students from all over the world, who were trained and well versed in the language, codes, and rhetoric of international negotiations. It is true that several parallel events allowed the audience to be a little further integrated: opening and closing ceremonies staged by the then director of the Amandiers theater Philippe Quesne; a series of conferences bringing together specialists in the issues under discussion; actors who served as mediators

MAKE IT WORK

Frédérique Aït-Touati, Bruno Latour, and raumlabor, *Theater of Negotiations*, Amandiers Theater, Nanterre, France, 2015

between the negotiators and the public. The fact is however that the negotiation itself remained very opaque for those who had not worked directly on these issues. Our experience was based on the conviction that the reality of technical negotiations could be shared, without needing to be fictionalized, let alone popularized, explained or transformed. A raw reality, as it were—that of a political assembly of negotiators, transformed by the venue in which it takes place, and confronted with the other assembly that constitutes an audience. We chose another path than the one Rimini Protokoll tried in the *World Climate Change Conference*, for instance, in which the public was invited to play the role of a delegate for a few hours. It has to be said that their approach was much more welcoming for the audience, even if the negotiation in this case does not "really" happen. These extremely different experiences allowed me to identify different ways of articulating fiction and political reality, and to understand the strengths and limitations of these different modes.

What I learnt from this experiment is that to "make assembly" in a theater, you have to be part of the process, not just the result. You have to be an agent of the action, not just a spectator. If you don't participate in the creation of the organization, in the reflection on the forms of the debate, in the pooling of arguments, it doesn't work. Either you include the audience in this active assembly, or it is better not to have one—which does not invalidate the strength of the device for the participants.

Florian Malzacher: I really appreciate how you've spoken through the things that didn't work. When we deal with assemblies in art, that's part of the game. It's bound to fail. It is an experimental situation, and as such is in a way like democracy: the assembly in theater is always still "to come." This, again, for me has to do with the paradoxical machine of the theater—it works a bit like Bertolt Brecht's alienation effect. It puts you in a situation where you are outside and inside at once; an observer but also a witness. You are co-responsible. This enables an involved and at the same time analytic view of the situation: who speaks and why, who speaks for whom, who does not speak, etc. What is my role in this? The question of representation in theater is very much linked to the question of representation in society.

The biggest project dealing with the concept of assembly I have been involved in was *Truth Is Concrete* at the steirischer herbst festival in Graz. We began working on it when the square occupations in Tunisia, Egypt, and Spain emerged. Of course we were also inspired by Occupy Wall Street. Preparations lasted for more than one and a half years—and when *Truth Is Concrete* took place in September 2012 a lot had changed already: there was a hard backlash in Egypt, Zuccotti Square in New York was evacuated—but there were new movements, in Istanbul or Moscow. Knowing that events in the context of art (but also in the context of activism) often have quite high thresholds, we were fascinated by how Occupy Wall Street allowed very different intensities of engagements: you could be there for an hour and then come back, or you could engage in a committee and come for a few hours a day. Or you could bring your tent and move in. We wanted to enable these different kinds of engagement also at *Truth Is Concrete*.

Truth Is Concrete brought together more than 300 artists, activists, theorists, and students for a 24 hours a day, 7 days a week marathon camp, structured by 170 hours of lectures, performances, productions, and discussions intended to pool together useful strategies and tactics in art and politics.[1] The core

1. See: Florian Malzacher and steirischer herbst, eds, *Truth is Concrete. A Handbook for Artistic Strategics in Real Politics* (London: Sternberg Press, 2014).

activities of the marathon were situated within a camp-like living and working environment—a social space with its own needs and timings. The vertical marathon itself was thus embedded in a horizontal structure of openness. Foregrounding these curatorial decisions was important for us in order to make clear that, in the end—with all its political ambition—*Truth Is Concrete* wasn't an activist event, but a curatorial one.

In an artistic context there are specific hierarchies at play. While we of course tried to minimize them, we also wanted to be very honest about where they remained. I believe assemblies within an artistic context have to be very honest about the curatorial framework, power relations, and institutional structures within which they're situated. For me this is not only an ethical question, it is also much more productive in pragmatic terms to make the existing rules visible, instead of pretending they don't exist. In *Truth Is Concrete* this was done through setting a very rigid timetable, within a marathon program which was running across seven days and nights. And in contrast to the open marathon and the surrounding camp which was much less regulated.

Piersandra Di Matteo: Yes, there is always this dialectic between the need to organize and the limits that this organization induces in participation. I would like to add another element: the assembly in the field of the performing arts can also become a space for giving a voice to people and questions that are not heard.

Frédérique Aït-Touati: You are right to remind us of the idea of unheard voices: it was at the heart of the *Theater of Negotiations* and, earlier, of Bruno Latour's notion of "parliament of things." The whole project could be summarized as an attempt to broaden representation, in all its meanings—political, scientific, artistic. The COP 21 was therefore an opportunity for us to test this philosophical concept:

what does it mean to give a voice to the unheard? To go from a concept to an experiment, you really have to create a device, as you mentioned. That's what theater can do; we had the framework, which was the COP, but to make other voices heard we had to break the rules, to negotiate the negotiation. The whole discussion was about the fact that we were moving away from reality, from the UN framework. Hence the following questions: whom do we invite around the table of negotiation? What does it mean to bring the living and non-living realms together? How do we include animal species and endangered territories? How do we move away from the nation-state assembly to include entities such as youth, the internet, or the oil that must stay in the ground?

Piersandra Di Matteo: How did you do that? How did you include these other entities?

Frédérique Aït-Touati: First, we totally revised and expanded the list of delegations which, in the COP 21 rules, was only made of nation states. We kept the general framework of delegations, discussions, and negotiations, but we changed their composition, their architecture and even their timetable. Within each delegation, we included scientific, economic, or political entities, in the hope that this heterogeneity would allow the delegations to break down from within and create new alliances between the agents of the different delegations. In the case of Antarctica, for example, we had companies, threatened territories, non-humans, and political representatives. Bruno Latour's aim was to "map the territories in struggle," as he called them, and to do this we wanted to follow the decomposition and recomposition of collectives in real-time. This was the most speculative and conceptual part of the project: beyond the negotiations, beyond the large-scale simulation game, it was about testing a hypothesis: the multiplication of political fronts of struggle around climate issues.

Jonas Staal, *New World Summit – Berlin*, Sophiensaele/7th Berlin Biennial, Berlin, Germany, 2012

We worked with the Berlin architects raumlabor and the task we gave them was to "create a negotiation space for human and non-human entities that would allow the creation of new types of alliances." raumlabor had a wonderful idea that encouraged moving around rather than sitting: no chairs, but high, irregular, hexagonal tables on which one could write, erase, start again, but also fold them up and use them as protest signs, reassemble them to make a reassemblage within the assemblage. They were invitations to ally differently, to remain vigilant, to act, to move, and not only to speak and negotiate through words. They were objects of negotiation, performative objects.

Piersandra Di Matteo: I'd like to go a bit deeper into the conditions of materiality you've touched on here, which can inform and create different possibilities for encounters. I am thinking about Jonas Staal's *New World Summit*. Space that acts as a tool for investigating the physicality of being together: a tactic to promote acts of embodiment that also shapes our ways of thinking, processing and practicing common experiences.

Jonas Staal, *Training for the Future*, 2021, Fondazione Sandretto Re Rebaudeng, Turin, Italy. Curated and co-programmed by Florian Malzacher

Florian Malzacher: Yes, a certain knowhow about the role of physical presence is another aspect theater can contribute. "It matters that as bodies we arrive together in public" as Judith Butler said in her famous speech at Occupy Wall Street. Obviously, that very much resonates with the performing arts. Jonas is a visual artist, but it is not by chance that the *New World Summit* often takes place in theater venues. Simply put, these are assemblies of people and organizations that are excluded from "democratic" discourse, often through their inclusion on state sanctioned terrorist lists. Jonas creates set-ups based on different architectural models of parliaments—and again: they are very real and very artificial at the same time.

There are also limits to what assemblies can achieve—especially when the discourse has become antagonistic. This is why in recent years Jonas and I became interested in the concept of "training" and developed the ongoing program *Training for the Future*. The program was structured on the basis of a concept you were already referring to, Frédérique: that of pre-enactment. These are provisional training sequences, for something that is yet to come. The

Jonas Staal, *New World Summit – Utrecht. Stateless Democracy*, Utrecht University, Utrecht, Netherlands, 2016

Democratic Nation
Secularism
Democratic Autonomy
Commune
Democratic

notion of the training—with its military overtone—is of course not unproblematic: it suggests a particular hierarchy. Joining those trainings—which were held by artists and activists from all over the world—meant accepting this temporary division of roles and power, and following instructions, even if one does not entirely agree with the particular practice proposed. It is to take the form of embodied practice first, and verbal reflection second, knowing that this temporariness also means that adopted roles within this framework are, if perhaps not arbitrary, then certainly interchangeable. Trainers could become the trainees within any other given training.

P*iersandra* D*i* M*atteo*: In this respect, performativity and its "reality-making" capacity—whether generated through performances, participatory practices, actions in the gaps of urban life, or long-running workshops—has become a key space through which tensions and urgencies can emerge. It has become a site where it's possible to embrace the kinds of conflict, uncertainty, and friction such actions entail. But do assemblies really produce change, or is this sense of change reliant on the way such events are later narrativized?

F*lorian* M*alzacher*: Well, when an assembly "works," it can be understood as performative. It not only offers the possibility of imagining and testing a different future, it becomes a space where things are actually done differently. It creates a temporary reality. The question is: how can this transformation become structural and sustainable? This was the crucial point for the *Artist Organisations International*, that the artistic/activist work takes the form of an organization, in order to create new schools, institutions, and collectives that can function differently whilst also working on a bigger change in society.

F*rédérique* A*ït*-T*ouati*: Fiction has been very important in my research on the history of science, even before I began to think about its performative significance in theater. My study of fiction is linked to the cosmological change of the seventeenth century in which it was used specifically to reconfigure the cosmological structure of the world through the creation of new images. This connection between my work as a historian and as a theater practitioner soon became clear: I conceive and practice theater as a force for reconfiguring reality, combining fiction and performativity. I use it as a heuristic, modeling and fictional space—not in the sense of lying or unreality, but as a means of creating new images that can then be transferred back into the real world (or not). Theater is a place for testing thought experiments—a laboratory, in the very precise sense articulated by Bruno Latour in his 1983 article, "Give Me a Laboratory and I Will Move the World."[2] The laboratory, he explains, is at once a place of visualization, of testing, and of reversing forces. To conduct an experiment (on a virus, on a physical phenomenon) is to imitate it, to reproduce it, or to transfer it into the lab in order to be able to control it, understand it, measure it, etc. The difference is that in the theater, while we can experiment, we never control the outcome and the impact it will have. Its quality as a heterotopia (to use Foucault's conceptual term) gives it a great deal of freedom to rearrange agencies. It's a model: a place where we can test new ways to assemble, test new political powers at a small scale. This tension between performativity and fiction is at the heart of our discussion, as it reveals both the limits and the political impact that the performing arts have to reconfigure our vision and understanding of reality, hence to open up the potentialities of the future.

2. Bruno Latour, "Give Me a Laboratory and I Will Move the World," in *Science Observed: Perspectives on the Social Study of Science*, eds. Karin Knorr and Michael Mulkay (New York: SAGE Publications, 1983), 141–70.

II.

Patrick Boucheron

Dis-assembling

the Civic Square

How does a political assembly take shape? What does it take for speaking bodies to assemble, discourse, deliberate, and decide? One will generally talk of "customary places," the most common expression used in the regulatory texts of the Middle Ages to designate the urban forms—squares, forecourts, crossroads or any type of widening or spacing of the roadway—that can accommodate the crier.[1] A crier who, through his authorized speech, will shape the space of the information ceremony, that is to say, a space of the representation of power which, at any moment, and thanks to the gathering it provokes, is likely to turn into a space of protest or deliberation.[2] This would be the first medieval form of political assemblies: a "customary place" which would also be, in rhetorical terms, a common place.

But what is a common place, if not a place that puts in common those who gather there, and that consequently arouses not so much adherence as recognition—or the immediate feeling of identification? This is why the common place, to preserve the fluidity and lability of its meaning, necessarily includes implicitness. We can even go further and say that the banality of the topos configures a cultural community: all those who accept as banal the notion of public space have something essential in common.[3]

The common place of political deliberation is, in France at least, the revolutionary assembly—or more precisely, the moment it becomes revolutionary. On June 20, 1789, three hundred deputies of the Estates General swore, in the Salle du Jeu de Paume in Versailles, not to break up before they had given France a constitution. They formed a body, that is to say, faced with the absent body of the sovereign, they imposed the presence of the body of the people as national sovereignty. In doing so, they set a date with themselves and

1. Veronika Novák, "L'Espace du cri à Paris aux XIV-XVIe siècles: recherches sur les 'lieux accoutumés,'" *Revue historique* 4, no. 696 (2020): 61–86.
2. Didier Lett and Nicolas Offenstadt, eds., *Haro! Noël! Oyé! Pratiques du cri au Moyen-Âge* (Paris: Publications de la Sorbonne, 2003).
3. Jocelyne Dakhlia, "La Question des lieux communs. Des modèles de souveraineté dans l'Islam méditerranéen," in *Les Formes de l'expérience. Une autre histoire sociale*, ed. Bernard Lepetit (Paris: Albin Michel, 1995), 39–61.

the future of the nation. In the morning, they were hesitant; in the evening, they became revolutionaries.[4] The place of the *conjuratio* (alliance) has no particular quality—it is because they found the doors to the Hôtel des Menus-Plaisirs closed that the deputies of the Third Estate filled the Salle du Jeu de Paume. Here too, therefore, there is talk of a displacement and, even more so, of a break-in.

David captured this by depicting the wind rushing through the windows of his famous unfinished picture and showing the possibility of assembled bodies to institute politics. It is not only a group portrait, even if it is clearly structured by a hierarchical principle placing Jean-Sylvain Bailly at the top of a triangular composition; it is a sheaf of individualities, forming the memory of the ongoing event. For this event is inseparable from the image it creates, and this image is immediately commemorative. This image becomes inseparable from its place. Compelling the viewer to be present in the part of the room not occupied by the deputies, as if the "match" were only being played in one part of the court. For history continues, and we who contemplate it are always its contemporaries.

Why begin this way? For three main reasons. First, to show how I intend to take seriously the very notion of representation in order to undo the links between places and spaces; second, by dismantling the false obviousness that the visual presence of certain places of assembly in European cities induces in the conception, if not of institutional durability, at least of political duration; lastly, by suggesting that the history of political assembly is also the history of its disassembly, that it must be discontinuous and heterogeneous, and that it must write itself on the motifs of in-between time and spacing. Revolutionaries always drape themselves in ancient togas to deliberate and, as always, historians must be wary of this dread of origins—in this case, of the Greek agora. Hence the need to speak not of the

4. Timothy Tackett, *Becoming a Revolutionary: The Deputies of the French National Assembly and the Emergence of a Revolutionary Culture, 1789–1790* (University Park, PA: Pennsylvania State University Press, 2006).

Trial of the Duke of Alençon, Tours, ca. 1459–60, full page frontispiece in Giovanni Boccaccio, *Des cas des nobles hommes et femmes* [1373], Munich, Bayerische Staatsbibliothek

Middle Ages, but from the Middle Ages, which is what I shall try to do here.

What Serves as a Deliberation

If the history of medieval assemblies makes it possible to complicate a genealogy of modernity which, from Greek democracy to contemporary regimes of parliamentary representation, draws a line in the sand, its knots are nonetheless the milestones of another history—that of the excluded third.[5] We know what the juridical motor of this is: it is on the grounds of the principle of Roman law *Quod omnes tangit* (what concerns everyone must be discussed and approved by everyone) that the representative assemblies of the kingdom's states could acquire, from the thirteenth century onwards, if not sovereignty, at least *plena potestas* (full powers).[6] From this stems a state mechanism historians are familiar with: the royal State comes into being when it goes to war; to finance the war, it levies taxes; to justify the tax, it convenes assemblies.[7] From the British Parliament to the constitutional monarchy, another genealogy is drawn, which we must also unravel.[8]

To do so, we can recall that the figurative and political meanings of the very notion of representation are closely intertwined in the system of symbolic powers in the Middle Ages.[9] Consider, for example, the miniaturist Jean Fouquet's famous depiction of Charles VII's *lit de justice* (bed of justice) at the Parliament of Paris established in Vendôme

5. Henry Babeau, *Les Assemblées générales des communautés d'habitants en France du XIII*^e^ *siècle* à *la Révolution* (Paris: Arthur Rousseau, 1893).
6. Caroline Decoster, "L'Usage de la *plena potestas* dans les assemblées médiévales," *Cahiers de recherches médiévales et humanistes* 31 (2016): 31–42.
7. Michel Hébert, *Parlementer. Assemblées représentatives et échanges politiques en Europe occidentale* à *la fin du Moyen* Âge (Paris: De Boccard, 2014); and *La Voix du peuple: une histoire des assemblées au Moyen* Âge (Paris: Presses Universitaires de France, 2014).
8. Jean-Philippe Genet, *La Genèse de l'État moderne. Culture et société politique en Angleterre* (Paris: Presses Universitaires de France, 2003).
9. Jean-Philippe Genet, Dominique Le Page and Olivier Mattéoni, eds., *Consensus et représentation. Le Pouvoir symbolique en Occident, 1300–1640* (Paris/Rome: Éditions de la Sorbonne and École française de Rome, 2017).

in 1458. Here, no wind lifts the heavy draperies of the space of representation; everything here is in its place, immutably, hierarchically arranged around the sovereign body, partitioned in order to keep a perfectly contained crowd at bay. This figurative order, in which the head represents the entire body politic, is governed by the implacable laws of symmetry—the King's gaze is, literally, his vanishing point, which assembles the space through the perspectival system.

Such an image should make us take seriously the question of structural homology, following Marcel Detienne's programme of "plural comparatism": is there a specific geometry of deliberation, is it really necessary to gather in a circle to produce the emotional epiphany of the collective will?[10] To return to the source of such a belief in the immediate effectiveness of the very form of the assembly, where the space itself would determine in advance our capacity to deliberate, we should go back to the famous Bororo village analyzed by Claude Lévi-Strauss, where the position of the huts in relation to the central spaces of collective use—*Maison des hommes* (house of men), *Aire de la danse* (dance area)—"once and for all" determined a social system that governed kinship, engaged social behavior in general, constrained power relations and represented the cosmological order.[11] This type of interpretation—in which the arranged space is the transfer on the ground of the actors' idea of their own society—inspired much of the architectural semiology that has dominated the field of urban studies since the 1970s.

Political history has obviously benefited from this type of approach: consider Jean-Pierre Vernant's reflection on the political space of the Greek city, where the equidistant relation of the city's different parts to the agora constructed the isonomy constitutive of the democratic

10. See: Marcel Detienne, ed., *Le Genre humain*, no. 40–41, "Qui veut prendre la parole?" (Paris: Seuil, 2003); and Marcel Detienne, "L'Art de construire des comparables," *Critique internationale* 1, no. 14 (2002): 68–78.

11. Claude Lévi-Strauss, "Contribution à l'étude de l'organisation sociale des Indiens Bororo," *Journal de la société des américanistes* 28, no. 2 (1936): 269–304.

Ambrogio Lorenzetti, *Effects of Good Government in the City*, ca. 1337–40, fresco, *Sala dei Nove* (Hall of the Nine), Siena, Palazzo Pubblico

bond, where "in order to make it impossible to appropriate power, it is 'deposited in the center.'" Whether they claim it explicitly or implicitly, historians of urban development almost always take up this type of hermeneutics: in medieval history, the classical analysis of the formal regularity of city plans—from tenth-century Baghdad to the "ideal cities" of the Renaissance, by way of the famous orthonormal plans of the medieval foundation cities postulate an immediate and intuitive effectiveness of the urban form that would spontaneously "speak" a political language.[12]

However, this tendency seems to pay little attention to the political semiology of the relation between space and place in the Middle Ages. What we see here is the *reductio ad unicum* (reduction to unicity) of space, entirely squared by its "ministers of vision" which, for Alberti, are the lines of perspective.[13] The city delivers one and the same language, its language, the great urban phrase. However, the city gives us something else to hear, something which Jean-Christophe Bailly has described. Not the univocal unfolding of a single urban phrase—what the city says about itself—but the polyphonic choir of words that resound in it: "everything that is said in the city, the mass of everything that the city—even without being aware of it—propagates within itself."[14] Even stronger than the force is this incidental and discreet propagation that spares itself the vehemence of propaganda: what the fresco painted by Ambrogio Lorenzetti in the public palace of Siena in 1338 shows—a fresco painted in defense of the deliberative political regime of the Nine—is the multiplicity of the places of deliberation.[15]

12. Patrick Boucheron, "Corps cinglants et langages assemblés. L'Espace public en puissance," *Le Visiteur* 24 (2019): 7–18.
13. Leon Battista Alberti, *On Painting: A New Translation and Critical Edition*, ed. and trans. Rocco Sinisgali, (Cambridge: Cambridge University Press, 2011 [1436]).
14. Jean-Christophe Bailly, *La Phrase urbaine* (Paris: Seuil, 2013).
15. Patrick Boucheron, *Conjurer la peur. Sienne, 1338. Essai sur la force politique des images* (Paris: Seuil, 2013).

Places before space: not a space and a *historia* (story) in the sense that Alberti would give a century later in his *De Pictura* to this art of ordered persuasion that painting had become, but places, bodies and stories. From this point of view, we could say that Ambrogio Lorenzetti's pictorial universe is fundamentally Aristotelian, in the sense that it represents nothing other than "the sum of places occupied by bodies."[16] For Aristotle's *locus* is defined as "the primary container of each body."[17] Undoubtedly inspired by the arts of memory, this conception of space, which predates the Albertian reduction through which a unified space will unite with a single story, is that of a juxtaposition of places where figures and stories take place. This has nothing to do, of course, with the beautiful symmetrical arrangement of a civic square where one could assemble politically. Nor does it have anything to do with the falsely welcoming architecture of the thirteenth-century Lombard civic palaces in Piacenza, Brescia, Cremona, and elsewhere. These palaces, in which sat the council that forms the communal executive, were raised on arcades that outline, on the ground, the space available to house the assembly of citizens from which they originate. Theoretically sovereign, but rarely convened in actual fact (except, in the case of conflicts, to renew the oaths establishing the commune as a *conjuratio*), the assembly of citizens is designated by this empty space, rather than welcomed there.

This, therefore, is my proposal: to start from this Italian civic square where all the architectural, political, legal, and philosophical qualities of public space seem to be ideally superimposed and to try to disassemble them, and to desecrate, on the very site of its apotheosis, this false visual evidence which acts as a trap for the gaze, but also as an interpretative net.

16. Daniel Arasse, *L'Annonciation italienne. Une histoire de perspective* (Paris: Hazan, 1999), 59.
17. Aristotle, *Physics,* IV, 209b1.

Palazzo del Comune, Cremona, Italy

It was in central and northern Italy that the communal experience was brought to its maximum degree of social intensity, and as early as the twelfth century. By communal experience I mean the social production of a new mode of governmentality accompanying urban emancipation, based essentially on the election of magistrates, the deliberation of citizens, the collegiality of decisions, and the control of the elites—all of which can be seen as an alliance, that is to say, a political community bound together by an oath taken jointly. Two points need to be made in this regard. The first concerns the Italian specificity in this process which, to varying degrees, influenced the whole of urban Europe. An accentuation rather than an exception, it deserves to be compared with other heightened forms of the same phenomenon, as in the cities of Flanders.[18] The second concerns the urban effectiveness of the previous formulation: an experience which can be seen as an alliance of the gathered wills. For the public spaces referred to here are much more than just the setting for this political scene which, in order to be effective, must constantly be replayed; they are in fact one of its

18. John Watts, *The Making of Polities: Europe, 1300–1500* (Cambridge, Cambridge University Press, 2009).

Giuseppe Zocchi, *The Piazza della Signoria in Florence*, first half of the eighteenth century, private collection

main protagonists. In other words, in this theater of power, the city and its material forms play, if not the leading role, then at least one which in reality makes and breaks the social meaning of the places whose architectural qualities are always renegotiated by the practitioners of the city.

For it was indeed the deliberative practices of the urban assemblies (in particular the civic assembly called *arengo* in central Italy and *parlamentum*, *concio*, *comune colloquio* in northern Italy) that precipitated the creation of their own place, the civic square—which was envisaged as a place for political speech, a place of exchange and confrontation that welcomes and encourages the deployment of a public space that could then spread across the city, insofar as the communal system was characterized first and foremost by its institutional plurality and its urban polycentrism.[19] Indeed, the public power of the communal institution was not limited to its central councils but was disseminated across several public offices, in the "parties" and in the government of the trades—all places of power that gave rise to their own

19. Élisabeth Crouzet-Pavan, "'Pour le bien commun'... À propos des politiques urbaines dans l'Italie communale," in *Pouvoir et édilité. Les Grands chantiers dans l'Italie communale et seigneuriale*, ed. Élisabeth Crouzet-Pavan (Rome: École française de Rome, 2003), 11–40.

assemblies and were distributed across the urban space. The accentuation of the solemnity of places was also a way of depoliticizing these public places and of blocking the deployment of a true public space. This was the case of the Italian cities with a communal tradition but which came under the control of a seigniorial or princely authority in the fourteenth century. This was the case for the *Broletto* (i.e. the civic square) in Milan, whose monumental setting had been fixed since 1228. The lords of Milan also occupied this space, but fictitiously, magnifying it with their monumental presence: a space of political deliberation became the place of dynastic celebration through a soft strategy of semantic inversion.[20] The same could be said of the Piazza della Signoria in Florence under Medici rule, where a crowd of statues was gathered at the very moment when the deliberative practices of the great collective assemblies that constituted the matrix of communal regimes were drying up.

A Theory of Spacing

It is therefore necessary to take up this story the way Chris Wickham suggests: tentatively, since those who instituted the Italian commune did so not without thinking about it, but in any case without *foreseeing* it, contending themselves with the already considerable task of expanding the possible.[21] The year is 1117, in Milan, and an earthquake has shaken the whole of northern Italy. The chronicler Landulf Junior, Landulf of Saint Paul, relates a gathering of the people on the initiative of the archbishop and the consuls. So the consuls were there, and they acted. They acted to ward off the anguish of the people. The people all went outside "for fear of the ruins and rubble"—it is said that one exposes oneself when one comes together, but one can also protect

20. Patrick Boucheron, "Espace public et lieux publics: approches en histoire urbaine," in *L'Espace public au Moyen Âge. Débats autour de Jürgen Habermas*, eds. Patrick Boucheron and Nicolas Offenstadt (Paris: Presses Universitaires de France, 2011), 99–117.
21. Chris Wickham, *Sleepwalking into a New World: The Emergence of Italian City Communes in the Twelfth Century* (Princeton: Princeton University Press, 2015).

oneself from collapsing buildings. But Landulf specifies that the people were "waiting for vices to be extinguished and virtues to be reborn." All the people? Yes, but two platforms had been erected: one for the archbishop with his suffragan bishops (Milan was establishing itself as a metropolis at the time), the abbots, and the most important monks; the other for the consuls and "the legal and customary scholars" (in other words, the jurists). Here, then, we have a staging of the Gregorian bipartition, at the origins of the structure of pre-communal society. Urban emancipation at the time was the continuation of the Reformation of the Church by other means: the instituting cleavage is here theatricalized, like the *stasis* (standing, stoppage) in the Greek world, overlapping moreover with the separation between law and theology.

For this staging was indeed a theatricalization. Let us listen to Landulf: "the archbishop and the consuls had two *theatra* set up." This is not just a way of saying that the acts of the first consuls of the Milanese commune were taken up in the *theatrum civitatis*, that is to say, most probably, in the ruins of the ancient theater of the Roman *Mediolanum*—near the present-day Piazza Cordusio. Can one infer a historical continuity from this topographical superposition, from this insistence on places? Medievalist historians have looked for precedents for the first communal assemblies in the Carolingian *plaids* (general court of justice) or public assemblies which also reused ancient memories: the testament of Bishop Anspert, dated September 10, 879, refers to the "public forum, known as the *Assemblatorio*," where these large gatherings were organized. The entire nineteenth-century historiography attempted to establish a continuity between the ancient *municipia* (municipalities) and the medieval communes, between the forum and the *arengo*. But it failed: beyond the Carolingian revival (or recharge), the thread is broken.

It is therefore in the ruins of the Roman world that the future of the medieval West was invented—this is true from the conceptual point of view (whether we think of Roman law or the liturgical heritage), but it is also true from the point of view of the material framework of cities. Lorenzo Tanzini rightly reminds us that the development of communal Italy can also be explained by the physical presence of the monumental setting of the Roman city, which is still active—like a great symbolic machine that has been put to sleep but which is always capable of being restarted, of beginning again.[22] To account for this in-between time, I would like to make a somewhat theoretical proposal: a place of deliberation is only possible thanks to an act of emplacement, that is to say, the capacity of a place to turn itself around, to rise up, to become something other than itself. From this point of view, what I here call an act of emplacement is not far removed from what Benoît Goetz called *dislocation* (dismemberment).[23] In this case, it should be understood that spacing is what makes room for the freedom of women and men, that is to say, what makes room for them and gives them a place, insofar as this place will never be assigned in advance and once and for all. The space of the square—not only the public square where one can assemble, but the political act of emplacement, and therefore the place of deliberation—is that place where one becomes visible, open to a mixture that is not a melee. This is what "forbids one to remain in place, and to stick to *a* place, to *one's* place, determined since time immemorial by a narrative that neglects space. To give space a place is to cancel in one place the power of these identifying narratives," writes Benoît Goetz.[24]

It is, in short, to take the side of an architecture that draws the void in the city far more than it imposes eloquent objects on it, it is to choose an art of spacing that has to do with the politeness of the Greeks that Gilles Deleuze speaks of, "an art of establishing appropriate distances between men, not hierarchical, but geometrical," an art that consists of "being neither too close nor too far away, in order to avoid giving or

22. Lorenzo Tanzini, *"A consiglio." La vita politica nell'Italia dei Comuni* (Bari: Laterza, 2014).
23. Benoît Goetz, *La Dislocation. Architecture et philosophie* (Lagrasse: Verdier, 2018 [2011]).
24. Goetz, *La Dislocation*, 233.

receiving blows."[25] One could identify many historical situations to support the political philosophy of the assembly whose performativity Judith Butler rightly reminds us of: occupying the public space is more than taking a stand or exercising pressure, it is instituting the political by exposing one's own vulnerability.[26] There are many examples in the history of medieval urban commotions that describe this direct effectivity of the bodily occupation of public space. The Flemish cases show this most eloquently. In Ghent, for example, on June 28, 1467, Charles the Bold was unable to make his princely entry into the city because it was occupied by an assembly mobilized to defeat the ritual by force of numbers. What constitutes the revolt in the Middle Ages, what establishes the crowd as a political force, is related less to its level of violence than to the physical pressure exerted by "the great support of the people"—a gathering rather than an uprising. Regardless of their repressive capacities, the powers generally do not resist for long.[27]

But we must also remember that the most political moment of any assembly is always that of the dispersal. Maurice Blanchot articulated this thought in these memorable lines: "One must not last, one must not take part in any duration whatsoever. This was understood on that exceptional day: no one had to give us the order to disperse. We separated out of the same necessity that had brought the innumerable crowd together. We broke up instantly, without any remnants, without any of those nostalgic after-effects by which the true demonstration is altered by the pretense of persevering in combat groups. The people are not like that. The people are there, they are no longer there; they ignore the structures that could stabilize them."[28]

25. Gilles Deleuze, *Périclès et Verdi. La Philosophie de François Châtelet* (Paris: Minuit, 1988), 14.
26. Judith Butler, *Notes toward a Performative Theory of Assembly* (Cambridge, Harvard University Press, 2015).
27. Élodie Lecuppre-Desjardin, *La Ville des cérémonies. Essai sur la communication politique dans les anciens Pays-Bas bourguignons* (Turnhout: Brepols, 2004).
28. Maurice Blanchot, *La Communauté inavouable* (Paris: Minuit, 1983), 56.

Richard Banégas,
Florence Brisset-Foucault
& Armando Cutolo

Street Parliaments:

Public Spaces for Speech and Citizenship in Africa

"Patriotic agoras" in Côte d'Ivoire, "Standing parliamentarians" in the Democratic Republic of Congo (DRC), "People's Parliaments" in Nairobi and Eldoret in Kenya, *ebimeeza* and other "Listeners' forums" on Ugandan radio stations, *grins* in Mali, Côte d'Ivoire, and Burkina Faso: over the past twenty years throughout Africa, forums for debate, discussion, and public speech have been springing up, bringing together dozens, sometimes hundreds of people. Some have developed into lasting structures and have become institutions—after drawing up statutes, codes of conduct, and written procedures to structure the debates—whilst others have had a more fleeting existence.

How are we to interpret these popular gathering places, which often present themselves both as spaces of "plebeian public opinion" (*plebejische Öffentlichkeit*), and as "alternatives" to the dominant public space?[1] Should they be perceived as sites within which one can confront the authorities, or as tools for the dissemination of the authorities' diktats? Should we understand them as counter-hegemonic, "proper places" conducive to citizen emancipation,[2] or as instruments of depoliticization and subordination to a dominant order—even if that order is newly deliberative? The research carried out on these "street parliaments" in Uganda, Côte d'Ivoire, the DRC, Kenya, South Africa, and Burkina Faso provides contrasting and nuanced answers to these questions, prompting us to revise the ways in which we approach these assemblies.[3]

Previous page: *Mambo Bado* (What's New?), an *ekimeeza* broadcasted on CBS radio, Kampala, Uganda, 2008

1. Jürgen Habermas, "Préface à la seconde édition," in *L'Espace public. Archéologie de la publicité comme dimension constitutive de la société bourgeoise* (Paris: Payot, 1993).
2. On "proper places" and speech during social mobilisations, see Michel de Certeau, *Arts de faire. L'Invention du quotidien* (Paris: Gallimard, 1980); and Michel de Certeau, "Pour une nouvelle culture. Le pouvoir de parler," *Études* 408 (2008): 628–35.
3. See the dossier "Parlements de la rue. Espaces publics de la parole et citoyenneté en Afrique," in *Politique africaine* 127, no. 3, eds. Armando Cutolo, Richard Banégas, and Florence Brisset-Foucault, (2012); Richard Banégas, "Putsch et politique de la rue au Burkina Faso. Quand les étudiants débattent du Régiment de sécurité présidentielle," *Politique africaine* 139, no. 3, (2015): 147–70; and Florence Brisset-Foucault, *Talkative Polity: Radio, Domination, and Citizenship in Uganda* (Athens, OH: Ohio University Press, 2019).

Rather than portray African street parliaments as mere replicas of a worldwide movement (whether by framing them as akin to Occupy Wall Street, to the Arab Spring, or to a broader "global participatory turn"), our research stresses that each of these phenomena are part of their own distinct, singular, and yet globally interconnected histories. Without denying either the similarities between them or the global circulation of models of deliberation—in itself central to understanding, for example, the transnationalization of movements such as *Y'en a marre* (Enough!) or *Balai citoyen* (The Citizens' Broom) in French-speaking Africa—and without, of course, exoticizing these phenomena, we defend an approach that unpacks the singular meanings of these practices with regard to their historical contexts and the specific (even if of course globally connected) imaginaries of citizenship that they reflect and produce.

These phenomena lead us quite naturally to discuss the notion of "public space" which often arises in conversations about street parliaments, and which usually follows the version theorized by Jürgen Habermas. Several anthropologists and sociologists working on the theme of the "public space" in Africa have, on the basis of this formulation, detailed spaces subject to the power of chiefs, of the administration, and of NGOs, concluding that public space "could not be found" south of the Sahara, and that it was difficult to distinguish from community or religious spheres.[4] Other authors, who take a philosophical and normative approach, have developed reflections on endogenous models of the public space, invoking in particular the

4. Jean-Pierre Olivier de Sardan, "L'Espace public introuvable. Chefs et projets dans les villages nigériens," *Revue Tiers-Monde* 157 (1999): 139–67; Michèle Leclerc-Olive, "Arènes sahéliennes: communautaires, civiles ou publiques?" in *Les Sens du public. Publics politiques, publics médiatiques*, eds. Daniel Cefaï and Dominique Pasquier (Paris: Presses Universitaires de Fance, 2003), 157–76; and Michèle Leclerc-Olive, "Sphère publique religieuse: enquête sur quelques voisinages conceptuels," in *L'Islam en Afrique: vers un espace public religieux?*, ed. Gilles Holder (Paris: Karthala, 2009), 37–60.

"palaver"—presented as an African ideal of deliberation that encourages a return to the foundations of an Indigenous culture of democracy.[5]

Our research was complementary to normative approaches. It was not our intention to compare real situations to standardized ideals—whether the Habermasian ideal, the palaver ideal, or indeed any other. To us, such an evaluative approach seemed destined to fall into a problematic register of the "not there yet."[6] Based on the meticulous observation of street parliaments, we propose instead to reflect on the genealogy of emic conceptions of citizenship and deliberation, by taking seriously Habermas's initial methodological proposal. This proposal, which was also taken on by others,[7] consisted of considering these phenomena as empirical opportunities to study the imaginaries of good government, or of the ideal public space. The ways in which these assemblies are organized, the turns taken for speaking, the spatial arrangement of the audience, and the form and content of the speeches all reflect these ideals—whether intentionally or not. They are also indicative of the power relations and of the dynamics of sociopolitical inclusion and exclusion specific to any given society. Consider, for example, the *grins* in Côte d'Ivoire, where people gather in the evening over tea to talk about one thing or another. These places of sociability, which

5. This is the spirit of the text by Jean Godefroy Bidima published in this volume. See also: Jean Godefroy Bidima, *La Palabre. Une juridiction de la parole* (Paris: Michalon, 2000).
6. See on this register the introduction of Dipesh Chakrabarty, *Provincializing Europe. Postcolonial Thought and Historical Difference* (Princeton: Princeton University Press, 2000).
7. Indeed, this approach is not only Habermasian: authors such as Dipesh Chakrabarty on Bengal, Maurice Agulhon on France, Edward P. Thompson on England, or the authors gathered by Maurice Bloch in rural African contexts already started from the idea that the analysis of assembly and sociability practices give precious indications on local debates about good government. See: Dipesh Chakrabarty, *Provincializing Europe. Postcolonial Thought and Historical Difference* (Princeton/Oxford: Princeton University Press, 2000); Maurice Agulhon, *Le Cercle dans la France bourgeoise 1810–1848. Étude d'une mutation de sociabilité* (Paris: Armand Colin, 1977); Edward P. Thompson, *The Making of the English Working Class* (London: Penguin, 1991 [1963]); and Maurice Bloch, ed., *Political Language and Oratory in Traditional Society* (London: Academic Press, 1975).

Parlement La Réflexion (The Thinking Parliament) in South-Yopougon, Abidjan, Côte d'Ivoire, June 2021

exist throughout the Manding cultural space of West Africa, became highly politicized in Côte d'Ivoire during the civil war of the 2000s, and became informal mobilization structures for Alassane Ouattara's camp against the patriotic agoras of President Laurent Gbagbo's camp.[8] By facilitating the relatively secure self-expression of "Northerners," these micro-assemblies enabled the claiming of both moral and political respectability, and the affirmation of social categories formerly stigmatized by the autochthonist/southern ideology of Ivorianness. But close observation of the modalities of expression within the grins shows that, while they are presented as open assemblies of free expression, they are governed by strong statutory hierarchies (between elders and juniors, "old fathers" and "good children," and also gender relations, since women are virtually absent),

8. Present in many Sahelian countries, particularly in Mali, Burkina Faso and Niger (*fada*), the institution of the tea grins in Côte d'Ivoire brings together mainly members from the country's northern regions, who identify with a form of solidarity based on identity (*dioula* in particular) and politics (the grins having become strongholds of Alassane Ouattara's party during the crisis). Practices of sociability and the ways in which people speak out reconstruct this imagined northern moral community in the cities of the south.

Patriotic Parliament of Yopougon, Abidjan, Côte d'Ivoire, January 2019

and by implicit rules of access to the floor. These implicit rules are not only tied to inequalities in cultural capital, but also to relations of patronage and seniority which, far from encouraging challenges to the established order, promote its reproduction.[9]

On the Emergence of Street Parliaments

How can we explain the emergence and development of these parliaments across the continent? Several hypotheses deserve to be examined here. When we look at the timeline of their appearance, we see a strong overlap with the "transitions" of the 1990s. It is therefore tempting to interpret African street parliaments as by-products of the "Third Wave" of post-Cold War democratization. Many of them are indeed linked to media liberalization, since in Benin, the DRC, and Kenya they developed directly through the collective reading and commenting of radio bulletins and

9. See: Sarah Vincourt and Souleymane Kouyaté, "Ce que 'parler au grin' veut dire: sociabilité urbaine, politique de la rue et reproduction sociale en Côte d'Ivoire," *Politique africaine* 127, no. 3 (2012): 91–108.

Niangon Parliament of Yopougon, Abidjan, Côte d'Ivoire, June 2021

headlines from the press often exclusively sold and read in the street—giving rise to the well-known phenomenon of the *titrologues*, groups who gather to discuss the news based on the *titres* (or headlines) posted at newsstands. In Uganda, the *ebimeeza* were the product of the newly-established private radio stations, some of whose producers sought to position themselves within the political arena. Other spaces of speech were deployed on the basis of the local reinterpretation of transnational NGO and donor initiatives, which aimed at promoting "participatory democracy" and "accountability."[10] The repertoires of legitimacy invoked and staged in these spaces reflect the centrality of the democratic question. However, an overly mechanistic relation of cause and effect between "democratization" (often understood in a very generic way) and the emergence of these spaces of expression runs the risk of overlooking some of their specificities in relation to the production of political

10. Florence Brisset-Foucault, "La Cité radiophonique. Démocratie de chantier, domination technocratique et patriotisme bureaucratique en Ouganda," *Sociétés politiques comparées* 40 (October–December 2016), http://www.fasopo.org/sites/default/files/varia1_n40.pdf.

cultures. Case studies show that these street parliaments can be spaces for celebrating the sovereignty of the people as much as they are spaces for reinforcing, or even enhancing, certain inequalities in accessing the floor—that they are just as much "proper places" for resisting power as they are arenas for mobilizing in support of a hegemonic social or political project.

To consider these street assemblies as manifestations of the vitality of African "civil societies" would be to neglect their complex links with the State, and what these street assemblies can therefore reveal about the changes in the latter, or its anchor-points in society. This remains true both in the formulation of rules that strongly regulate speech (but that are not necessarily experienced as a constraint by the speakers), and in the very significant presence among the speakers (in Uganda and Côte d'Ivoire, in particular) of representatives of the ruling parties, and of the clientelistic dynamics that have shaped and informed the links between governing elites and certain sections of society in these two countries. Moreover, although they are not institutionalized in the sense that they are not integrated into public policies, the street parliaments are nonetheless often very bureaucratized, and are characterized by the highly procedural nature of the exchanges—underlining the importance of the state imaginary in these assembly practices, which nevertheless often present themselves as spontaneous and informal.

To what extent are these parliaments the heirs of older practices of speaking in assembly? The image of the "palaver tree" mentioned above is not only used by philosophers; it is also used by some of the actors in these assemblies who identify it as the origin of today's street parliaments. If we wish to pursue this genealogical perspective, it is necessary to carefully follow the transfers from one space of speech to another. We can do so, on the one hand, through the analysis of speeches, ways of speaking, vocabulary—and, on the other, through the biographies of the speakers. The invocation of the palaver by the actors themselves also prompts us to examine the ways in which they project themselves into this reinvented imaginary of tradition. As the example of the Abidjan grins shows, the reference to a tradition of authority and to a common origin, to the reproduction of the village of common ancestors, makes it possible—in the very singular context of the civil war—to reimagine and stage a "northern" community whose urban assembly constitutes a local representation and a temporary achievement.

With this in mind, one of our concerns during our collaborative research was to take into consideration the high level of porosity between various spaces of speech, and the potential conversion/diffusion of oratory skills running between them. There are indeed many connections between street parliaments, electoral meetings, trade union assemblies, village assemblies, seminars, and participatory events organized by NGOs and religious sermons—all of which are places where people learn to speak publicly. This integration has a decisive influence on the unfolding of the exchanges and on their status. The meticulous reconstruction of these reciprocal influences, based on in-depth field research, makes it possible to avoid reducing the explanation of the emergence of these spaces to an enchanted or sentimental discourse on their spontaneous success after the lifting of repressive lids, to the reproduction of more or less reimagined traditions, or to framing their existence as the result of the lure of profit of the participants—some of whom indeed get paid for their performance by politicians. Our approach here aims to reinsert them into intersecting histories of change in the urban space, the labor market, education, the media, party and union structures, ethnic patriotism, and religious mobilization. The links between street parliaments and oratory practices in religious spaces and the tensions that run through the latter are indeed fundamental components that must be taken into account. In Côte d'Ivoire, the influence of Pentecostal churches on patriotic agoras evidences these effects of diffusion, as do the links between the grins and certain imams.

One of the central findings of our comparative research is the fundamental influence of school and university environments on street parliaments, particularly in Kinshasa, Abidjan, Eldoret, and Kampala: the "parliamentarians" are often students or former students, "frustrated intellectuals" who hope to recover in the parliaments the networks, pleasures and resources (at once intellectual, social and financial) they once enjoyed on campus. In the former British colonies, the speakers are often former champions of school debate clubs, spaces which in turn replicate the debate procedures entrenched in the parliamentary debates at Westminster. The links between the emergence of these spaces, the massification of higher education and university political culture, and the devastating effects of structural adjustment plans and economic crises on skilled employment prospects, are self-evident. The "people's parliaments" then become spaces of social distinction in which to cultivate one's identity as an intellectual, from which the attendant moral stature of the model citizen is supposed to follow—they are not spaces in which to celebrate the democratization of speech.

Speech, Political Subjectivation and Social Exclusion

There are also direct links with electoral and party dynamics. This is particularly evident in the case of Côte d'Ivoire, whether for the patriotic agoras or the network of grins: political and electoral competition directly influenced their development and structure, revealing the extent to which the political battle was played out in the speeches and the control of urban space. Similarly, in Kinshasa, the "standing parliamentarians" were massively mobilized by the political parties, particularly the UDPS of the late Étienne Tshisekedi.[11] In multiple countries, political parties encouraged and even actively trained speakers to stand up for the party views in street parliaments. But interestingly—and this is particularly the case in the DRC, Uganda and Côte d'Ivoire—these

11. Camille Dugrand, "'Combattants de la parole': parlementaires-debout et mobilisation partisane à Kinshasa," *Politique africaine* 127, no. 3 (2012): 49–69.

Coca-Cola
Big Beer
Big Taste

BUY
ROMPS
HERE
MTN

spaces, however marked they may be by a party identity, are not simply sounding boards for the party leadership's watchwords. They are also spaces of internal dissent, where intra-party competition is played out within "proper places" of social retaliation for certain sub-groups and factions among the young and among subaltern categories.

In Uganda, for example, the *ebimeeza* have highlighted and even been the driving force of the re-partisanization of political life after twenty years of "no party democracy" under the regime of President Yoweri Museveni. Far from being the product of top-down strategies, however, the partisanization of the debates occurred from the bottom up, because the people's parliaments provided the means for very junior agents of these parties to acquire a modicum of political weight, and to compensate for their lack of economic and social capital: they were therefore the driving force of this partisanization process. Moreover, by serving as a direct channel between these small, under-resourced subordinate agents and President Museveni, who relies on such networks in order to bypass traditional elites, the Ugandan people's parliaments also contributed to the presidentialization of political life. In Côte d'Ivoire, under the Gbagbo regime, street parliaments have accommodated a whole generation of speakers within which students from the university union (FESCI) rubbed shoulders with grassroots activists from the ruling party, the Front Populaire Ivoirien—but also with militiamen from the "patriotic galaxy," Pentecostal pastors, and other actors from the working-class neighborhoods of Abidjan. In these spaces, public speaking soon went beyond its instrumental role of supporting the regime and defending the republic, then under attack from the rebellion. It became a way of life, and a significant lever of power for these new speech workers—young downtrodden people who had become semi-professional speakers organized in a national federation, and who moved from one assembly space to another recounting Gbagbo's patriotic and anti-colonial efforts. Interpreting and explaining, day after day, the political and religious meaning of the Ivorian crisis

Previous page: *Simbawo Akatii* (Information Point), an *ekimeeza* broadcasted on Radio Simba, Kampala, Uganda, 2008

through an active hermeneutic work of "unveiling" the truth, these young speakers made an important contribution to the moral subjectivation of the citizens participating in the "work" of the parliaments and to their own category-specific emancipation. However, our research underlines the ambivalence of this process of subjection (in the dual Foucauldian sense of subordination and subjectivation) which took place within the framework of a constraining device of professionalization of the patriotic speech.[12]

Another striking commonality between these different street parliaments is their almost exclusively male character. Women are not completely lacking in presence, but they often appear in an almost clandestine manner, and the few who dare to speak are experienced activists generally linked to one or another party apparatus. This gendered segregation is indicative of the models and imaginaries of citizenship that are staged in these spaces. Women often embody a kind of "counter-model" of citizenship—stigmatized, associated with emotionality and with local, everyday concerns, they represent in a caricatured way everything that a "parliamentarian" should not be. While they can sometimes constitute spaces for the emancipation of social juniors, street parliaments often reassert dominant social identities. Indeed, it is not just at the level of gender that these parliaments create hierarchies. One of the common denominators of these different parliaments is the value attached to formal education, and in particular to a university degree, as well as to a method of information research that is very thorough and that precedes the act of speaking. Besides underlining classic inequalities within access to political speech, we wanted to demonstrate, above all, that in these forms of discrimination, competing (and sometimes antagonistic) visions of the political and moral conditions enabling an individual to claim the right to speak were also at play.

12. Armando Cutolo and Richard Banégas, "Gouverner par la parole: parlements de la rue, pratiques oratoires et subjectivation politique en Côte d'Ivoire," *Politique africaine* 127, no. 3 (2012): 21–48.

It is often more a citizenship of distinction that is staged and practiced in street parliaments than a radically democratic vision of citizenship.[13] One of the striking commonalities of many of these street assemblies is their strong mimetic dimension with regard to national parliaments. In many cases, "parliamentarians" do not seek to assert that "anyone" could be a parliamentarian, but rather that they are far from being "anyone." By presenting themselves as spokespersons for the working classes, these street speakers paradoxically celebrate the representative, rather than the participatory model of democracy: one speaks in "parliament" not (definitely not!) as a "common man," but to represent, or even "educate" others, as an intellectual and potential leader. This ambivalence calls for not approaching "people's parliaments" with participatory blinders on, but rather for questioning the hybridizations between participatory *and* representative conceptions of democracy.[14]

These spaces are often repressed. Through the discourses of justification that often accompany them, these repressive episodes promote, as a counterpoint, a model of popular speech and citizenship that is honorable in the eyes of the State. It is also in this respect that street parliaments are heuristic. It is significant that, in most cases, the street "parliamentarians" try to counter their bad reputation, and the accusations of idleness, vulgarity and alcoholism they attract. Instead, street parliamentarians aspire to display their respectability—to demonstrate adherence to a certain model of governing both the self and others based on the valorization of rationality, self-control, individuality, and respect for formal procedures.

However, the qualities required to speak in people's parliaments are not only proper morality and education: it is also a matter of displaying courage and strength. This in

13. Florence Brisset-Foucault, "A Citizenship of Distinction in the Open Radio Debates of Kampala," *Africa: Journal of the International African Institute* 83, no. 2 (2013): 227–50.

14. Samuel Hayat, "La Représentation inclusive," *Raisons politiques* 50, no. 2 (2013): 115–35.

part because speaking out in many African contexts is also a great risk. But it is also because the politics of street assemblies can be linked to violence. The public space as imagined and staged in these spaces is not always a space for "the civilizing of behavior."[15] On the contrary, these spaces are sometimes the crucible of modes of self-engagement and political subjectivation that also involve the valorization of force and verbal or physical violence. What Camille Dugrand's work on the "standing parliamentarians" of Kinshasa in particular shows, as well as the analysis of the agoras of Abidjan, is that the imaginaries of violence and the imaginaries of deliberation are articulated in a complex combination that mixes the valorization of the figure of the intellectual with that of the militiaman, of force and of risk—what we can call the "speech fighter."

Regardless of their origins and future, these street assembly practices are indicative of the ingrained debates over citizenship that characterize African societies. It is in these socially situated spaces—in terms of the social and gendered status of the participants—which are more or less politicized and more or less constrained by measures of control and by repression, that discourses and debates on civic virtue and the conditions of belonging to the nation (as in Côte d'Ivoire) or to an ethnic group (as in Uganda) are developed. Through their day-to-day performances, their debates about which rules to instate and to follow, who to admit and who not to admit, and the right and wrong ways to express oneself, street parliamentarians participate in broader and often fierce controversies—controversies about the boundaries of the political community, and about what one is to expect from a "good citizen." While the conflicts affecting many countries on the continent remain "citizenship wars," street parliaments offer an opportunity to capture the political, social, and moral depth of these controversies.

15. As drawn from Norbert Elias, *The Civilizing Process: Sociogenetic and Psychogenetic Investigations*, rev. ed. (Oxford: Blackwell Publishers, 2000).

Laurent Jeanpierre

The Ideal Assembly

of the
Worker-Poet
Constant Hilbey

A TOUS LES MEMBRES DES Clubs Démocratiques.

CHEVREMONT

Profession de foi du citoyen

Constant Hilbey.

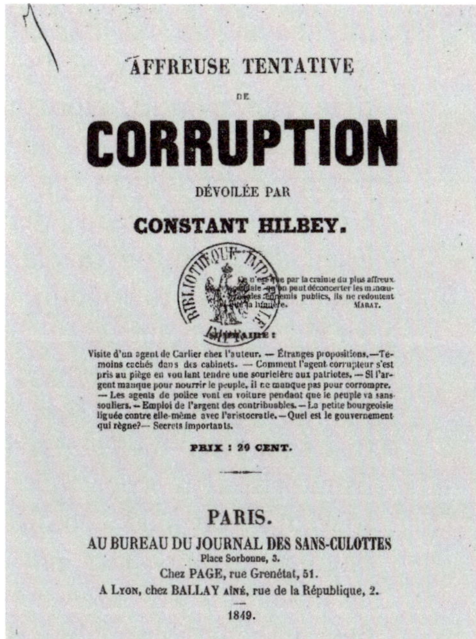

AFFREUSE TENTATIVE DE CORRUPTION DÉVOILÉE PAR CONSTANT HILBEY.

Visite d'un agent de Carlier chez l'auteur. — Étranges propositions.—Témoins cachés dans des cabinets. — Comment l'agent corrupteur s'est pris au piège en voulant tendre une souricière aux patriotes. — Si l'argent manque pour nourrir le peuple, il ne manque pas pour corrompre. — Les agents de police vont en voiture pendant que le peuple va sans souliers. — Emploi de l'argent des contribuables. — La petite bourgeoisie liguée contre elle-même avec l'aristocratie. — Quel est le gouvernement qui règne? — Secrets importants.

PRIX : 20 CENT.

PARIS.
AU BUREAU DU JOURNAL DES SANS-CULOTTES
Place Sorbonne, 3.
Chez PAGE, rue Grenétat, 51.
A LYON, chez BALLAY AÎNÉ, rue de la République, 2.
1849.

À tous les membres des Clubs Démocratiques (To all members of democratical clubs), anonymous poster with Constant Hilbey's statement to be elected at the National Convention, 1848, Paris, Bibliothèque Nationale de France

Affreuse tentative de corruption dévoilée par Constant Hilbey (A hideous attempt of corruption, unveiled by Constant Hilbey), frontispiece (Paris: Page, 1849)

On February 25, 1848, just after three days of insurrection in Paris that led to the overthrow of the July Monarchy, the following recommendations for forming assemblies could be read on walls around Paris:

> "Establish clubs, demand that a National Convention be formed, and that the hall be big enough to hold at least four thousand spectators, so that you may always have eyes on your representatives; this is the most important point, and for that reason, the one that they will attempt not to grant you."[1]

The poster was signed Constant Hilbey, a working-class tailor from Normandy who had come to Paris some years earlier

1. The author thanks Jacques Rancière for having pointed out to him Constant Hilbey's unique project and for having encouraged him to begin investigating into him. A more extensive version of this research will be proposed in another context.

after having been dismissed by his first supervisor, and who wrote plays, poetry, and political pamphlets in his spare time. A few months before the 1848 Revolution, he published a pamphlet against the poet Alphonse de Lamartine (who was also opposed to the monarchy) and his *Histoire des Girondins*, a well-read interpretation of the history of the French Revolution in eight volumes intended to entertain, as well as to contain, rising public anger. Imprisoned for having denounced the book and defamed its author, as well as for having criticized Lamartine's call for repression when the population rose up against hunger, Hilbey nonetheless drafted the February 1848 placard upon his release from prison, in order, this time, to alert the French people to what he deemed a confiscation by the bourgeoisie of the ongoing revolutionary movement. To avoid this usurpation, he thought it was necessary, while there was still time, to fight with all their might against "fake Republicans," "timid reforms," and to completely revamp "the code of laws."

The main goal of public mobilizations, according to Hilbey, was to set up a new "National Convention," similar to the one that condemned Louis XVI in 1793 and established a new Constitution. At the same time, they were supposed to re-establish and expand political clubs, those deliberative micro-societies that had developed before the French Revolution and that were reborn following the advent of the Second Republic at the end of February 1848. Even more important, for the worker-poet, was the architecture of the new national assembly he dreamt up: the debate space had to be big enough to welcome "at least four thousand spectators," a number much greater than the number of parliamentarians. The latter would benefit from being seen by the public and, for this reason, some people say that Hilbey had envisioned placing them in a pit, as with an orchestra, with a large audience looking down on them from above. In this ideal parliament, it was a matter of preventing any kind of "betrayal" of the people that may result from a parliamentary oligarchy, inevitably produced by representative democracy. The worker-poet planned to turn parliamentarians elected

N° 16.

Lith. Gosselin Editeur r. St Jacques 71

CLUB FÉMININ.

Nous demandons 1° Que le jupon soit remplacé par la culotte.
2° Que les maris s'occupent de l'intérieur au moins trois fois par semaine.
3° Enfin qu'il n'existe entre l'homme et la femme aucune autre distinction que celle qu'il a plu à la nature de leur accorder.

E.B., Club féminin (Women's Club), second half of the nineteenth century, lithograph, Paris, Musée Carnavalet

by "universal" suffrage (though we know that women were excluded) into servants of the people by placing them under permanent scrutiny, and by highlighting both their minority status and the transitory nature of their terms.

Hilbey belonged to the wing of what some historians call the democratic and social Republic that was opposed, between February and June 1848, to the more moderate Republic of the temporary government of the National Assembly.[2] He demanded that the people keep control over their representatives and participate directly in collective decisions. We can see why he published, between May 1848 and March 1849, a paper titled *Journal des Sans-culottes* which borrowed its name from a heading appearing during the French Revolution, with an epigraph that remained in their memories of some: "The souls of Emperors and those of cobblers are thrown into the same mold." Hilbey was also an admirer of Marat—a "friend of the people" as he was famously called in reference to the newspaper that the revolutionary doctor had himself created—and dedicated several brochures to him before 1848. In one of them, we find several reflections on the architecture of assemblies, a subject that was rather rare among the radical Republicans of the time, but that warranted without a doubt the particular attention of the author.[3]

Here is what Hilbey reported. During the September 25, 1792, session of the National Convention, several representatives accused Marat of wanting to put in place a "dictatorship," to break away from the assembly, and to cause bloodshed in the streets of Paris, as the "September massacres" he was then accused of planning were supposed to confirm. During this session, he who was singled out by the other representatives stated that, since its beginnings, the Revolution had been violently threatened, that it had to

2. Samuel Hayat, *1848. Quand la République était révolutionnaire. Citoyenneté et représentation* (Paris: Seuil, 2014).
3. Constant Hilbey, "Séance de la Convention nationale du 25 septembre 1792, extrait du *Journal* de Marat. Précédé d'une introduction et accompagné de notes par Constant Hilbey (ouvrier)" in *Les Grands orateurs de 1830 et un imbécile de 93* (Paris, 1847).

defend itself, sometimes with violence, against those who might betray or threaten it, and that not to do so would be naïve. But never did the idea of going against the democratic ideal of the Convention cross his mind. Marat displayed, on the contrary, unbridled rationalist faith in deliberative exchange and reminded the representatives that his positions on these issues had always been public and printed in his newspaper:

> "How could clearly unabashed opinions subject to the consideration of readers be regarded as offences? No, no doubt; had they been false, they would never be but mere errors; had they been extravagant, their author would appear to be nothing but a blindman or a fool. [...] I subjected my opinions to the consideration of the public; if they are dangerous, it is in combatting them through solid reasoning, and not in condemning me to anathema, that my enemies must proscribe them."[4]

Hilbey tells that this session was influenced by a particular commotion going on in the galleries. One of the parliamentarians demanded that the session chairman call them to order, because they were "allowing themselves whispers" and "had tyrannized the assembly for far too long."[5] During the session, Marat accused two other parliamentarians, Élie Guadet and Jean-Pierre Brissot, of having organized a plot against him by printing a fake issue of his newspaper and of having him followed by hitmen on a mission to kill him. During the debates, the galleries of the Convention stood up for Marat and became agitated by "a great fermentation," to the point that, according to one witness, there would have been "heads cut off" if he had been attacked.[6] "Look at the people *tyrannizing* its representatives!" concluded Hilbey about all these episodes. "They were thus not representing, since their opinions differed from [the people]. Marat,

4. « Discours de l'ami du peuple, prononcé le 25 septembre à la Convention nationale. Complot de le faire égorger par des brigands », in Hilbey, 7.
5. Ibid., 11.
6. Ibid., 13.

N° 54. Intérieur d'un club.

N° 169. Séance du club démocratique.

Inside of a political club, in *Journées illustrées de la Révolution de 1848* (Paris: Aux Bureaux de L'Illustration, 1848).

on the contrary, *had the galleries on his side* [...]."[7] Marat was no tyrant, he "tyrannized the tyrants," claimed his Norman admirer, who goes on to question the use of the term "tyranny" to describe what he understood to be true democracy.[8]

In emphasizing, in his February 1848 poster, this issue of the size and role of the galleries in parliamentary deliberation, Hilbey was taking up a subject that had enthused the revolutionaries of 1789 as well as the architects of parliament, and that had resurfaced from time to time since 1789. Emmanuel Joseph Siéyès had established a position in imagining infinite galleries: "The rows of spectators," he wrote, "must extend to all those who are behind, to the entire nation," in order for them "to be true judges of what is going on the center."[9] In practice, this desire to extend the democratic arena outside the walls of parliament depended on the idea of an active press relaying the debates of the National Assembly and instituting a court of public opinion. As for Robespierre, he compared the edification of assembly chambers to that of opera houses, lamenting the fact that the latter are usually built much more quickly than the former.[10] But the fear that the galleries might transform the representatives' benches into a theater stage was the basis of the most recurring criticism.[11]

Under the Revolution, representatives had already wanted to get rid of them, evoking the example of galleries where "no mark of approval or disapproval" was allowed "in the courtroom."[12] During the reconstruction of the Palais Bourbon, following the degradation of the Hall known as "of the Five Hundred" at the end of the 1820s, spaces reserved for the public within the precinct of parliament were

7. Ibidem.
8. "Poor orators who were tyrannized by those who did not want to listen to their absurdities and their impostures! Like that, tyranny can be found everywhere!" Ibidem.
9. AN 284 AP5 (Archives nationales), cited in Jean-Philippe Heurtin, *L'Espace public parlementaire. Essai sur les raisons du législateur* (Paris : PUF, 1999), 48.
10. Heurtin, 110.
11. Ibid., 119–23.
12. Archives parlementaires, 1ère série, vol. 26, cited in Ibid., 120.

criticized for arousing passions and emotions to the detriment of reason. There was outrage over the transformation of representatives of the people and elected officials of the nation into vulgar stage actors, forced to please the audience and to seek to produce an *effect* rather than to deliberate with serenity. There was complaint of applause and booing that risked inhibiting orators, and of a twisting of the nature of debates and the exercise of judgement. This is why the ban on applause in the tribunes has been a constant in French parliamentary regulation since 1790. And this is why Hilbey's proposal carried with it a hint of scandal.

The other cause of this scandal came from the promotion of clubs, which came, in contrast, from numerous other voices during the revolutionary flareup of 1848. Their number, in Paris, between February and June 1848, is estimated at around 450, including the Club de la Montagne de 1848, for whom Hilbey was an important figure. He feared that their number be reduced or that they be banned, as was the case for the Parisian sections of the *sans-culottes* in 1795. The audience of the galleries of the parliamentary assembly was therefore not a mere abstraction: it was made up, precisely, of members of clubs, who were used to deliberating and exercising their judgement. And the political architecture of the republic that he called for and desired was even more complex than that of the National Assembly. It was, first and foremost, to be a space in which the established distribution of roles in society could be questioned, where workers could also become poets, and where poets, ministers, and elected officials of the nation were more often than not traitors or corrupt.[13] And second, it was to take on an unstable, fragmented form thanks to which representatives obviously no longer occupy neither the main role,

13. "Tailor, stand still!": Hilbey retained this impression that profoundly hurt him in the response that Lamartine had given with respect to his writing, accompanied by an admirative letter, when he arrived in Paris. In Constant Hilbey, *Vénalité des journaux. Révélations accompagnées de preuves* (Paris, 1845), 22. On the centrality and primordial nature of the issue of the distribution of places (i. e. social positions) in some of the discourses of workers, see Jacques Rancière, *La Nuit des prolétaires* (Paris: Fayard, 1983).

nor the advantage that notoriety is supposed to confer on them, and where parliamentary galleries are now in fact spread out throughout society and become genuine scenes of democracy.

With his revolutionary exhortations, his apology of clubs and of direct participation and his plan for the architectural reform of the National Assembly, Hilbey's poster did not have much success. It was quickly torn off and burned in the streets of Paris. Its author and printer were pursued and physically threatened. This was not the first time the worker-poet had been in danger; he was used to scandals and trials. In three years, he amassed several convictions for his placards and brochures deemed defamatory or seditious. He made of these trials what must be called, yet again, public *tribunes* for the ironic denouncing of the incoherencies of the justice system and the unfairness of power, often by publishing a *verbatim* along with his own comments. It was therefore not by chance that, during one of these trials, the president of the court accused him of seeking the approval of the public and of stirring up emotion.

Hilbey had become a specialist at denouncing institutions. One of his brochures questioned the venality of the press at the time, reporting on the sums that the author had had to pay to journalists and newspaper owners in order to obtain a positive critique of a play he had put on, or of a collection of poems he had published. Another text tells how the director of the Théâtre royal de l'Odéon had asked him as naturally as anything for a sum of money in order to put on one of his comedies.[14] Hilbey then took on the role of an avenger, revealing hidden facts to the masses regarding the powerful, and demonstrating a certain degree of truth-seeking courage. But behind these revelations as to the corruption of the organs of public opinion or of cultural institutions, and as to the sense of impunity among the elite, Hilbey targeted, above all, the deeply fundamental lie that

14. Constant Hilbey, *La Manière de faire recevoir une pièce au Théâtre royal de l'Odéon* (Paris: Chez Lehougais Libraire, 1845).

Ignace-François Bonhommé, *15 mai 1848, envahissement de l'Assemblée* (May 15, 1848, invasion of the National Assembly), lithograph, Paris, Musée Carnavalet

instruments of representation are doomed to incarnate. Politics is no exception.

Although it had been destroyed a few months earlier, might the call that Hilbey had plastered have been heard when, on May 15, 1848, the crowed invaded the session chamber of a parliamentary precinct? In any case, it contributed to the spirit of the times; ideas similar to his circulated among the Parisian masses and among those belonging to clubs. Victor Hugo describes the scene of this famously insurrectional day as follows:

> "The invasion of the 15th of May was a curious sight. Let the reader picture the confusion in the Senate. Swarms of ragged individuals descending, or rather streaming, down the pillars of the lower tribunes, and even of the upper ones, into the hall, the thousands of flags waving in all directions; the women frightened, and supplicating; the rioters perched in the reporters' gallery; the crowded corridors; heads, shoulders, howling mouths, extended arms, clinched hands, everywhere; no one speaking, everybody yelling; the representatives motionless; and this going on for three hours! The president's desk, the secretary's platform, the tribune, had disappeared, and were nothing but a heap of men. Men were seated on the back of the president's chair astride on the brass griffins, standing on the secretary's table, on the short-hand writers' desks, on the double staircase, on the velvet of the tribunes."[15]

The episode made a lasting impression. It was the crystallization of the confrontation between the two republican programs that faced off during these months of 1848. It also marked the end of the idea of clubs as purveyors of popular sovereignty in competition with the elected constituent assembly, or even as replacements for it.[16] Indeed, in the

15. Victor Hugo, *Things seen*, trans. Tom Taylor (Boston: Estes and Lauriat), 209–10.
16. Samuel Hayat, "Participation, discussion et représentation: l'expérience clubiste de 1848," *Participations* 3, no. 2 (2012): 119–40.

wake of the demonstration, the leaders of the clubs were imprisoned, half the clubs were shut down, and the activity of political groups was regulated. In June, a few weeks after the invasion of the Palais Bourbon, the revolutionary crowd was massacred in the streets of Paris. But the Parisian scene of May 15, 1848—reminiscent of other more recent events coming from another place on the ideological spectrum, for example the assault on the Capitol in Washington D.C. by supporters of Donald Trump on January 6, 2021—reminds us that parliamentary assemblies can be invaded and *are* invaded by the people, and even more so, perhaps, since galleries are narrow and regulated, and since the assembly of elected officials of the nation is uncontested by other assemblies.

Even if his ideas have been condemned, the working-class tailor and poet from Normandy was not the most enraged of the ultra-republicans; he remained skeptical with regard to the socialists. He emigrated to Switzerland and took distance from the Paris Commune. We know much less about what he did under the Second Empire, with the exception of a long poem on the French Revolution. His name has been lost in history. But his poster still speaks; it established links between revolutions, those of the past, of the present, and those to come, through a thoughtful consideration of the material design of assemblies. It allowed us to see and to imagine a society of assemblies, in which elected representatives would remain subject to citizens and to their deliberations. And finally, it treated the form of these arenas as a highly recalcitrant core, and as the most inacceptable part of democratic power: this "most important point, and for that reason, the one that they will attempt not to grant you," as the ephemeral poster announced in February 1848.

Charlotte Malterre-Barthes
& Markus Miessen

New Sites for Assembly

In conversation
with Anne Davidian

Anne Davidian: "Each era has its spatial definition, a system of geometrical references in which a society fulfills itself," wrote architect Claude Parent and philosopher Paul Virilio in 1968.[1] This primary geometric substratum determines the social relations of a society. It would be interesting to think about a spatial definition of our age (or lack thereof), and how these original structures translate into the staging of one of the most versatile forms of political sociality—an assembly. But let's start with a slightly more general question: what can spatial organization, architecture, and design provide for convening and bringing people together? How can they enhance, or, on the contrary, hinder debate and collective decision-making?

Charlotte Malterre-Barthes: I would refer to Michel Foucault's interview with Paul Rabinow in 1984, in which he was asked about how "useful" design and space were, and responded that architecture can "resolve social problems and does produce positive effects, *when* the liberating intentions of the architect coincide with the real practice of people in the exercise of their freedom."[2] Grounded in Foucault's theories of power, this definition speaks of the possibilities that designed spaces can hold for benevolent action—that is, if some form of power is handed over to the people. This is not a default state, as many designed spaces serve quite the opposite function—they are in fact designed to oppress, to eliminate freedom. I would tie this to the conditionalities of influence: where citizens can voice and affect political processes and outcomes, and where empowering spatial programs take place. Their capacity to enact those things (and their efficiency in doing so) will depend on different

1. Claude Parent and Paul Virilio, "Architecture principe," *L'Architecture d'aujourd'hui*, no. 139 (September 1968): 75–80; our translation.
2. Michel Foucault, *Space, Knowledge, and Power (Interview with Paul Rabinow)*, *Skyline*, March 1982, trans. Christian Hubert, in *Architecture Theory since 1968, Columbia Books of Architecture*, ed. K. Michael Hays (Cambridge, MA: MIT Press, 2015), 451; emphasis not in text.

factors—including their territorial organization, social relevance, and architectural design. Take the example of public swimming pools. These are potentially empowering spaces, because swimming is a social marker that touches upon questions of gender, religion, income, and race. Programmatically, it provides vital skills and certain key experiences or senses vital for generating a sense of freedom (via sport, or body acceptance). Territorially, the location of the pool will both determine and reveal a great deal about whether it aligns with certain discriminatory policies or not—how accessible is the pool by public transport, is it well maintained, is it well managed? Its physical and infrastructural condition will reflect the kind of budgeting and care of which it is either afforded or deprived. In short, I wonder if it can ever be left solely to design to promote community and collective life, to "resolve social problems (or) produce positive effects."

Markus Miessen: Whether deliberately designed or not, any spatial setting creates a framework in which *Handlung*, a spatially-choreographed plot, can take place. If we think about the specifics of assembly, or convening, the spatial setting creates the fundamental backdrop that provides the conditions under which we are able to talk to one another. Chantal Mouffe's concept of agonistic pluralism—emphasizing the potential assets of non-violent forms of conflict—is relevant and interesting, but it must also take into consideration that even social interaction, which presents the most rudimentary form of political confrontation, never takes place in a vacuum, but rather in a space—physical or virtual—which is exposed to, or ruled by, spatial or legal constraints and forms of power distribution. It starts with the ways in which we position ourselves vis-a-vis one another whenever we enter a room.

Adolphus Pepper, *La Salle des séance en 1893* (Plenary hall of the Palais Bourbon), 1893, gelatin-silver print, Paris, Musée Carnavalet

Jacques Gondoin, *Description des écoles de chirurgie* (Description of the schools of surgery), pl. XXIX (Paris: Cellot et Jombert, 1780)

Anne Davidian: A circle, a semi-circle, a square that delimits a space ... What are the elementary forms of architectural vocabulary that design a place of assembly?

Charlotte Malterre-Barthes: One of the physical design components I would argue is exemplary here is the covering. The Marseille Canopy by Forster Partners, or the Metropol Parasol by Jürgen Mayer H. in Sevilla, are spaces of assembly—they are political spaces of sorts which enable people to find each other, and which group everyone literally under a roof; a roof that delimitates a space, and unites people by protecting them from rain and shine.

Markus Miessen: For me, the default form and format of seating in the context of spatial forms of assembly is the bench. A bench provides basic seating, and it can be placed in different layout formations assuming certain spatial oppositional rhetoric, even before a conversation has started. Depending on the space itself, a particular form of the bench may lend itself in a more productive way to creating a particular effect or affect of conversational politics.

Anne Davidian: Could you say a little more about these devices and positions that allow bodies to engage in the acts of assembling, speaking together, and listening? How are the separations staged, for example, between the spectators and actors, between those who speak and those who listen?

Markus Miessen: It depends whether one focuses on state power—as opposed to more general, more public or private forms of assembly. Of course, when we investigate different parliamentary systems, we find that there is a wide range of spatial layouts which were originally designed to facilitate debate at state level. Interestingly, the design of most parliamentary chambers across geographies is based on a stratification between speaker and audience, or between the speaker and the governing party. There are only very few exceptions globally. The two examples that really stand out are the British House of Commons and the British House of Lords. Not because of what they represent politically, but because of how they have used architecture and design as tools to shape conversations and political structures. Both chambers' curatorial and choreographic approaches are based on the concept of proximity—and therefore of confrontation—as well as the introduction of a central and physical core of the debate, a symbolic bonfire so to speak.

It is hard to find seating arrangements in which bodies are juxtaposed against one another, and in which the arrangement is not already always hierarchical, because depending on the size of the assembly, there are only very few formats that prohibit the introduction of hierarchy. This is the case for example with a number of citizens› assemblies, including Dewaniya in Kuwait. The circle of course is the most inclusive format, but is very limited both in terms of the number

Joseph Grima and Markus Miessen, *Dewaniya*, Kuwait, 2010
A project in collaboration with Zahra Ali Baba, commissioned by Harvard Graduate School of Design, exhibited at Harvard University, Cambridge, United States, and Storefront for Art and Architecture, New York City, United States.

of participants, and also in terms of what I would call a "brutal transparency"—in which participants are directly and consistently exposed. Many people prefer to not always be visible, to avoid sitting in the first row. This needs to be taken into consideration as well.

Anne Davidian: And what about the places of assembly across geographies that emerged independently of the State? Do they manage to challenge those hierarchies and to establish a space which could favor more egalitarian deliberation—oftentimes with a smaller community involved? Is the change of scale to one in which everyone seems to be within reach and visible important to you?

Markus Miessen: One interesting historical example for me is the concept and realization of the so-called Dewaniya, that I mentioned earlier, a form of assembly that originally stems from Kuwait. As a result of nomadic culture, the rare phenomena of crossroads were historically used to set up camp, creating a temporary space of exchange. This spatial-societal concept has survived throughout the process of urbanization, and today presents a contemporary architectural typology, which—depending on its urban context—can assume different levels of physical address, ranging from the very informal address of a street corner space, to a super-formal, purpose-built structure attached to the private house of an affluent family. However, the societal function always remains the same: it constitutes a form of democratic expression within a deeply rooted cultural tradition. The Dewaniya is a simple, four-sided room, with seating on each side, in which regular meetings are held. Historically, Dewaniya was exclusively for men, but today mixed gender Dewaniya and women-only Dewaniya also exist. There are thousands of those spaces across Kuwait City.

I have been working on a research fellowship at Harvard Graduate School of Design on this topic, together with Joseph Grima, since 2010. We discovered that Dewaniya is both a real thing and a metaphor; it is an architectural typology that embodies a precise historical role in defining a nation's political identity. Although they are considered an oppositional space, as in a parallel reality to the formal state-parliamentary system of Kuwait, these Dewaniya directly inform the upper levels of formal-political decision-making. These spaces are officially recognized, and are often visited by formal representatives of the parliament who come to inform themselves of political and social matters concerning particular geographies and sections of Kuwait City.

Landsgemeinde (canton assembly), Glarus, Switzerland, 2006

Charlotte Malterre-Barthes: Following on from that point, I would say that the design of places of assembly will always differ, as cultures do, but that common features tend to emerge, such as in religious spaces for instance, which are both spaces of power and of assembly, i.e., a speaker on a slightly higher ground, and an audience—some of whom have carpets to sit on while others have benches. Whatever the case, the forms of hierarchy at play will tend to reflect the power structures of that particular religion. So at times, the spatial organization of the assembly mirrors social structures.

In the Canton of Appenzell in Switzerland, for instance, the city's central square becomes a public space for the local public assembly, the *Landsgemeinde*. However, the so-called transparent, democratic premise of these open-air votings could also be understood as a kind of fraud. Who gets to vote? Appenzel was the last Canton to have given the rights to vote to women in 1991, and was forced by federal law, as the Canton argued it had the strongest form of democracy. The voting matter was first discussed "collegially" at home with the whole family, with the man casting the vote being considered the ambassador of that decision in the name of all other family members, including the women. It's a dated, patriarchal, and sexist argument that thankfully did not hold. Additionally, the visible voting system is in some ways also a form of social control, as it exposes the voter, and thereby indirectly coerces them into showing forms of allegiance and support for passing laws they might not agree with, but to which they might feel they have no alternative or choice in resisting. So I think it's dangerous to romanticize these so-called "direct democracies."

Anne Davidian: Through the ages, assemblies have embodied the ideas of popular sovereignty and democratic equality. But how precisely can we characterize a democratic space?

Charlotte Malterre-Barthes: I use the term "spaces of agency" to discuss these physical spaces in which a group or an entity (e.g., the State) either tolerates or has granted a certain amount of freedom to another group (e.g., the public)—and in which activities empowering that group are practiced—as the materialized version of a "political space." Typically, a library is a space with agency: a space programmed to educate, to hold, and to transmit knowledge. Perhaps, as with The Seattle Public Library or the Centro Cultural São Paulo (CCSP), there is an additional complexity that enhances the functions of the building through spatial solutions. The CCSP was designed by architects Luiz de Castro Telles and Eurico Prado Lopes, while Brazil was still under a dictatorship regime. Hence the building stands as a political gesture, a space for peace and coexistence. It occupies a difficult plot, a leftover created by the metro construction, a thin long strip next to the highway. Yet it is very accessible, right next to a subway station, with an open area that remains open at night, even when the cultural spaces are closed. A 500 meter-long structure over three or four levels, it has covered open spaces, a roof garden, and public restrooms, with a public interior street and bridges that connect all programmatic spaces (the canteen, showrooms, library, meeting rooms, study rooms, patio, print shops, workshops) to one another; with all exhibitions free of charge.

Another cultural center, the Rote Fabrik in Zurich, is similarly interesting because it was handed over to the youth of the city who revolted against a massive public funding project for the Opera of the city, which was perceived as a very unjust way of spending taxpayers money, a wealthy-pleasing choice to splash on a conservative bourgeois institution. After a series of protests and occupations resulting in violent repression from the police in May 1980, known as the Opera House Riots, the city repurposed this ancient factory into a cultural center, as a gesture of appeasement—but it was a victory following a long period of demonstrations and street fights.

It could also be that a space of agency lasts only for a brief moment, if and when it enables a major political breakthrough, because of its configuration, location, and capacity to accommodate revolted masses—as is the case with Tahrir Square in Cairo, or Plaza Baquedano (renamed "Plaza de la Dignidad") in Santiago.

Anne Davidian: Are there, nonetheless, structural commonalities between these different "spaces of agency"?

Charlotte Malterre-Barthes: If you look at these public spaces of agency, the key elements are often centrality, visibility, accessibility, and perhaps sometimes proximity to institutions of power. Public squares with a history of revolt such as Tahrir Square, Gezi Park, the Pearl Roundabout—all of which in their own ways are contested spaces—have a centrality of sorts, what we might call an "aggregating power." All of these examples have been either sanitized or demolished, which means that those in power are fully aware of how potent these spaces were. By extension, universities and schools of architecture are an interesting example of spaces with political agency, and the relocation of many to outward campuses after the 1960s also clearly evidences the authorities' awareness of their power. This is also one of the reasons why spaces of central government may be exfiltrated, with new capitals built outside of the cities (in Egypt, Indonesia, or Myanmar).

Anne Davidian: We have inherited classical Western forms of assembly with their parliamentary architectures, procedures, and rituals, which were stabilized in the eighteenth and nineteenth centuries. These forms, widely exported to other cultural areas, are still in use today. How do they reflect certain forms of social order, distributions of power, or political cultures? Should they be dismantled, or could they be readapted and transformed? What could be the new sites and ways of assembling that resonate with our contemporary aspirations?

Markus Miessen: The oddity is that there is no normative or logical link between the set-up of parliamentary spaces across the globe, and the political systems or populations that they claim to represent. Of course there are certain typologies of parliaments, such as the more traditional assembly, the half circle, or the class-room-like setting, as pointed out by David Mulder van der Vegt in his brilliant book on Parliaments[3]—but one cannot infer from them the democratic or otherwise practices that are taking place within each respective assembly. The point is that even for a non-democratic or para-autocratic regime, it comes as a great representational and public relations

3. David Mulder van der Vegt, *The Parliament Book* (Amsterdam: XML, 2016).

asset to "own" and inhabit such spaces, which have—historically speaking—held strong connotations with democratic practices. But the reality is that as long as a given space does not perform these democratic values, its spatial setting—at least to a certain extent—is, or becomes, useless. Now what is crucial, at least from my point of view, is to ask how these spaces perform—how do they suggest, or indeed exacerbate, certain democratic and discursive practices? These questions also refer to a spatial and democratic culture, which is why I have been calling it "Cultures of Assembly."

In the City of Esch, which is my home turf as the Chair of Urban Regeneration in Luxembourg, we are just building a small satellite and project space, a gallery of our programme, in the pedestrian area of the city center. Within this space we will also start to host formal political events, such as urban planning commissions, and discursive formats of programming such as what we term an "agonistic monthly." Again, the point is to understand the role proximity plays in the context of political conversation culture, and hence in decision-making.

For me, a new model and site for a parliamentary assembly would have to be a hybrid that consists of three strategic changes, of which only one is spatial. First: a distributed, politically formalized, but socially informal assembly as socio-political thermometer, which would be able to be more discursively inclusive and agile. The decentralized format would be based on a rotational system between a number of designated spaces in different cities and communities. Second: all members of the parliamentary assembly should be called into position via lottery-based, short-term national recruitment. And third: all parliamentary decision-making should be ratified by professional, long-term expert commissions, informing the temporary protagonists.

Charlotte Malterre-Barthes: If you are referring to representative architectures, those intended to host and project power, then their design and use does indeed convey the details of their constitutive hierarchies, but these things also point to one feature of incredible fragility they all bear: they all host almost all of the ruling elites, concentrated in one place, at the same moment. They encapsulate the tensions of our times, and the irreverence in which these spaces are held erupts in physical forms—attacks on sieges of power, wherever they are, are part of a political arsenal. From the Palais Bourbon in Paris in 1848 to the 2021 United States Capitol assault, the pattern is unaltered: discontent is brought before the unwilling eyes of those in power, and often then turns violent and destructive. The building might be the first victim, because in the eyes of those leading the insurgence, the building is not only the seat of the power—it *is* the power. For instance, the modernist siege of Hosni Mubarak's party located on a corner of Tahrir Square was set on fire during the Egyptian Revolution, and later demolished. This is obviously not to equate or equalize the agendas of the different political groups and factions planning and perpetuating these actions—they are of course motivated by entirely different principles. However, put simply—it is precisely because of the power and social structures these buildings represent that the threat of their demise always hangs in the air. They will be dismantled if the power structures they rely on collapse, and new ones will emerge.

This conversation was prepared in collaboration with Hannes Grassegger.

Spaces

Studio Miessen

# of Negotiation

On Site, a community Hub for content production, Gwangju Biennial, South Korea, 2011
Spatial design by Markus Miessen, Ralf Pflugfelder, and Magnus Nilsson
A typological framework, merging parliamentary, sacral and theatrical layouts, generated a certain density of use yielding a sense of programmatic friction.

Backbench, Manifesta 8, Murcia, Spain, 2010
Spatial design by Markus Miessen, Ralf Pflugfelder, and Magnus Nilsson
Based on the layout of the British Parliament, with its spatial and procedural protocols, the Backbench was conceived as an intense discursive forum that both enabled and structured the exchange of ideas.

Discursive Sauna, Artsonje Center, Seoul, Korea, 2014
Commissioned by Sunjung Kim, artwork by Liam Gillick
A micro-site for informal assembly whose scale explores the notion of proximity, tension and unease when it comes to social settings.

An assembly space is not only about its architectural and material manifestations, it is primarily about the people gathering within it. To think of an assembly space as an infrastructure for daily activities turns it into a reliable and recurrent gathering point—like a coffee corner or a newsstand. Why are those typologies relevant as assembly spaces? The system of assembly in those spaces does not operate in an institutional manner, but rather on its capacity to be part of a routine, a societal infrastructure.

Instead of creating a self-referential object, the ambition of the studio is to introduce a micro-platform for localized social life and infrastructure. Our proposal aims to avoid the traps of both formalism and beautification in contemporary public art, as well as the commercial rationalism of publicly-funded architectural projects.

The proposal should be understood as an urban infrastructure, which can be set up in a decentralized manner, like small kiosks or phone-booths, when those structures still existed in public space. Its essential characteristic is embodied by the ability to exist as a multiple, which starts to occupy specific local contexts in order to foster conversational formats in a setting beyond the normative.

The conceptual structure of the project is highly critical of the transformation of public space into a "post-public" category, in which the citizen is replaced by the customer. Our proposal explores the idea of bastardizing the programmatic contents of such privatized, post-public spaces of immaterial labor (examples include open air offices, normative co-working spaces, Wi-Fi zones et al.) with an autonomous forum referencing typological symbols of power in Western architecture—the Roman Senate, the Colosseum, the Victorian operating theater, the (inverted) Panopticon, or the nineteenth-century lecture theater. By hijacking a spatial template that is associated with multiple forms of control, institutional settings, and Western hegemony, we are attempting to corrupt its role and instead serve as a micro-polis, antagonizing the status of public space as a form of private enterprise within the urban context of a cultural institution. The project and space(s) would therefore be mobilized by agonistic practices as a tool for the construction of public space(s) and its associated and yet to be negotiated discourses.

When it comes to the physical design of an assembly space, we believe that *proximity*, both as a physical embodiment of scale and relational distance(s) as well as a condition that needs to be practiced, should be anchored as the core of any assembly-based practice. To expand on the notion of what an assembly space could trigger, the reduction of the distance between people results in a nowadays rare proximity. This proximity blurs the divide between the participants, enabling a discursive program that could benefit from friction as a productive conflictual force. The 360-degree bleachers provide a constant overview and awareness of the participants and activities within the space, enabling a visual and sound proximity, while leaving little room for easy exit-strategies.

In an assembly space, there is usually documentation and communication of what is happening within those spaces—a form of reflection and documentation of the discussions and decision-making, which is taking place within it. Informing and information culture is a task usually done and delivered by the media, taken over by the digital tools and means in the last decade. What would be a way to localize and emphasize the discussions held in a particular space, while also showing the passing of time and voices involved in it? The historic typology of the *Litfaßsäule* (an urban, cylindrical format of an advertising column) is a communication device located in public spaces throughout Germany and Europe. It was created by Ernst Litfaß in 1854 in Berlin, and still today, is part of the city's communication infrastructure for cultural events. Thinking of the lower part of the assembly space as an interface for narratives in a layered manner, allows for a continuous and ever-changing performative chronicle, working like a palimpsest, with no set messages, but rather open-ended for contributions. A protocol for "visual listening." It essentially becomes a local sounding board, both on its outer surface as well as its core.

F. G. Nordmann, *Berlin erste Litfaßsäule* (Berlin's first advertising column), ca. 1855, lithograph

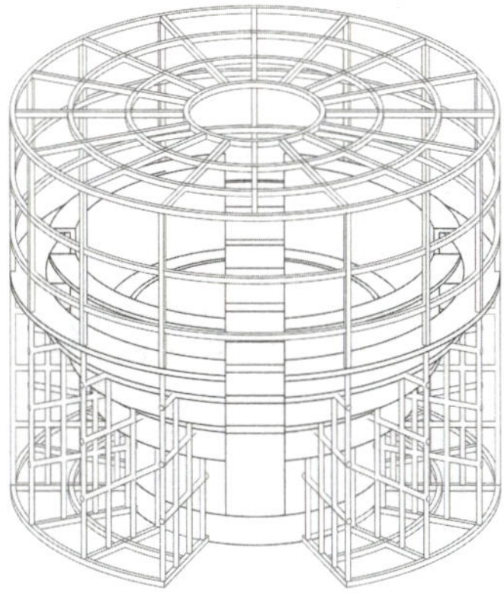

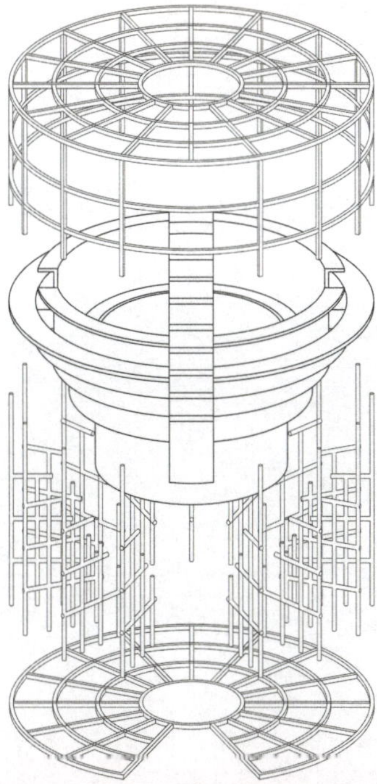

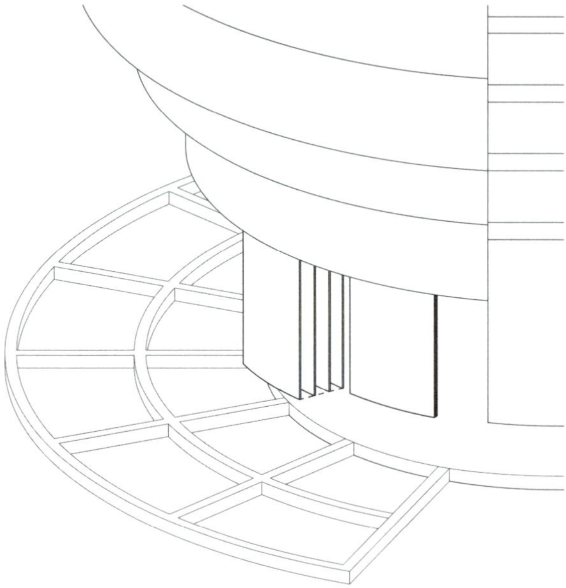

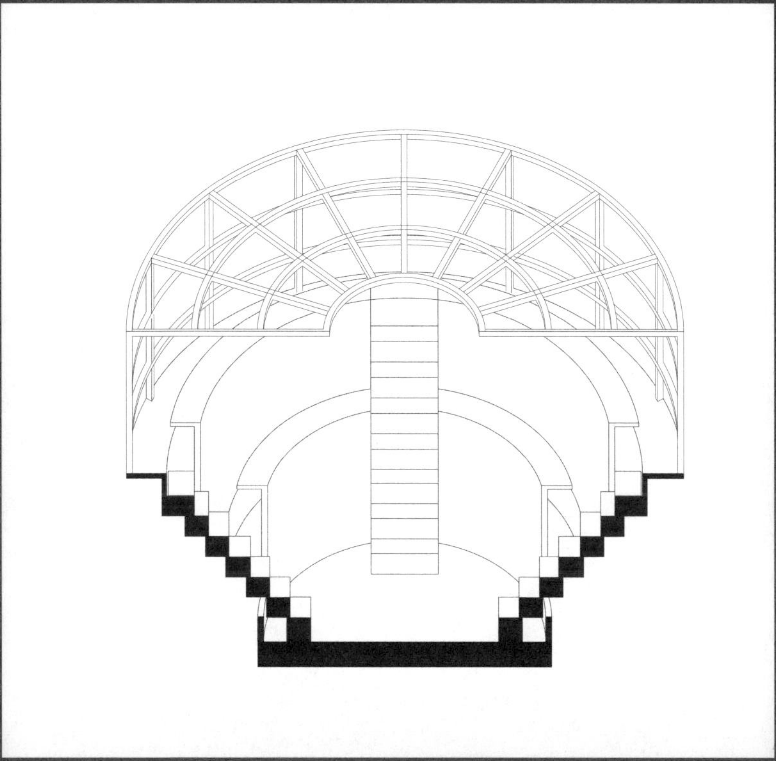

Text by Markus Miessen and Pablo Prado Serrano

Delphine Gardey

The Domestic Economy

of the French Parliament

Popular emotions led to the outbreak of the 1789 Revolution and produced, at least in France, the emergence of an unprecedented space: an assembly that was sovereign and deliberative first and foremost, before seeking to become truly representative. A collective sense of the Parliament as both the condition and central organ of democracy originates from popular fervor, but must ultimately aim to overcome that fervor and to define an "other," newly instituted and robust form of sovereignty if it is to endure. What were the ideal and practical dimensions that governed the production of this "counter-space," this "heterotopia" as Michel Foucault would say?[1] If, given its particularly turbulent nature, we might say that French political history is formed of sound and fury, our central inquiry here is to question the set of legal, material, and social processes required in order for a space as fragile as a parliamentary assembly to both emerge, and to become a durable, long-lasting institution.

A Work in Stone and Paper

Let me stress what it means to assign a building, and a territory, to an ideal. Or, simultaneously, to shape and produce a building and a territory that can host and bring into form a utopia. In the first French revolutionary assemblies, self-proclaimed representatives sat alongside the King; first in Versailles, and then in the Louvre. The transformation of the Estates General, convened by King Louis XVI at Versailles, into the National Constituent Assembly (1789–91) marked the first stage of an uncertain adventure that would falter on numerous occasions. The revolutionary project of bringing to life a deliberative, representative, and sovereign assembly is *utopian*; it is an uncertain project seeking a fragile achievement. The difficulty, then, is in necessarily arresting time, in

1. Foucault's heterotopia can be understood as a practical or physical utopia; as the materialization of another space. See: Michel Foucault, *Le Corps utopique, Les Hétérotopies* (Paris: Lignes, 2019).

inscribing this movement in a political form—a form which is both its expression and its offspring.

Having principles cast in stone is perhaps one of the most effective methods humans have developed for demonstrating what "instituting" actually signifies. Designing a hall, indeed a palace dedicated to the ideals of the Republic, was the mission the National Convention—the second parliamentary assembly, which sat between 1792 and 1795—had assigned to itself, despite wars and political and financial difficulties: "The National Convention felt it consonant with the French Republic's majesty to place its Senate in a vast and sumptuous edifice."[2] During the building's inauguration (which took place under the Directory[3]), the chief architect welcomed the future accomplishment of "this new sanctuary of laws." Soon, he said, "an Areopagus forever celebrated will honor this site with its presence and will make the vaults of the organ of justice ring out."[4] Words do indeed matter. Such design and pronouncement is about establishing a shelter, a protective place (but also a cultic one) for republican ideals. The edifice was erected "to the glory of the French people." Having pronounced these words, the President of the Assembly sealed a lead box containing a bronze plate recalling the decree creating the building[5] and showing its plan, along with two pieces of silver and two medals of the elected representatives. Having made known their "attachment to the Republic," the construction workers were then invited "to preserve that purity of mores that has always distinguished the useful and laborious class of workers." They were finally invited to join their voices with their hearts, singing "touching songs of liberty" and shouting: "Vive la République!"[6] The forms of interchange of qualities between text and buildings were thus multiple and were

2. Parliamentary Archives and Historical Research Department (Service des Archives et de la Recherche Historique Parlementaire, or SARHP), 17AN52: Bâtiments.
3. The Directory was the French political regime from October 26, 1795 to November 9, 1799.
4. SARHP 17AN52: Bâtiments.
5. Ibid.
6. Ibid.

frequently repeated. The ceremony surrounding the podium's foundation stone was intended to magnify the oratorical art, and to enshrine that essential figure of the parliamentarian as a tribune. They were meant to leave their mark in writing; both in stone, and in people's memories.

The Directory's edifice—which was finally inaugurated on January 21, 1799, the anniversary of the King's execution—no longer exists, but the significance of its chosen location was to be long-lasting. In immediate proximity to the Seine and the future Pont de la Concorde, the parliament was housed in an area consisting of two aristocratic palaces: the Hôtel de Bourbon, and the Hôtel de Lassay. Seized as national property during the Revolution, it was returned to the Bourbon dynasty during the Restoration and then eventually bought by the State in 1827. Administrators of the successive chambers had to sustain endless effort from one constitutional regime to the next in order to preserve the parliament's prerogatives on the building.[7] Despite political turbulence, the French MPs tried to produce and preserve a form of continuity: a sort of skeleton of the Chamber's processes that could persist over time, embodied in the buildings, furniture, archives, and committed staff. It is under the more "liberal" July Monarchy (1830–48) that the core architectural features of the Palais Bourbon were designed and consolidated, in particular with the current debating room—which was first rebuilt in 1832 in the form of a semicircle (the "Hemicycle") in order to revive the architectural and moral choices made by former revolutionary assemblies.[8]

The parliamentary order also needed to be invented as a dialogical space.[9] An assembly, by virtue of not being the State but rather a spatial form preserving itself from the power and excesses of the executive, counts as a counter-space.

7. SARHP, 17AN52; 17AN53: Bâtiments.

8. Jean-Philippe Heurtin, *L'Espace parlementaire. Essai sur les raisons du législateur* (Paris: Presses Universitaires de France, 1999).

9. Claire de Galembert, Olivier Rozenberg, and Cécile Vigour, eds., *Faire parler le parlement. Méthodes et enjeux de l'analyse des débats parlementaires pour les sciences sociales* (Paris: Librairie Générale de Droit et Jurisprudence, 2014).

Within even the earliest forms of assemblies, formal measures and procedures were transmitted and compiled. They aimed to define who would initiate the agenda, what the modalities were, who had the right to voice an opinion, how to organize the discussion, and so on. Parliamentary procedure took the form of a (voluminous) law, as encompassed by the publication of *Traités de droit parlementaire*[10] at the end of the nineteenth century—the equivalent of the Standing Orders of the House of Commons. Administrative and legislative jurisprudence were determining and the two were closely intertwined. They had a generative capacity; they could be mobilized in order to execute and perform the last incarnation of the reborn parliament, and to recover previous values and strengths erased by political reaction.[11]

The Right of Police

Structuring and ordering the National Assembly as a comprehensive counter-site also depends on police and military capacities. "Politics" cannot live without "policing." Here we follow Foucault's investigations into the double sense of "police": as a science of the State, or cameralism, and as an instrument of "order keeping."[12] There is no utopia (in this instance the National Assembly) without territory, no consecration of values without material settings. In other words, there is no political body without administration or without police. In order for there to be a Chamber (politics), it is necessary to regulate a space and *create* a territory, and with this a specific administration. Considerable effort was made in the history of the making of the French Parliament to produce and indeed to protect the National Assembly's territory as singular and exceptional by ensuring it remained disembedded from the *commun*; from the State and the city.

10. Eugène Pierre and Jules Poudra, *Traité de droit parlementaire* (Paris: Chambre des Députés, 1902).
11. Delphine Gardey, *Le Linge du Palais Bourbon. Corps, matérialité et genre du politique à l'ère démocratique* (Lormont: Le Bord de l'Eau, 2015).
12. Michel Foucault, *Dits et écrits. Vol. IV* (Paris: Gallimard, 1994).

Emanating from revolutionary assemblies, the right to enforcing internal discipline, as ascribed to the President of the Assembly, is the prerequisite for freedom of speech and voting liberties. Coextensive with the right to police is the right to security. Within the model of republican chambers, the remit of the military forces in charge of the security of the assemblies expires at the doors of the plenary hall, at which point bailiffs take over. Since the French Revolution, assemblies have maintained control over the military forces responsible for their security. They were formed of companies provided by the military but placed under parliamentary command and regularly replaced, to avoid dependence on the executive power. No police force—and much less external any military force—should be allowed to penetrate the ring-fence surrounding the Chamber's territory without authorization from the President. As for the plenary hall, its preservation from any violation or invasion remains an absolute priority. The wearing of swords and the instantiation of military rituals are used to signify that violence is suspended, and that the use of (legitimate) force is submitted to the authority of the Chamber.

The "right of police" is thus a fundamental prerogative that contributes to the parliamentary assemblies' capacity for self-determination. Beyond the policing of the plenary hall, it is in the French case the whole territory of the Palais Bourbon that is regulated. In a sense, one could see nested territories within the territory of the Assembly, organized in concentric circles, from the most profane to the most sacred,[13] the latter being the hall where the members of parliament sit. The law, rules, staff, and practices may vary from the attics of the Palais Bourbon to the corridors, the courtyards and the plenary hall, but none of the spaces that constitute the territory of the Chamber are left exempt from regulations or administrative and police control.

13. Philip Manow, *In the King's Shadow. The Political Anatomy of Democratic Representation* (Cambridge: Polity Press, 2010).

Roger Henrard, *Le Palais Bourbon*, 1957, gelatin-silver print, Paris, Musée Carnavalet

A City within a City

Foucault interrogated the historical and political links between "security," "territory," and "population."[14] Within the French Parliament, a social and a sanitary police was in place in order to delimit and regulate its whole population. Throughout its history, the Palais Bourbon has tended to remain closed off from the outside world. But these long-standing attempts at the enforcement of boundaries were rendered complex by the presence of the families of the various employees, all of whom lived within the space until the mid-twentieth century. As a city within the city, with its garrets housing the domestics of senior officials, lodging gas workers, workhands, and other laborers dedicated to maintaining the outbuildings, the Palais Bourbon appeared

14. Michel Foucault, *Sécurité, territoire, population. Cours au Collège de France, 1977–1978* (Paris: Seuil, 2004).

to be a complex and socially heterogeneous world which needed to be policed. The caretakers hunted down bags of coal abandoned under the stairs, forgotten trash cans, linen hanging in the attics. They kept an eye out for dogs and children whose presence did not chime with the image the institution wished to project. The caretakers were bound by the regulations to return to their parents "the children of all classes" who had either strayed into or were playing in the courtyard.[15]

This vigilant "social police" was supplemented by a form of sanitary regulation, which was particularly vigorous under the Third Republic. With the help of the physician attached to the parliament, the administrators deployed numerous examinations and vaccination campaigns in aid of the population of the Palais Bourbon, so as to preserve the national representatives from noxious air, infection, and epidemics. In the case of an old, confined, and poorly ventilated Hemicycle, the desire for openness to the public (a necessity for those who defend a liberal and then republican conception of parliamentarism) appeared in contradiction with the sanitary protection of the legislative body.[16]

A territory cut off from the city, detached from Paris, socially policed, sanitarily boxed off: the territory of the French Assembly and its palace was insular and clearly marked out. Contrary to the new open territory of economics, which historically characterized the emergence of liberalism and was described by Foucault as fluid, open and interpenetrated, the liberal (then republican) territory of modern politics paradoxically had to be preserved and separated from the vernacular.

When technological networks such as the telephone or electricity appeared, it was a primary concern for the Assembly to oversee their control. A power station was built inside the Palais Bourbon and administrators recruited "their" men (dedicated blue collars or technicians) as

15. SARHP, 17AN52; 17AN69: Sécurité du Palais Bourbon.
16. SARHP, 17AN13: Service médical; 16AN30 to 16AN37: Archives du secrétariat général de la Présidence: Rapports médicaux.

Jules-Louis Breton, *Salle de la buvette* (the Palais Bourbon cafeteria), 1912, gelatin-silver print, Paris, Archives de l'Assemblée Nationale

operators.[17] Meanwhile however, in order to avoid the presence of too many blue-collar workers, especially printing workers known for their class consciousness and their strong union traditions, the Assembly, upon returning from Versailles to Paris in 1879,[18] decided to move to a pneumatic system. Pneumatic technology helped to displace the printing workshop formerly located within the walls of the parliament where proceedings, resolutions, and laws were published.[19] The shorthand office was then directly connected to the national printing house some kilometers away.[20] In this instance a technological system appeared as a solution to preserve the Assembly from potential political and social threats posed by the integrated presence of the working class.

17. SARHP, 16AN107: Usine électrique. The alternative for the Assembly was to connect to the existing secteur rive gauche.
18. In order to flee the revolutionary turmoil of the Paris Commune, the National Assembly took refuge in Versailles in February 1871 and remained there until 1879.
19. SARHP, 16AN62: Impressions. Compte-rendu intégral.
20. SARHP, 17AN10: Sténographie et lignes pneumatiques; 16AN86: Lignes pneumatiques.

Salle de la buvette (the Palais Bourbon cafeteria), ca. 1905, postcard, photomechanical print, Paris, Archives de l'Assemblée Nationale

The Household of French Republican Parliamentarism

The presence of working class bodies, right on the premises of the Palais Bourbon, had to be linked to worker (under)representation within the legislative body. This was a key issue after the Paris Commune and under the Third Republic, in a context of fresh defiance generated by the labor movement and the simultaneously increasing tension with the parliamentary Republic. As a symbol of this defiance, the socialist representative Thivrier (1841–95), a former member of the Commune, attended all parliamentary sessions wearing worker's overalls, worn over his bourgeois costume. Thivrier's ironic cross-dressing[21] was a way to demonstrate the pretense of bourgeois parliamentary order and to address the impossible representation of workers.

If we are to consider here the representation of those who have been historically considered "outsiders" of French

21. First page of *Le Petit Journal*, February 18, 1894.

Eugène Devéria, *Le Roi Louis-Philippe prête serment de maintenir la Charte de 1830* (King Louis-Philippe swearing the oath to keep the Charter of 1830), 1836, oil on canvas, Versailles, Châteaux de Versailles et de Trianon

universalism (the working class, colonial subjects, women), we also need to consider the place that was reserved for them inside the walls of the parliament as audiences, workers, and civil servants. If we are to understand the machinery of the legislative body as a new theater of politics, we have to consider the invisible workers, both male and female, who constituted the parliament itself, as well as the anthropological milieu the newly elected MPs experienced in their daily life.

Let's consider for a moment the question of the long-term exclusion of women from democracy and parliaments.[22] Once they finally became voters and acquired the right to be elected, 33 women entered the French National Assembly for the first time in November 1945. Their stage entrance was discreet, and their subsequent presence remained so. French women remained a minority in the National Assembly, and between 1945 and 1997 never accounted for more than 7% of the elected representatives. The French chambers firmly resisted the feminisation of its body. It was this long-standing imbalance that was at stake in the 2000 movement for parity; a demand for equal representation that has still not been achieved.

The exclusion of women from democracy is one of the core paradoxes at the heart of the definition of universalism that has held since the French Revolution.[23] And throughout the nineteenth century, citizenship as republican institutions were actively produced as masculinist spheres. Strangely, the situation seemed more open in terms of gender issues in parliamentary monarchies.[24] In the aristocracy-dominated representation of the eighteenth century, another gender arrangement prevailed via the presence of the house of the King, women, and children. The influence of the ladies, and

22. Catherine Achin and Delphine Gardey, "Gender and Parliaments," in *Handbook of Parliamentary Studies: Interdisciplinary Approaches to Legislatures*, eds. Cyril Benoît and Olivier Rozenberg (London: Edward Elgard Publishing, 2020).
23. Joan W. Scott, *Only Paradoxes to Offer. French Feminism and the Rights of Man* (Cambridge, MA: Harvard University Press, 1997).
24. Geneviève Fraisse and Michelle Perrot, "Histoire des femmes. Le xixe siècle," in Histoire des femmes en Occident. vol. 4, eds. Georges Duby and Michelle Perrot (Paris: Plon, 1991).

the culture of the Enlightenment salons, was felt both in private and public political spheres.

The republican model operated a radical split between the public and the private sphere, and invented a parliamentary scene that organized a genuine "gender theater." The republican order was based on bourgeois conventions which organized and delimited positions in the political space according to both gender and class. Shaped as it was by private spaces and active demonstrations of masculine sociability (i.e., the fencing hall, the smoking room, the *salons,* and the library), the Palais Bourbon was modeled on dominant bourgeois social uses and behaviors. The architectural arrangement followed the model of the theater, which strongly influenced the architectures of many parliaments. The gender roles assigned within this were clear: the ladies were in the balcony among the general public, whereas the scene of action, speech and discussion were contained within the male spheres. Passiveness and activity, speaking and listening, seeing and being seen were organized along gender lines.

One can see a striking parallel between the strictly masculine world of representation, in all political contexts and regimes, and the strictly masculine world of administrative jobs that held form until the mid-twentieth century. The Palais Bourbon is a male territory: MPs in suits (*costumes*), then in formal wear (*habits*); military men and public servants in uniform (*tenue*); blue collars and caretakers. This was a lasting state of affairs. The laundresses and needlewomen, who maintained the linens and curtains, were the only female workers at the French Parliament from the Revolution to the beginning of the twentieth century.[25] Typically wives or widows of male employees, these women were members of families dedicated to the upkeep, the protocol, and the administration of the Chamber. From the beginning of the nineteenth century through to the 1950s, the Assembly surrounded itself with faithful and reliable personnel:

25. SARHP, 17AN17: Personnels; 16AN88: Lingerie.

domestic employees, civil servants (with a specific status) who were under the Assembly's sole authority and who were part of professional dynasties reaching back several generations, including stenographers for the parliamentary debates, as well as caretakers and bailiffs. The prevention of women working as civil servants was in that respect more vivid in the French Parliament than in any other private or public administration preceding it.

While the first female MPs made their humble appearance in 1945, the Chamber's administrative tasks, and in particular those affording access to the plenary hall, remained closed to them. It took a court trial in 1972[26] for the first women to be given permanent positions as stenographers for debates in the Chamber. Female bailiffs first made an appearance in the Hemicycle in the early 1990s. In France therefore it was not only the republican and democratic institutions that excluded women from voting rights and eligibility for elected political office—both of which were acquired in 1945—but the entire territory of the Palais Bourbon, a territory that had been defined as a masculine space, immune to female penetration.

This arrangement persisted because it was central to the republican parliamentary order and rituals.[27] In other words: in order to exist and persevere, the institution had to adopt conservative precedents. A social and material study of parliament allows us to explore the everyday enactment of the paradoxes of republicanism, as well as how abstractions like the universal masculine became highly effective forces within quotidian activity. Here we move from the material setting to that which underpins them: domestic arrangements. The "material" referred to here encompasses not only cold, inanimate, or technical components (as is often the case in Actor Network Theory and in Bruno

26. Delphine Gardey, "Turning Public Discourse into an Authentic Artefact: Shorthand Transcription in the French National Assembly," in *Making Things Public. Atmospheres of Democracy*, eds. Bruno Latour and Peter Weibel (Cambridge, MA: MIT Press, 2005), 836–43.

27. Emma Crew, "An Anthropology of the House of Lords: Socialization, Relationships and Rituals," *The Journal of Legislative Studies* 16, no. 3 (August 2020): 313–24.

Latour's ontologies[28]), but also includes bodies; their real and symbolical presences as living entities, people of flesh and meaning,[29] sex and gender. As finally constituted, the parliamentary order held something of the order of a household. Have we sufficiently paid attention to the *domestic economy of politics*[30] defining Western democratic institutions?

Focusing on rules, rituals, and symbolic dimensions of parliamentary cultures, in addition to technological and material settings, is vital to considerations of the anthropological tissue that constitutes parliamentary orders, and to questioning what counts as "modern" in the definition of parliamentary democracies. It assists with addressing the question of how the "invention of tradition" occurs, as well as how parliamentary institutional culture processes both political continuity and institutional change. It renders visible the theoretical and political questions of representation as being both descriptive *and* substantive. It makes explicit that the legislative body, even when aligned with "universal" and "republican" absolutes, has been conceived and reiterated as a conservative, inhospitable ideal and concrete territory. Would it not be time to trouble that legacy, and to stake a claim for more hospitable parliaments?

28. Delphine Gardey, "Bruno Latour: Guerre et Paix, tours et détours féministes," in *Sous les sciences sociales, le genre. Relectures critiques de Max Weber à Michel Foucault*, eds. Danielle Chabaud-Rychter, Virginie Descoutures, Eleni Varikas, and Anne-Marie Devreux (Paris: La Découverte, 2010), 203–18.
29. Donna Haraway, "Modest Witness: Feminist Diffractions in Science Studies," in *Modest_Witness@Second_Millennium. FemaleMan©_Meets_On coMouse™* (New York: Routledge, 1997).
30. Christine Delphy, *The Main Enemy: A Materialist Analysis of Women's Oppression* (London: Women's Research and Resources Center, 1977).

François Antoine Vizzavona, *Une séance à la Chambre des députés by René Rousseau-Decelle* (A session in the National Assembly), 1907, postcard, photomechanical print, Paris, Bibliothèque Historique de la Ville de Paris

re des Députés, par René Rousseau-Decelle
VILLE DE PARIS
ND. Phot

Tallulah Frappier

Civic Technologies:

Reshaping the Public Space

Speaking or writing of political assemblies tends to evoke the action of people gathering to deliberate, or the spaces in which this deliberation might take place. One thing that is often overlooked, however, is the fact that these spaces can be digital. Online assemblies have become more widespread in recent years; from the first Web forums, to civic technologies specifically designed to host collective political debates. As digital services affect our possibilities for political mobilization and participation, I will here attempt to define the qualities specific to online assemblies, and to identify several patterns and continuities in the design features of civic technologies offering online spaces for debate.

The Spread of Online Assemblies

Since the creation of the internet, digital spaces have been considered to be fruitful grounds for the creation of assemblies. In 1962, Doug Engelbart, then the director of Stanford's Augmentation Research Center, presented several uses for the computer. This demonstration, subsequently named "The Mother of All Demos,"[1] insisted on the possibility of computers becoming tools for collaboration and enhancing collective intelligence. Digital pioneers often held the belief that technology would help them change society without needing to acquiesce to existing power structures, or to devise and enforce new ones. As digital pioneer John Perry Barlow stated in his 1996 "Declaration of the Independence of Cyberspace": "We are creating a world where anyone, anywhere, may express his or her beliefs, no matter how singular, without fear of being coerced into silence or conformity."[2] If these claims seem a little simplistic or indeed even naive today, they also help us to understand how digital tools have long-since been both imbued

1. Doug Engelbart, presentation at the Fall Joint Computer Conference on December 9, 1968, San Francisco. See: https://www.dougengelbart.org/content/view/374/464/#2.
2. John Perry Barlow, "A Declaration of the Independence of Cyberspace," February 8, 1996, https://www.eff.org/cyberspace-independence.

with and invested in the capacity to create new vehicles for collectively discussing ideas.

In 1985, *The Well*, one of the first and most famous online communities, was created. It was hosted by a specific form of discussion site: the internet forum. Originally inspired by bulletin boards, these sites differ from discussion chats as their structure is asynchronous. Forums spread online under slight variations, enabling individuals and communities to gather around particular topics. I decided here to identify them as assembly spaces due to the nature of their user-audience, their component functions, and their architecture. In simple terms, these sites aim to gather a large group of people together in order to discuss specific topics, within dedicated areas. Sometimes these discussions also result in a voting process, in which pre-posted messages can be voted on by other users, then ranked to reorganize content so the most "relevant" messages (as determined by this voting) appear first.

The central argument of "A Declaration of the Independence of the Cyberspace"—that the internet enables the creation of an alternative space that cannot be governed by any outside force—has been rapidly eroding since the late 1980s. Through observing increasing interferences in the internet ecosystem led by both the state and corporations alike, digital activists have grasped the intertwining of cyberspace with civil society, leading them to instead invest their time and energy in fields such as education, or political representation.[3] Creating alternative, liberated democratic spaces on the internet was never going to be possible if the existing order of the offline world was not also simultaneously changed. Therefore the goal of digital activism is currently more closely focused on creating ways to complete, fix, or challenge an overall political macrocosm. It is with this aim in mind that "civic technologies" have emerged. This term embraces various kinds of initiatives

3. Nicolas Auray and Samira Ouardi, "Numérique et émancipation. De la politique du code au renouvellement des élites," *Mouvements*, vol. 79, no. 3 (2014): 13–27.

that use digital resources to change political rules, or to intensify political engagement.[4] They attest to an increasing crisis of confidence in representative democracy, and revolve around the place of digital technologies—both in institutions and counter-power organizations. Academic and non-academic literature has referred to civic technologies from both government-centric and citizen-centric perspectives.[5] When civic technologies are government-centric, they "enable top-down change through the promotion of government transparency, accessibility of government data and services and promotion of civic involvement in the democratic process,"[6] and they can also be described as citizen-centric; as "platforms and applications that enable citizens to connect and collaborate with each other and/or with the government."[7] Online collective deliberation therefore constitutes a significant challenge in government-centric and citizen-centric initiatives, and many civic technologies offer services for people to debate together about specific issues, whether in public or in private contexts.

However, these technologies' purpose is not to promote specific democratic subjects, but to intensify democracy through their functionalities. They induce a procedural vision of politics in which good procedures allow for good democracy, driven by the central question: "How do we make democracy work?" Examining the structure of these online assemblies is therefore fundamental to understanding the democratic conceptions they have come to materialize.

4. Dominique Cardon, *Culture numérique* (Paris: Presses de Sciences Po, 2019), 277.
5. Jorge Saldivar, et al., "Civic Technology for Social Innovation," *Computer Supported Cooperative Work* 28, no. 1 (2019): 169–207.
6. The Knight Foundation, *The Emergence of Civic Tech: Investments in a Growing Field*, February 26, 2014, https://knightfoundation.org.
7. Manik Suri, "From Crowd-sourcing Potholes to Community Policing: Applying Interoperability Theory to Analyze the Expansion of 'Open311'," *Berkman Center Research Publication* 2013, no. 18 (August 2013): 1.

Online, every moment of action and interaction is authorized and delimited by technical resources. This phenomenon led Lawrence Lessig to famously state that "Code is Law,"[8] arguing that architecture—taken here to mean the physical traits and qualities of any given space—is the primary source of regulatory principles online. This assertion has since been qualified,[9] but it remains the case that technical choices and determinant necessities online can drastically affect the "canonical" shape of the assembly and of one of its intrinsic social practices: deliberation.

If we return for a moment to the notion of the "forum"—its name, as is well known, directly evokes the Latin *forum*, a public place for commercial and political exchanges. However the term itself is more likely drawn from the conception of the traditional public forum in the United States Constitutional Law, in which a "forum" is understood to be a public place dedicated to assemblies and debate. It's interesting to note that, while being differentiated from the synchronous chat, the forum has drawn its name from a space reliant on a common temporality. The most significant aspect of the forum highlighted online is therefore its spatial quality, its interlinking functions as they evoke another term: "synchorization." Synchorization is the spatial counterpart of synchronization, and has been described by Boris Beaude as a "process consisting in having a common place for being and doing,"[10] that allows people to interact.

This asynchronous aspect of the assembly induces a drastic change of the traditional conception of debate. Debating is no longer a purely back-and-forth, responsive

8. Lawrence Lessig, *Code and Other Laws of Cyberspace* (New York: Basic Books, 1999)
9. Françoise Massit-Folléa, Cécile Méadel, and Laurence Monnoyer-Smith, eds., *Normative Experiences in Internet Politics* (Paris: Presses des Mines, 2012).
10. Boris Beaude, *Internet: changer l'espace, changer la société* (Paris: Éditions FYP, 2012).

practice. Online, one has to wait to read a counter-argument. The online forum debate is constructed over a long period of time—over days, weeks, or even years. This time dilation can function as a mechanism encouraging constructive dialogue, but it can also make communication harder.[11] Helpful protocols and procedures like speaking turns or time management no longer hold relevance, as everyone can express themselves at any time. If a selection of content has to be made it happens after debate, and is qualitatively assessed according to questions like: "Is it relevant to the subject?" or: "Has it already been articulated?" Moderation, however, can take place either before or after the publication of a post—whether this is channeled through the decision of an administrator, or through reports from the community.

Synchorization is therefore enabled by online representation—you cannot be "physically" online, but rather you are represented by avatars, names, visualizations, and the words you write. Deliberation is no longer about speech, but about written practice. To analyze parliamentary assemblies' architectures, French political scientist Jean-Philippe Heurtin highlighted the fact that the multiple verbal and nonverbal interactions that take place between points of views, bodies, and facial expressions have shaped the course of interpersonal debate.[12] Online, the interactions of these key elements disappear. One could perhaps argue that this change is for the best: it could help debate to become more rational, and redirect the focus on the content of the argumentation itself. Sometimes, it can even lead to "benign disinhibition,"[13] where people are more inclined to be kind to people they can't physically see. But it can also complicate the identification of a common

11. Amanda Baughan, et al., "Someone Is Wrong on the Internet: Having Hard Conversations in Online Spaces," *Proceedings of the ACM on Human-Computer Interaction* 5, no. CSCW1 (April 2021): 1–22.

12. Jean-Philippe Heurtin, *L'Espace public parlementaire: essai sur les raisons du législateur* (Paris: Presses Universitaires de France, 1999).

13. John Suler, "The Online Disinhibition Effect," *Cyberpsychology & Behavior: The Impact of the Internet, Multimedia and Virtual Reality on Behavior and Society* 7, no. 3 (July 2004): 321–26.

ground,[14] and boost cyberbullying,[15] trolling,[16] and incivility.[17] Heurtin also evoked a "theater of glances" in order to describe amphitheater-shaped assemblies as glance-organizing machines that frontally oppose the spectator and the one speaking. Online assemblies constitute an opposite model. Within an online debate, internauts are deprived of any specific points of view, as they all see the same interface. It's only when they submit a form of writing (or act through voting) that they identify themselves as being involved in a debate. Beyond these particular forms of action, they can stay "pure spectators,"[18] which is to say, should they wish to, they can remain fully disengaged.

Heurtin also described an absence of endodeterminism within parliamentary space: the universal audience is outside of the assembly, and people who debate have to "talk to the windows." Online, the universal audience is potentially within the assembly, but we still have to talk to it through windows, albeit browser windows. Online assemblies are not closed spaces. Their openness is underlined by their structure of hyperlinks. Discourses might also consist of the aggregation of copy-paste texts, and almost every issue can be shared on other platforms and communities thanks to dedicated icons.

These assemblies also showcase their assemblage nature. Each space is a knot of technical layers, of diverse functionalities, of people, organizations, links, topics, sources, etc. As for the debate itself, since it is asynchronous, everyone

14. Maciek Lipinski-Harten and Romin W. Tafarodi, "Attitude Moderation: A Comparison of Online Chat and Face-to-face Conversation," *Computers in Human Behavior* 29, no. 6 (2013): 2490–93.
15. Hinduja, Sameer, and Justin W. Patchin. "Cyberbullying: An exploratory analysis of factors related to offending and victimization," *Deviant behavior* 29.2 (2008): 129–56.
16. Justin Cheng, et al., "Anyone Can Become a Troll: Causes of Trolling Behavior in Online Discussions," *Proceedings of the 2017 ACM Conference on Computer Supported Cooperative Work and Social Computing* (February 2017): 1217–30
17. Porismita Borah, "Does It Matter Where You Read the News Story? Interaction of Incivility and News Frames in the Political Blogosphere," *Communication Research* 41, no. 6 (2014): 809–27.
18. Jean-Philippe Heurtin, "Architectures morales de l'Assemblée Nationale," *Politix* 7, no. 26 (1994): 109–40.

participating is already immersed within a completely different physical background, with varying affects on each user. As time goes by, debate winds into an increasingly tight knot of circumstances—one person will read a part of the debate, but never all of it, and will never be connected to another user at a specific time without ever reading the following argument. The act of deliberation is therefore obviously intertwined with outside places and moments.

		OFFLINE ASSEMBLIES	ONLINE ASSEMBLIES
WHERE	Place	Local	Distributed
	Synchronicity	Synchrone	Asynchrone
WHEN	Time continuum	Time density	Time dilation
WHO	Scale	A sample of people	Virtually everybody
HOW	Type of practice	Speech practice	Written practice
	Point of view	Specific	Not specific
	Representation	Bodies	Images
	Identify as an actor	By being in the assembly	By acting in the assembly

Comparative table of online and offline assemblies

As I touched on earlier, these "civic technologies" gather together various kinds of initiatives that use digital resources to change political rules, or to intensify political engagement. Directories of civic technologies can be found online and can help users identify which civic tools are proposing online assemblies as services.[19] Analyzing their interfaces can also help determine patterns in their designs. Though they all include debate features, these technologies are diverse. Some can be used in a specific timeline and with a specific community, instantiated by public or private authority (Assembl, Consul, Decidim)—while others are accessible to all and are not meant to deliver results to any particular sponsor (DebateArt, DebateIsland, or Communecter). This could indicate that we will face a wide range of debate features' designs.

First, the online forum appears to be a blueprint for their debate tools, presenting as they do the same core characteristics: they are asynchronous; they are organized in threads, posts and comments; and they present the same specificities that bear the potential to overturn the necessary conditions for deliberation.

Each of these selected debate interfaces follow roughly the same pattern of display. The top of the page is framed by an area dedicated to the topic containing a title, a small blurb, and sometimes a visual accompaniment. This is followed by an interactive space, offering users the option to vote either "for" or "against" the topic at hand, and typically displaying a running percentage of votes so far received. Sometimes this is just a posting area, with space to elaborate a small commentary on whether the user is for or against the topic, which might result in deliberation being part of a voting process. The lower part of the interface displays the deliberative space and its arguments. This conception seems

19. See: https://civictech.guide; http://civictechno.fr/civic-theque; and *Démocratie ouverte*, which gathers "democratic innovators," https://www.democratieouverte.org.

somewhat counterintuitive when considered in comparison to typical processes of deliberation, in which voting takes place *after* a process of deliberation. Moreover, as the voting results are most of the time displayed, you see them even before reading the very core of the topic.

However, some of these platforms do not follow this form, such as DebateArt, or debate.org. Similar in form to some of the aforementioned oldest forms of cyberspace activism, these sites aim to actively foster deliberation between people, and are not linked to any institutional decision-making process. Each topic leads to two people arguing on opposing sides, and passes through several rounds. External users can then comment and vote for particular arguments, before a "winner" is finally declared.

Within other interfaces, placing the voting process ahead of the deliberation space seems strange: why debate if your decision has already been made? These interfaces demonstrate multiple voting functionalities—from the vote on the main proposition, to votes on arguments and comments. This prioritizing of the vote can also be crucial for articulating and promoting debate results and fostering participation from users, particularly when the given technology is supported by sponsors who require visible results. Voting results are an easier form of data to count and to reorganize than arguments are—they can be understood quickly and can facilitate swift reporting and decision-making processes, though of course they lack the subtlety that analysis of a range of arguments can generate. Furthermore, as numerical functionalities, they assimilate very well with digital environments and can be easily implemented. However, civic technologies that are not instantiated by sponsors but rather are animated by communities of citizens also present a profusion of voting functionalities. This could be prompted by a real need from the users, perhaps to have an overview of opinions on a debate—or by the fact that voting functionalities are typically constituted by a pattern instigated by the designers. Nevertheless this prioritization of voting functionalities often leads these forms of assembly to appear more like survey tools than deliberative spaces. I must note that some of them tend to minimize the significance of voting, by making voting buttons smaller or less central than other platforms, or by sequencing deliberation into phases of debate and phases of vote.

Two major design patterns can be identified in the display of arguments: the first gathers platforms resembling traditional internet forums, whereby deliberative arguments form “posts” appearing as comments within threads. A second pattern is a poll-like, two-column feature in which users choose between a “pros” and a “cons” column before posting their arguments. Some platforms combine these two patterns—with arguments placed in threads, and tagged as either pros or cons throughout. Each of these patterns reveals different concepts of deliberation, and emulates various democratic practices. The first forum-inspired design involves an approach where participants can comment on an issue, but the common construction is challenging. The second, poll-like pattern polarizes the debate between the pros and cons and maintains the deliberation on a pre-established binary scale.

The second pattern (and the overall presence of votes) is also linked to arguments that online assemblies bear the potential to facilitate the exacerbation of opposing views. This potential for increased antagonism is fostered on two levels: first through the framework establishing that an argument has to be registered as either for or against an initial affirmation or question. Second, through the presence of voting functionalities attributed to questions or comments, usually signified by a like or an unlike, a plus or a minus. This seems to give legitimacy to an argument following an aggregative logic: the more people agree with it, the more so-called relevance it accrues. Certain configurations slightly differ from this binary positioning, such as Assembl—which follows the same poll-like pattern, but also bears a third column dedicated to alternative propositions—or Kialo, which enables space for more nuanced reactions to an argument’s quality. However, online debate predominantly takes form through the opposition of arguments, and tends to be symbolically resolved through a vote between opposing sides.

These civic technologies thus display a very limited range of design patterns. There are several possible explanations for their aesthetic homogeneity (lots of white edges, touches of blues, reds and green colours, sans serif types). The first is technical; some of these platforms may be built using preexisting material, such as snippets of code used to streamline their construction. Secondly, designers often aim to make every new user's journey intuitive and to lower the entry threshold. Using the visual codes of known traditional social media platforms, such as Facebook, greatly assists with developing the capacity for effortless interaction. Though efficient, these variously traced design consistencies are, however, arguably somewhat counterintuitive—as the platforms they serve are and will likely always be used in diverse contexts, on diverse subjects, and emerge from diverse initiatives.

Nevertheless, these initially plain-looking interfaces, which seem to fit any context, present a readable assemblage of democracy's normative theories. Moreover, their relative consistency makes sense when considered in terms of a deliberative and participatory democracy approach, whereby deliberation can grant a form of legitimacy to processes of decision-making. However the omnipresence of voting functionalities they utilize connects them to survey tools and follows an aggregative logic, in which the majority of individual votes dictates the ultimate legitimacy of any given decision. Furthermore, the highlighting and emphasizing of opposition in these online assemblies conveys an agonistic conception of deliberation, which in turn illuminates the irreducible nature of conflict within democracy.

Analyzing online assemblies' design patterns helps us question ways of materializing specific conceptions of democracy such as aggregative, deliberative, and agonistic democracy. Furthermore, pursuing new pathways of analysis in line with these deliberations could help to seize design spaces not-yet seized or invested in by civic technologies, and open avenues for new forms of assemblies online.

III.

Experiments

Parliament of Bodies,
documenta 14, Athens, 2017

Andreas Angelidakis

DEMOS

On the hill of Pnyka in fifth-century Athens, a set of steps provided a higher vantage point for the speaker of the *demos*, a Greek word referring to "the people." The combination of speaker, audience, and steps was called the Ecclesia of Demos, often translated as "assembly," a group of people gathered together in one place for a common purpose. If you google the word "assembly," you might see that in our world of screens, it could also refer to the name of a "construction code language for a computer, or other programmable device." It is a language in which modules are combined as parts to form a variable architecture—a "*demo* architecture," as in "demonstration," a test run for a software, a piece of music, or even a street protest. An architecture in which to try out different spaces, or to produce a variety of Ecclesiae—a typological series for the gathering of the people "in one place for a common purpose."

On the occasion of the documenta 14 in Athens (2017) and following the brief for a Parliament of Bodies by Paul B. Preciado, a module for this "demo architecture" was proposed: a single soft step, referencing the timeless stones of the hill of Pnyka and the concrete slabs of contemporary Athens, which is in fact light enough to be lifted—a step where one can stand up to speak, or sit down to listen. The module is multiplied into copies and variations of itself, just like "a construction code language for a computer or other programmable device." First the module is placed along the entire perimeter of the space. As people gather and sit on opposite steps, they look at each other as much as they look at the programmed event. The Ecclesia of Demos has been inverted—it is no longer a central plinth to provide visibility to one, but a gathering for all. The next time the people gather, the space shifts into two exedras of opposition. On another occasion they find a single mountain of steps, with the seating facing outwards.

The exhibition space of Parko Eleftherias, which housed the public program of the documenta 14, is treated as a historical artefact, the site where democracy reached its lowest point in contemporary Greek history. During the dictatorship (1967–74), it was used by the military police as a detention center. As the Demos begins to develop its definitions, the building shell itself begins to negotiate its own history, sporadically removing layers of exhibition walls, uncovering parts of the space that witnessed its use as a headquarters for the military police, the famous EAT/EΣA torture chambers. Smaller gestures begin to appear, perhaps wall panels are removed to uncover windows blocked by metal bars, or ceiling panels are shifted to allow for lighting and projection hardware.

Demos creates a space as a programmable device with which to negotiate the relation between stage and audience, between performer and participant. As the public program unfolded over time, the modules gradually formed a language. Each variation is a demo for a possible Parliament of Bodies. Each demo is demolished to make way for the next demos.

Hans Asenbaum

Democratic Assemblage

A wave of democratic renewal is spreading across the globe, from participatory budgeting in Brazil and the Indian Gram Sabha village councils to global citizens' assemblies. A great variety of these participatory assemblies and their constitutive activities can be encapsulated by the term "democratic innovations." Democratic innovations have been conceptualized as meticulously designed institutions.[1] In his recent book *Democratic Design*, Michael Saward claims: "Design—the intentional creation of plans to solve a problem—is the key to understanding today's and creating tomorrow's democratic governance."[2] Via intentionally designed assemblies, participatory and deliberative democrats attempt to pre-structure—and to a certain extent pre-determine—human interaction. The intent of design is undoubtedly rooted in deep democratic convictions. Pre-structured assemblies can enhance the voices of the marginalized.[3] But expert design may also stifle democratic energies. It bears the potential to forestall democratic serendipity—the playful and spontaneous exploration of the unforeseen in democratic engagement.[4]

Democracy, as I will argue, is more than institutional design, more than assembly. It is *assemblage*. Democracy is not only constituted by carefully planned processes, but also by the many things—human and non-human—that assemble in ever-novel and unforeseen configurations.[5] Rather than being an institutional arrangement, democracy is a moment in which material objects, sentient bodies, and performative expressions align in a manner that affords freedom and equality. The term *democratic assemblage* does not only denote a formation that realizes democratic core values, but also the very process through which such a constellation is brought into form. Democratic assemblage is both a state and a process of becoming. When understood as a

1. Graham Smith, *Democratic Innovations: Designing Institutions for Citizen Participation* (Cambridge: Cambridge University Press, 2009).
2. Michael Saward, *Democratic Design* (Oxford: Oxford University Press, 2021), xiv.
3. Hans Asenbaum, "Facilitating Inclusion: Austrian Wisdom Councils as Democratic Innovation Between Consensus and Diversity," *Journal of Public Deliberation* 12, no. 2 (2016): 1–11.
4. Hans Asenbaum and Frederic Hanusch, "(De)Futuring Democracy: Labs, Ateliers, and Playgrounds as Democratic Innovation," *Futures*, 134 (2021): 1–11.
5. Andrea Felicetti, "Learning from Democratic Practices: New Perspectives in Institutional Design," *Journal of Politics* 83, no. 4 (2021): 589–1601.

subjective experience, democracy is felt in these moments when freedom and equality align to mutually actualize each other.[6] These moments are part of fluid processes of a becoming democracy; a living assemblage that is ever in the making.[7]

This might sound quite abstract. So, what does it mean for democracy to consist of many components that come to assemble? How do these things come together? How does assemblage work in practical terms? Here I will face these questions and outline a theory of democratic assemblage. I will argue that democratic assemblage brings material objects, sentient bodies, and performative expressions together in three ways: through natural forces, through affect, and through cognition. This explanation applies to any instance of assemblage. But I speak here specifically of *democratic* assemblage when such (be)coming together instantiates freedom and equality.

The approach I suggest does not do away with design. It merely shows that democracy encompasses more than planning and intentionality. Assemblage thinking is in itself radically democratic. It aims to overcome the exclusion of non-humans by proposing a flat ontology.[8] Assemblage brings together human and non-human animals, plants, microbes, artefacts, events, concepts, emotions, and performances. I mention this not to draw false equivalences, to suggest that all these things are the same. They are indeed very different. But all of them are relevant for democracy, interdependent and prone to interacting with one another in unforeseen ways. Design may be a part of these assemblages that pull and push us in different directions. Human agency is essential when our aim is to assemble democratically. Democracy is a regulatory ideal that can be engendered in and through assemblage. All struggles towards freedom and

6. Sheldon Wolin, "Fugitive Democracy," *Constellations* 1, no. 1 (1994): 11–25.
7. Different from Jacques Derrida's democracy to come, my proposal of a "becoming" democracy does not relate to the future. It rather focuses on the current fluid nature of ever assembling and reassembling democratic configurations. Jacques Derrida, *Rogues: Two Essays on Reason* (Stanford: Stanford University Press, 2005).
8. Levi Bryant, *The Democracy of Objects* (Ann Arbor: Open Humanities Press, 2011).

equality necessitate human agency. My argument, however, is that rather than attempting to gain mastery over assemblage, we should engage with assemblage through open curiosity, humility and respect. We need to listen and learn before we judge. We need to acknowledge all that we are enmeshed within and recognize our own limitations in our pursuit of radical democracy.

What is Democratic Assemblage?

The project of radical democracy creates new spaces for participatory engagement which reinvigorate and transform existing democratic frameworks. Such spaces include both formalized institutions such as citizens' assemblies and social movements' organizations, occupations, and protest formations.[9] In Judith Butler's words: "In wresting that power, a new space is created, a new 'between' of bodies, as it were, that lays claim to existing space."[10] These democratic innovations "can challenge the existing institutional order."[11] Against the neoliberal credo suggesting that there is no alternative, they demonstrate that things can be otherwise.

Employing assemblage theory as an analytical lens, our initial query is: What do democratic spaces consist of? The spaces that facilitate new forms of participation consist of material objects such as walls, pavements and chairs. They include tools such as flip charts and whiteboards in facilitated democratic processes; megaphones and banners in street demonstrations; microphones and lecterns in citizens' assemblies; and the smart devices that enable digital and hybrid democratic spaces. These physical infrastructures are populated by sentient bodies that relate to each other in contingent constellations of power structures,

9. Andrea Cornwall, "Spaces for Transformation? Reflections on Issues of Power and Difference in Participation in Development," in *Participation: From Tyranny to Transformation?*, eds. Samuel Hickey and Giles Mohan (London: Zed Books, 2004), 75–91.
10. Judith Butler, *Notes Toward a Performative Theory of Assembly* (Cambridge, MA: Harvard University Press, 2015), 85.
11. Smith, *Democratic Innovations*, 3.

sexual attractions and emotional ties. Here not only humans, but all sentient organisms interact. Natural events,[12] non-human animals,[13] and viruses[14] can become participants in democratic assemblage. Consider, for example, Eva Meijer's insightful work on interspecies democracy. With regards to a conflict over living space between seagulls and humans, she argues for material deliberation: "humans can make proposals to which seagulls can respond, to which humans can in turn respond, and so on."[15] To facilitate interspecies dialogue within cities, Sue Donaldson suggests installing "animal agoras" with reduced human traffic and increased free spaces for non-human animals to negotiate their own decisions.[16]

Lastly, democratic spaces are not only populated by material objects and sentient bodies, but by their performative expressions. When participants express something, they create some *thing*. Their words, sounds, or gestures become objects of contention or agreement. Their performative acts, their sighs, nods, silences, chants, songs, dances, artistic articulations, the clothes they wear, the images they share on social media all become part of democratic assemblage.[17] This also goes for the performative expressions of non-humans. The rainfall, birdsong, and smartphone notifications all affect these intricate constellations of engagement. Democratic assemblage, then, goes beyond intentional design. Attending to democratic assemblage highlights the many things that rearrange democratic formations, often

12. Romero Javier and John Dryzek, "Grounding Ecological Democracy: Semiotics and the Communicative Networks of Nature," *Environmental Values* 30, no. 4 (2020): 407–29.
13. Eva Meijer, *When Animals Speak: Toward an Interspecies Democracy* (New York: New York University Press, 2019).
14. Lucy Parry, Hans Asenbaum, and Selen Ercan, "Democracy in Flux: A Systemic View on the Impact of COVID-19," *Transforming Government: People, Process and Policies, 15*(2), 197–205, 2021. https://doi.org/10.1108/TG-09-2020-0269.
15. Meijer, *When Animals Speak*, 212.
16. Sue Donaldson, "Animal Agora: Animal Citizens and the Democratic Challenge," *Social Theory and Practice* 46, no. 4 (2020): 709–35.
17. Ricardo Fabrino Mendonça, Selen A. Ercan, Hans Asenbaum, "More than Words: A Multidimensional Approach to Deliberative Democracy," *Political Studies*, 70(1): 153–72, 2022. https://doi.org/10.1177/0032321720950561.

in unforeseen ways. Democratic assemblage respects and includes all the things that make up the temporary realization of democracy. As has likely become clear by now, democratic assemblage does not necessarily describe different democratic processes to those to which the term assembly refers—it simply illuminates them differently. It identifies more and more detailed elements of these processes, explores the distributive agency of the many things at play, and opens the perceptive conditions for serendipitous becoming.

Democratic assemblage also draws attention to the contingent boundaries of democratic space. When understood as *assemblage*, a citizens' assembly is not confined to a fixed location or time. Rather it attunes us to the fact that participants carry many things into and out of the physical assembly space. They circulate ideas, arguments, sentiments, and impressions within the wider public sphere. Media reporting both online and offline disperses assembly contents, images, and sounds.[18] Democratic assemblage extends to the psychological rhythms and thinking patterns of participants, who rearrange impressions as they form and connect them to their previous experiences. Thereby, just as participants are part of a becoming democracy, democratic assemblage is also part of participants' personal becoming.

The Politics of Becoming

A becoming democracy, then, consists of ever-changing constellations of sentient bodies, who are themselves constantly changing. Identities of participants—who they understand themselves to be, and who they are seen to be by others—are themselves formed as assemblages. The body appears as a collection of muscles, blood vessels, hormones, bones, skin, and hair. The assemblage of the body simultaneously interacts with discursive concepts of gender, sexuality,

18. Marie Paxton, *Agonistic Democracy: Rethinking Political Institutions in Pluralist Times* (New York: Routledge, 2020).

race, and class, as well as with political affiliations, personal experiences and desires. These concepts relate to social practices and performances, including gendered or racially coded body language and culturally coded objects such as clothing.[19] The subject, then, appears as a multiple, shifting self.[20]

Conceptualizing the democratic subject as a mosaic, temporary configuration allows us to think about how the self can be re-invented within democratic spaces.[21] This politics of becoming has far-reaching consequences for the composition of democratic assemblage. The relationship between participants and democratic assemblage is dialectic. As participants constantly produce the assemblage they are part of, so too does assemblage produce participants. Various components of the assemblage—objects, bodies, performances—bring out different sides of the multiple self. Who we are in any given moment is partly afforded by the constellation of things of which we are a part. At the same time, the momentary identity of democratic subjects changes democratic assemblage. Alteration of participants' identities alters the entire assemblage.

How does Democratic Assemblage Work?

Assemblage theory claims that all things bear some kind of agency and liveliness. Even inanimate things affect us. A chair affords a certain usage. A thunderstorm might wake us up at night or chase us down the street to seek refuge. Assemblages, hence, have been explained as compositions of multiple things of different nature, wielding multiple agencies, and cohering through the interaction of diverse forces.[22] Elsewhere I have articulated my skepticism about the

19. Iris Marion Young, "Gender as Seriality: Thinking about Women as a Social Collective," *Signs* 19, no. 3 (1994): 713–38.
20. Jon Elster, ed., *The Multiple Self* (Cambridge: Cambridge University Press, 1986).
21. Hans Asenbaum, "The Politics of Becoming: Disidentification as Radical Democratic Practice," *European Journal of Social Theory* 24, no. 1 (2021): 86–104.
22. Jane Bennett, *Vibrant Matter: A Political Ecology of Things* (Durham, NC: Duke University Press, 2010); Diana Coole and Samantha Frost, eds., *New Materialisms: Ontology, Agency, and Politics* (Durham, NC: Duke University Press, 2010);

hardly substantiated claim that all things are alive.[23] Here I will try to demystify some of these claims and contribute to more clarity. So how do assemblages assemble? What are the forces that draw and keep material objects, sentient bodies, and performative expressions together?

The value of assemblage theory lies in its ontological inclusivity. While positivists conceptualize reality as an external condition, which can be approximated through empirical methods, and constructivists conceptualize realities as products of linguistic construction, performance and socialization, assemblage thinking offers a middle ground. Its critical realist ontology claims that while there is an external reality, we can only ever gauge its qualities through our socially configured senses.

> "Critical realisms ... marries the positivist's search for evidence of a reality external to human consciousness with the insistence that all meaning to be made of that reality is socially constructed ... It is impossible to step outside our own perspectivism and so the gap between the real world and our knowledge of it can never be closed."[24]

This ontological positioning of assemblage allows us to find a new appreciation of matter, substance, objects, and artifacts, without understanding them as fixed or predetermined. Through this lens we can "see a physical and biological world operating not according to fixed laws and blueprints, but rather one teeming with dynamism, flexibility, and novelty. Such a world is not determined; rather it is constantly in the process of its making."[25]

and Manuel DeLanda, *Assemblage Theory* (Edinburgh: Edinburgh University Press, 2016).

23. Hans Asenbaum, "Rethinking Digital Democracy: From the Disembodied Discursive Self to New Materialist Corporealities," *Communication Theory*, 31(3): 360–79, 2021. https://doi.org/10.1093/ct/qtz033.
24. Carolyn Oliver, "Critical Realist Grounded Theory: A New Approach for Social Work Research," *British Journal of Social Work* 42, no. 2 (2012): 372–74.
25. Victoria Pitts-Taylor, ed., *Mattering: Feminism, Science, and Materialism* (New York: New York University Press, 2016), 4.

The critical realist ontology allows us to identify at least three forces that bring and hold the assemblage together: natural forces, affect, and cognition.

Think of any democratic assemblage—a citizens' assembly, an occupied public square, a classroom discussion. What keeps the walls, chairs, and bodies in place, and what allows them to move about, is gravity. The attractive force of gravity is not only what keeps every material object, including sentient bodies, from drifting into space; gravity exists *between* any material being or thing. There is gravity between physical objects and between living bodies. These bodies and objects internally are made of uncountable particles which are held together by cohesive forces. Not only are our bodies internally made of blood vessels, traveling hormones and cells that convert nutrients into energy, form connections, and heal tissue; any object is made of particles that are constantly in motion, form new connections, or repel one another.

The second force that enables assemblage is affect. "Affect, at its most anthropomorphic, is the name we give to those forces—visceral forces beneath, alongside, or generally *other than* conscious knowing, vital forces insisting beyond emotion—that can serve to drive us toward movement, toward thought and extensions."[26] When in a citizens' assembly, the story shared by a participant causes another participant's sadness; this is the result of affect. We might be under the impression that affect is a force outside the body. The sadness of one body has moved to another. And indeed, Sweigworth and Gregg explain affect as "the passage (and duration of passage) of forces or identities. That is, affect is found in those intensities that pass body to body."[27] I take issue with this kind of explanation. Can anger, for example, really exist outside the human body? If anger arises in one body and cause anger to arise in another, has the same anger moved from one to another body? In contrast, I understand

26. Melissa Gregg and Gregory Seigworth, "An Inventory of Shimmers," in *The Affect Theory Reader* (Durham, NC: Duke University Press, 2010), 1.

27. Ibid.

affect as an often sudden, visceral response to some occurrence. Each affect occurs *within* its own body. There may be a causal relationship between the two, but there is no exchange or transmission of forces.

A third force completes the picture. It is the force of cognition. Democratic assemblage is brought together by our subjective interpretations. As participants or observers of participatory processes, we sense other participants, their performative expressions, and the material surroundings and objects of the process. We make sense of discursive expressions and embodied performances. In our minds, we bring these many elements, processes, and gestures together. This cognitive process is what Martina Löw calls synthesis.[28] Cognition means making sense of things and establishing connections between them. In so doing, we assemble them. This means that the constitution of democratic assemblage is subjective. The same participatory event is perceived differently by everyone observing or participating in it.[29]

Understanding democracy not in terms of assembly but in terms of assemblage opens new perspectives and avenues of thought. Rather than focusing on carefully developed expert designs, striving for democracy instead entails attending to serendipitous processes of becoming, including human and non-human participants. This does not mean that we have to surrender to forces beyond our control. Distributive agency does not entail giving up on political responsibility or indeed personal agency. On the contrary, the concept of democratic assemblage suggests that society and the self can be infinitely rearranged and recombined. As an analytical tool, the perspective I am proposing offers the possibility of detecting the many components that constitute democratic assemblage, as well as the forces that hold them together. This form of analysis enables us to assemble things

28. Martina Löw, "The Constitution of Space: The Structuration of Spaces Through the Simultaneity of Effect and Perception," *European Journal of Social Theory* 11, no. 1 (2008): 25–49.

29. Hans Asenbaum, "Rethinking Democratic Innovations: A Look Through the Kaleidoscope of Democratic Theory," *Political Studies Review*, 0(0), 1–11, 2021. https://doi.org/10.1177/14789299211052890.

differently. By saying something unexpected, by breaking conventions, by interrupting the established order of things, entrenched configurations can be disturbed. These interruptive moments can be used to destabilize established hierarchies and to assemble democracy anew.

Alana Gerecke
& Laura Levin

Choreographic Deliberations

in Pandemic Times

In our co-authored article *Choreographies of Assembly*,[1] we asked how can "different choreographic arrangements of public assembly shape and reshape the social, the aesthetic, and the political?"[2] We grounded our inquiry in a twinned focus on protest and performance, in order to explore how the structure of an assembly determines its possibilities and its limits—how the formal and physical characteristics of gathering and sharing space are inextricable from the social and political possibilities of a given event. As we are both trained as performance scholars and performing artists, we are keenly attuned to and focused on the power of moving bodies in shared space. The analysis of assembly articulated here is therefore funneled through the kinesthetic, the relational, and the material. We hope that our focus on the materiality of the body is a useful contribution to a broader discussion of deliberative assembly which has, as political theorist Amanda Machin reminds us, tended to absent the body from a theorization of the political processes of assembly.[3] We echo Machin's insistence that "Bodies can agitate or accelerate the supposedly smooth and steady process of public reasoning, with an awkwardly placed elbow and a subtly raised eyebrow. By sighing or shrugging; by turning one's back or shaking a hand."[4]

Alana Gerecke: I'm curious to see how Performance Studies could energize the concepts of both deliberation and of assembly—how the field might reorient our discussion of these terms to emphasize the production, scoring, and performance of a range of cultural practices, as well as the productive possibility of improvisation. Whereas deliberative assembly is concerned, broadly, with the process of coming together to make choices about a common

1. Alana Gerecke and Laura Levin, "Moving Together in an Era of Assembly," *Canadian Theater Review* 176 (Fall 2018): 5–10.
2. Gerecke and Levin, 5.
3. Amanda Machin, "Deliberating Bodies: Democracy, Identification, and Embodiment," *Democratic Theory*, vol. 2, no. 1 (Summer 2015): 42–62.
4. Machin, 47.

action, a performance focus spotlights the subtle, physical, and non-verbal choices we make within the process of *coming together* itself. In this way, a performance frame "may yet inform current understandings of both what counts as democratic politics and the particular role of the body therein."[5] The unspoken, embodied deliberations undertaken by bodies as they move into and out of assembly enable and affirm (or foreclose) a sense of collectivity and determine the contours of any assembly. I'm reminded of dance theorist Randy Martin's insistence that "Politics goes nowhere without movement."[6] Shifts in orientation, proximity, and gesture function to either align or distance members of a group. These micro-positionings of bodies in space—in alignment, unison, counterpoint, or tension—enact a rippling, stuttering, and constantly shifting embodied negotiation of what it is to assemble.

An exploration of the function of physical and gestural elements of assembly (beyond their status as addendums to the deliberative speech act) yields choreographic questions. How many bodies gather? Which height-levels do they occupy: do they sit, stand, walk? Where do they face: towards, away, or otherwise? How close together are the bodies within the space? Are there any prescribed gestures that reach across bodies? How do these gestures signify differently on different bodies—with all their raced, classed, gendered, and other historical and geographic contingencies?

Laura Levin: Writing in the fall of 2021, a year and half into the COVID-19 pandemic, I'm curious about what the distancing mandates of the pandemic have taught us about the nature of assembly pre-, during,

5. Emily Beausoleil, "'Only They Breathe': Identity, Agency and the Dancing Body Politic," *Constellations*, vol. 21, no. 1 (2014): 112.
6. Randy Martin, *Critical Moves: Dance Studies in Theory and Politics* (Durham, NC: Duke University Press, 1998), 3.

and post-pandemic. It is significant that we are revisiting the choreographic politics of assembly at a moment when assembly itself has become so challenging—when restrictions have limited the movement of publics across populations, when the technologies of assembling have shifted into the digital sphere, and when we are only just beginning to move back toward in-person gathering.

Alana Gerecke: I agree. The pandemic has functioned as a kind of aperture that allows us to examine the constituent elements of embodied assembly beyond this historical moment. What would you say you've noticed about how performers and audiences are navigating this renewed engagement with physical copresence during your recent return to "live" performance?

Laura Levin: I've been working as a dramaturg on an art exhibition delayed by the pandemic, which finally launched in September 2021 once restrictions in Toronto had been relaxed. The show is a retrospective of Jess Dobkin's performance art work, a Toronto artist who has shaped feminist and queer performance in Canada. Our opening event was a big party where exhibition visitors gathered outdoors to celebrate the show, but also to celebrate the very fact that we were able to assemble in person again. It was the first IRL art event most of us had attended in nearly two years.

This assembly was met with a mixture of pure joy and acute physical awkwardness. After months of Zoom interactions we struggled to know how best to place our bodies relative to one another within a live space. Individuals shifted forward and backward gauging distance, face masks were put on and removed at random in what looked to me like a tense, almost vaudevillian kind of dance. The partnered movement was *deliberative* as interlocutors silently interpreted desires for social distance while making embodied decisions about how best to engage: to embrace or bump elbows? Spread out or huddle in? Linger or rush along? Physical improvisation is a constitutive feature of assembly, as we routinely make choices (conscious and unconscious) about where to place ourselves within a larger "scene." But the edges around these improvisatory deliberations felt especially jagged on this occasion, and left many feeling physically exhausted by the end of the evening.

Still, overall this return to assembly was really joyful and moving. The event reversed the sharp separation of public and private life, on and offline, material and immaterial that has defined the pandemic, and reminded us of the power of physical copresence. I'm thinking here of theorist Jill Dolan's idea of "utopian performatives": moments where assembled groups find in the live encounter "a processual, momentary feeling of affinity, in which spectators experience themselves as part of a congenial public constituted by the performance's address."[7] The event reminded me that the ethical-political stakes of bodies coming together is the decision to form a "temporary community," or as Dolan puts it, "to feel themselves citizens of a no-place that's a better place, citizens who might then take that fccling into other sites of public discourse."[8]

And speaking of utopian spaces—it's interesting that the event was choreographed in a park adjacent to the gallery, and not in the gallery itself. This made us feel like we were suspended in a "no-place" unanchored by gallery walls; it was like we were moving on the moon. I know that you've been researching movement in impromptu gathering spaces over the last year. What kinds of thinking has it prompted for you about choreographies of assembly?

Alana Gerecke: Like you, I'm seeing a stilted, unspoken negotiation between bodies during this

7. Jill Dolan, *Utopia in Performance: Finding Hope at the Theater* (Ann Arbour, MI: University of Michigan Press, 2005).
8. Dolan, 15.

moment of return to a more regular sharing of physical spaces. For a snapshot of deliberative bodies in assembly during these times of physical distancing, we can look to the recent Canadian federal election (September 2021). Canada's COVID-19 safety guidelines during the election meant that assembly was spaced and staggered throughout voting day, and that bodily placement in line-ups and at polling stations throughout the deliberative exercise was, itself, extremely *deliberate*. The voting experience was not identical across the country—nor even within a polling station across the span of voting day—but some common characteristics included the now familiar ground spacers in public line-ups that indicate a safe, two-meter distance; the delicate, back-peddling steps that correct an accidental transgression of the invisible two-meter boundary; or the responsive shuffle forward, a footwork calculation that accommodates an overly close body arriving in line behind. The minor choreography of the precise and repeated mask adjustments was another movement signature: hand to face to pinch—thumb to pointer finger—at the bridge of the nose; a gentle tug downward from the chin; and the comb of fingers behind ears or neck to tighten or loosen fit. There was a quality of vigilant precision that structured my experience of the federal election, small and responsive adjustments articulated by the furthest extremities (fingers and feet) that functioned to maintain distance.

Dance scholar Kate Elswit calls this renewed attention to the space around one's body, the two-meter physical distancing bubble, a "coronasphere."[9] Her term plays on the choreographic language of the *kinesphere*—the perimeter around the body defined by the potential reach of fully extended limbs without

9. Kate Elswit, "Dancing with our Coronasphere to Navigate the Pandemic," *Dance Magazine* (21 July 2020). https://www.dancemagazine.com/six-feet-distance-2646412593.html?rebelltitem=1#rebelltitem1.

locomotion. It's notable that the "coronasphere" is more than twice the size of the typical "no touch zone" built into North American sidewalk corridors—an urban design formula that accounts for an invisible perimeter of a few inches around each moving body.[10] In order to assemble during the pandemic, we have had to work against the built design of many public spaces, diverting off the sidewalk in order to facilitate the safe passage of a neighbor, or pushing toward the edges of a park plaza to maintain the invisible boundary between groups. The shuffling, corrective negotiations we've been making during the pandemic remind us that we are always already responsive to a larger "scene." As a *New York Times* dance critic recently observed of pandemic mobility: "When you walk outside, you are responsible for more than just yourself. We are in this together, and movement has morals and consequences—its own choreographic score, or set of instructions—in this age of the coronavirus."[11]

Laura Levin: This is so true, Alana. I have seen both professional colleagues and groups of friends ripped apart in the last year because decisions about *where* to gather (in or outside, crowded or empty venue), *how* to gather (arrangement of bodies in space), and *with whom* to gather (with vaccinated folks, those in/out of bubbles, etc.), have become freighted with heavy moral meaning—eliciting judgment from some about what constitutes the "right" way to assemble. There is a new deliberative intensity surrounding acts of coming together in person and the consequences of making the "wrong" choices can be stark. I'm thinking here of all of the politicians who were publicly admonished in the past year for gathering with family members for birthdays or dinners (even funerals).

10. Nicholas Blomley, *Rights of Passage: Sidewalks and the Regulation of Public Flow* (London: Routledge, 2011), 43.
11. Gia Kourlas, "How We Use Our Bodies to Navigate a Pandemic," *The New York Times* (March 31, 2020).

Alana Gerecke: Instead of a notion of a *me* over here, and a distinct *you* over there, we have a more finely tuned awareness of how the space between us constitutes us: the air you exhale (with its aerosols and droplets) is the same air I inhale. This is not unique to the pandemic, of course, but it puts a fine point on pre-pandemic notions of enmeshed bodily boundaries and "constitutive relations."[12] We've been cast into a set of protective choreographies that function to fabricate a degree of separateness within assembly. And yet, simultaneously (and conversely), we also see an opposing impulse in the sphere of digital assembly: in these past months, we've been invited into a range of digital contexts that seek to foster a sense of togetherness despite simultaneously enduring purposeful, physical separation.

Laura Levin: Assembling daily on Zoom over the last year has been a challenge, though it's clear digital assemblies in universities are here to stay. Incessant videoconferencing makes me appreciate the textures and contexts produced by other bodies when we assemble together in person. When you sense the person next to you shifting in their seat, this impacts your understanding of how they are reading an event. Zoom is insistently frontal; it obscures your colleague's orientation, preventing you from seeing what they are leaning towards, what's capturing their attention. In-person gatherings allow us to choreograph alliances and personal status through bodily decisions about where to locate oneself. Do you sit near the front or back of a room? Next to a particular person (a political ally perhaps), or definitively on your own? Performing positionality is harder to achieve physically on Zoom, especially since a scene can be viewed

12. Judith Butler, *Notes Toward a Performative Theory of Assembly* (Cambridge, MA: Harvard University Press, 2015), 130.

in speaker or gallery view, and we can choose to move the little human-filled boxes around on our screens.

Assembling on Zoom can often be dehumanizing in cutting us off from the sensory experience of mutual contingency that is an unspoken characteristic of embodied presence ("the space between us constitutes us," to echo your words). This feeling is exacerbated by participants' choices to keep their video off at meetings, creating the uncomfortable spectacle of individuals speaking passionately into an indifferent, dark void. The reassuring sounds of assent and laughter, on which speakers instinctively rely as the basis for building support, are lost when participants are muted *en masse* to prevent distractions. Without the same visual scope for reading bodily cues (we're typically cut off at the shoulders), and subject to a "host" who uses digital controls (spotlighting/muting) to shape who is foregrounded/backgrounded, Zoom assemblies can breed mistrust and misunderstanding, making even the warmest participants appear cold or aloof.

But even as I worry about the loss of embodied connection in digital spaces, I'm excited about new possibilities that are opened up through assembling online. We've become much more aware of our physical emplacement within domestic spaces, as platforms like Zoom have given new ways to choreograph our relationship to the environments we inhabit. Peering into these mini worlds of humans enmeshed with fragments of material culture (objects, artworks, books, framed photos, and more appearing as background) is a reminder that deliberative assembly is an act not only of positioning our bodies relative to other people, but also of blending into material environments. To assemble is to become entangled in more-than-human (and more-than-professional) *assemblages*[13]—webs of connection that the pandemic has made visible in all-too painful ways. But I'm also interested in how these material entanglements can help ease the formality of deliberative assembly—for example when the deadly seriousness of a dissertation defense or a faculty meeting is punctured by the unexpected sound of a garbage truck backing up, a kitten dancing across the keyboard, or the sudden appearance of a child. These lively and enlivening moments, forming what I've referred to elsewhere as the "environmental unconscious," can in fact also counter the sense of detachment that is often produced by the digital meeting.[14]

However I am of course also mindful that each of these moments or forms of choreographic interruption reveal, in their own ways, the cultural, gendered, classed, and geographic digital divides that shape our use and experience of digital spaces, the many fault lines of inequality the pandemic has laid bare. Who, for example, has the luxury of appearing solo in the Zoom assembly, and who is physically negotiating with dependents (for example, small children) popping in and out of the video frame? Similarly, a Zoom assembly generally presupposes that each interlocutor has adequate technology and a stable place from which to participate, a set of staging requirements depending upon socioeconomic factors such as access to housing (a room of one's own), computers, and reliable broadband service. In this sense, interruptions here pose key questions about spatial privilege: who has the privilege of making their private home or work environment visible and using it as a platform for staging public identity? When does the impossibility of

13. Jane Bennett, *Vibrant Matter: A Political Ecology of Things* (Durham, NC: Duke University Press, 2010).
14. Laura Levin, *Performing Ground: Space, Camouflage, and the Art of Blending In* (Basingstoke: Palgrave, 2014).

certain bodies physically appearing mark differentiated access to assembly?

Alana Gerecke: Agreed, yes, that really resonates for me. We've also seen an expanded expression of assembly emerging during the pandemic, including the use of cars to facilitate physically distanced protests; experimentation with drive-in and bike-through performances; and models for assembly-at-a-distance through sonic space (like Clap for Our Carers or the early proliferation of balcony music flash mobs). Social movement theorist Paolo Gerbaudo has posited the pandemic as an unlikely but effective instigator of public assemblies, noting that the prolonged suspension of daily social routines yielded a paradoxical "surge of mobilization" in the midst of a "severe reduction in travel and mobility."[15] Gerbaudo proposes a taxonomy of pandemic protest that organizes assemblies by their relationship with state-sanctioned contagion containment measures: from socially distanced assemblies, to anti-lockdown protests, to "pandemic riots."[16] A key consideration along this spectrum is the placement of bodies in relation to one another, to authority figures, and to space.

With Gerbaudo's observations in mind, consider the physical arrangements that structured a handful of different pandemic assemblies. On one hand, we could think of the static and home-based assemblies that animated Clap for Our Carers, a participatory social gesture that filled neighborhoods with applause for front-line health care workers each evening during the height of the pandemic. On the more mobile end of the spectrum we might think of the traveling, shoulder-to-shoulder procession of thousands of protesters who took up the Black Lives Matter cause. Protesters reclaimed public spaces for the

15. Paolo Gerbaudo, "The Pandemic Crowd: Protest in the Time of COVID-19," *Journal of International Affairs,* vol. 73, no. 2 (2021): 62.

16. Gerbaudo, 63.

duration of each event—often in downtown cores that had been underused during pandemic months—sharing a common directional orientation and signature gestural vocabularies ("hands up, don't shoot") as they moved forward through the streets.[17] Of course, the different stakes of these forms of assembly and the coding of the bodies (both physical and symbolic) that enact them are inextricable from the physical vocabularies each movement adopts. The static, sub/urban clapping action attaches itself to the subdued safety of the home-space, and the distanced gesture of audience applause; whereas the BLM human rights campaign embodied by, and enacted in support of, Black bodies traverses city streets, pushing the boundaries of pandemic gathering protocol while performing a critique of the Black body as always-already vulnerable to public violence.

That the stakes of these choreographies are accentuated and exacerbated by the risks (and benefits) of coming together during a pandemic is what makes this moment a useful touchpoint for thinking about assembly. The disparity of vulnerabilities across bodies in assembly is cast into relief. This pandemic has forced us to innovate new ways of assembling, whilst also asking us to attend more closely to the bodily and environmental coordinates of traditional forms of gathering. It has allowed us to see more clearly how the location, movement vocabularies, orientations, and gestures that characterize a given assembly are shaped by the issues that drive the assembly, and how these choreographies are intrinsically connected to which bodies show up to participate or to witness.

17. Anusha Kedhar, "Hands Up, Don't Shoot: Gesture, Choreography, and Protest in Ferguson," *The Feminist Wire* (October 6, 2014). https://thefeministwire.com/2014/10/protest-in-ferguson/.

François Cooren

Assembly

as Social Ventriloquy

I have found that in the study of interactions—whether undertaken from within interlaced academic fields, or experienced as live communication analysis—I am often struck both by their complexity and their relative orderliness. As conversation analysts have demonstrated and explored for the past 50 years, interacting within the context of even a simple conversation requires that people speak one at a time (in other words, they usually take turns), that they use both verbal and nonverbal methods for selecting and agreeing on who will speak next (for example by looking at the next chosen speaker, or by indicating where their attention falls with their body language and orientation), or that, once selected, the person designated as the next speaker attends to what has previously been said.[1] These are just some of the general rules that interlocutors implicitly follow—all the while knowing, of course, that these rules can always be breached (for instance, overlapping can take place, or an interlocutor can decide to ignore whatever has been said to them). These breaches, however, provoke accountability; that is, people can ask their interlocutors to account for what they consider to be a deviation from expected conversational norms, which can lead to various forms of repair.[2]

Assemblies and meetings are, in this regard, a little different. They are usually characterized by the existence of formal rules and procedures that have been purposely designed to regulate how participants intervene, but also to designate certain people—a chairperson, a president, etc.—to be in charge of making sure that these rules are abided by.[3]

1. Anita Pomerantz and B.J. Fehr, "Conversation Analysis: An Approach to the Analysis of Social Interaction," in *Discourse Studies: A Multidisciplinary Introduction*, ed. Teun A. Van Dijk (London: Sage, 2011), 165–90; and Jack Sidnell, "Basic Conversation Analytic Methods," in *The Handbook of Conversation Analysis*, eds. Jack Sidnell and Tanya Stivers (Malden, MA: Wiley-Blackwell, 2013), 77–99.
2. Makoto Hayashi, Geoffrey Raymond, and Jack Sidnell, eds., *Conversational Repair and Human Understanding* (Cambridge, UK: Cambridge University Press, 2013); and Emanuel A. Schegloff, "Repair after Next Turn: The Last Structurally Provided Defense of Intersubjectivity in Conversation," *American Journal of Sociology* 97, no. 5 (March 1992): 1295–1345.
3. Anita Pomerantz and Paul Denvir, "Enacting the Institutional Role of Chairperson in Upper-management Meetings: The Interactional Realization of Provisional

In France, the *Règlement de l'Assemblée nationale* (Rules of procedure of the national assembly) stipulates, in its Article 52, that "The president opens the session, directs the deliberations, enforces the regulation, and maintains order; s/he may, at any moment, recess or adjourn the session." In its Article 54, it also specifies that "the deputies who wish to intervene register with the president, who determines the order in which they will be called to take the floor, subject to the provisions of Article 49 and Article 95, paragraph 2."[4] While small meetings can sometimes manage to function more or less informally, assemblies, because of their size and the often-polemical character of their discussions, have to be, whether we like it or not, regulated and organized. We also have to consider the possibility that such assemblies are not necessarily the locus where the most interesting or generative debates occur. For instance, the French National Assembly has its plenary sessions, but it also has committees whereby more dialogic forms of communication are given the chance to take place. Indeed, plenary sessions tend to be marked by the monological character of their interventions. When the members of the National Assembly take the floor during these public sessions, they certainly talk to each other, but they also, and perhaps most crucially, talk both to and for their constituents, as well as to and for the population.

Could we imagine other forms of assemblies, in which more constructive dialogues could take place and be organized? Where interventions would be made in a register beyond simply the making of a point, without necessarily attending to what has been previously said? This is a difficult question, and it is not my ambition to answer it in this essay. I would like, however, to examine a specific feature of communication—what I call its *ventriloquial* dimension[5]—in order to explore the possibility of alternative

Authority," in *Interacting and Organizing: Analyses of a Management Meeting*, ed. François Cooren (Mahwah, NJ: Lawrence Erlbaum, 2007), 31–52.

4. *Règlement de l'Assemblée Nationale*, art. 52–1 and 54–2 (Paris, 2019 [1959]). Translation mine.

5. François Cooren, *Action and Agency in Dialogue: Passion, Incarnation, and Ventriloquism* (Amsterdam: John Benjamins, 2010); and "Communication Theory

types of assembly in which new forms of collective thinking, speaking, and acting could be practiced. If (deliberative) politics always has to be organized, and if organizing always involves questions of politics,[6] then we first need to better understand *how communicating works*, as it is the only way the organization of assembling and disassembling can be facilitated.[7]

So, what is communication? According to John Durham Peters in *Speaking into the Air*, two competitive answers tend to exist.[8] For the *dialoguians*, communication is a matter of exchanges, debates, and discussions—that is, it is about action and reaction, a back and forth or an intercourse that evokes a certain form of eroticism and can sometimes lead to the possibility of *co-construction*. According to this dialogical view, communicating thus allows people to assemble in order to co-identify a situation and co-define what to do about it. For the *disseminators*, however, communication is more a matter of propagation, diffusion, and proliferation, which is to say that communicating does not always necessarily imply the possibility of an answer. Like a star that communicates its presence to us from a remote galaxy, we can communicate something even if nobody communicates back to us. Communication, in other words, can also be a one-way street.

Examining the ventriloquial dimension of communication can be understood as a potential means to reconcile dialoguians and disseminators. It acknowledges that even in a situation of interaction, diffusion and propagation always take place. We are indeed ventriloquists, because whenever we communicate, we are consciously or unconsciously *making other beings say things through that we ourselves*

at the Center: Ventriloquism and the Communicative Constitution of Reality," *Journal of Communication* 62, no. 1 (February 2012): 1–20.

6. Dennis K Mumby, "Organizational Communication," in *The Encyclopedia of Sociology*, ed. George Ritzer (New York: Blackwell, 2007).
7. François Cooren, *Organizational Discourse: Communication and Constitution* (London: Polity, 2015).
8. John Durham Peters, *Speaking into the Air: A History of the Idea of Communication* (Chicago, IL: University of Chicago Press, 1999); and *The Marvelous Clouds: Toward a Philosophy of Elemental Media*, (Chicago, IL: University of Chicago Press, 2015).

articulate—that is, we ventriloquize them. In this regard, politicians can be said to be the ventriloquists *par excellence*, as they often excel in making others say things whenever they speak in public. A politician will, for instance, speak on behalf of her constituents whenever they state, implicitly or explicitly, what they think, want, or need. In other words, they will ventriloquize what those constituents in question think, want or need—whether the latter like it or not.

Diffusion thus takes place precisely because any speaker, writer or communicator systematically becomes a *medium*—a conduit through which others come to express themselves. Incidentally, I believe this is also why politics tends to be so contentious; as listening to a politician always amounts to paying attention to someone who claims to be speaking in our name, or in the name of someone or something we may either want or not want to hear from. While this ventriloquation appears acceptable when we recognize ourselves in what is being said, things become a little more intense when we feel betrayed by this rendering of what we allegedly think, want, or need. No wonder politicians can acquire such a bad reputation, whether or not they deserve it. They are in charge of an impossible task: they have to speak on our behalf, whilst also speaking in the name of what they believe should be done in any given situation.

But ventriloquation should not be reduced to effects of political representation, that is, effects by which politicians claim the voices of their human constituents. As pointed out by Michel Callon, speaking is also a matter of factual representation, as whenever we articulate the conditions of a particular state of affairs, we are enabling the core, factual components of that situation to be seen, heard, and known.[9] This is especially important within assemblies, given that these gatherings are always meant to allow people to talk about the current state of a situation in order to decipher

9. Michel Callon, "Some Elements of a Sociology of Translation: The Domestication of the Scallops and the Fishermen of St Brieuc Bay," in *Power, Action and Belief: A New Sociology of Knowledge?* ed. John Law (London: Routledge & Kegan Paul, 1987), 196–233.

and reach a decision on the most appropriate collective action. It is indeed not by chance that the term "thing"—let's call it "thing 1"—initially meant, in Old English, a meeting or assembly in which various topics were discussed (we still find this original meaning in the term *Althing*, which is the name of Iceland's general assembly).[10] It is only from the 1300s onwards that the word "thing"—let's call this new term "thing 2"—began to refer to the content of discussion within those meetings or assemblies. An assembly is therefore a "thing 1" where people talk about "things 2."

But why do assemblypersons talk about various "things 2" that are supposed to define a situation? Precisely because each of these "things 2" are either implicitly or explicitly presented as *saying something* about what should be done about the situation people are allegedly facing. Assemblies therefore give their participants the opportunity to discover the multiple facets of a situation, as each assemblyperson becomes a potential *medium* through which various elements of a context can express themselves. Assemblies can thus be seen as generators of complexity, as they allow not only human constituents to be heard, but also constitutions, laws, precedents, scientific studies, the state of ecosystems, ideologies, gods, ancestors, etc., to *say something* about a given situation. In other words, these gatherings constitute *phonation devices* through which participants can collectively define *what a situation dictates* or *requires*.

Debates become, of course, a little complicated when people end up disagreeing about the factual nature of the situation under review, which is what is happening in the current political climate of the United States. Prior to the election of Donald Trump, while Republicans and Democrats typically disagreed about what had to be done regarding a situation, they could still occasionally reach a minimal agreement about the nature of the situation they were facing. This meeting ground of agreement is now becoming

10. See: Bruno Latour and Peter Weibel, eds., *Making Things Public. Atmospheres of Democracy* (Cambridge, MA: MIT Press, 2005).

increasingly volatile, whether the topics concerned relate to global warming, the safety of vaccines, or the results of presidential elections. While previous discussions focused on what mattered the most to each party (free market vs. regulations, limiting immigration vs. welcoming needed workforce, cutting down government vs. investing in infrastructures, etc.), congresspersons and senators (as well as the constituents they are supposed to represent) now seem to question the very *existence* of what matters most to the opposing side.

The question then becomes what happens to "things 1" (assemblies) when people cannot even agree about the "things 2" (elements) that supposedly constitute a situation? Is it still possible to assemble when we appear to live in two different worlds—let's call them A and B—that appear to call for opposite interventions? In world A, which for the sake of argument we could say the Republicans live in, the fraudulent stealing of an election dictates that a past president be reinstated as the new president. While in world B, that of the Democrats (but also the world of all the judges, including judges allocated by Trump himself, who were asked to adjudicate about this question), the alleged election fraud did not in fact take place.

In world A, there is no place for climate change or, at least, for a human-caused one—which means that nothing needs to be done to alter our means of production and transportation. While in world B, the world of Democrats—but also the world in which the immense majority of scientists and, let's be real, most of the world's population live—the existence and origin of climate change is overwhelmingly demonstrated and calls for huge changes in our ways of producing and consuming energy. As we see through these (US-centric) examples (as the United States unfortunately seems to be one of the only countries where such a "debate" can actually be taking place), factual ventriloquation matters a great deal, as it constitutes the ground from which collective decisions can reasonably begin to be made. If we all agree that climate change is a fact, and that this fact keeps being ventriloquized not only by scientists and environmentalists, but also by journalists, politicians, industrialists, and mere citizens, the only thing we can disagree on remains what to do about it. I'm not saying that this type of disagreement is superficial, but in the circumstances I'm describing here, it would at least be true that we collectively *found a way of allowing our planet to articulate something concrete about its current state of jeopardy.*

Can we imagine forms of assemblies in which this factual ventriloquation could be minimally consolidated and organized? I am not asking for any form of certainty, as what defines political and scientific representation is precisely the possibility that it be called into question. I am asking for organizational and political mechanisms that would give assemblypersons a chance to agree on the elements that may end up *counting* or *mattering* in any given situation. This idea is not that new because it is, I believe, one of the political consequences of pragmatism, as initially proposed by Charles Sanders Peirce in the second part of the nineteenth century,[11] and prolonged by John Dewey in the first part of the twentieth.[12] What defines pragmatism is indeed, by my interpretation, an attitude that consists of exploring *what a situation dictates, commands or requires*, knowing of course that this dictation, command or requirement is always colored by the way this situation expresses itself through our sensors, senses and words.

Nothing will ever eliminate bad faith, Machiavellianism or power relations, whether in politics or elsewhere, but can we give ourselves the chance to *start from* what is taking place or happening, not because such a meeting ground would constitute the absolute origin of any decision, but because it would allow us to get in touch with what should/could matter in our world. If something *matters*, it should *materialize* in our debates as a specific *concern*, and if this *concern* materializes in our debates, there is a chance that

11. Charles Sanders Peirce, *The Essential Peirce: Selected Philosophical Writings* (Bloomington, IN: Indiana University Press, 1998).
12. John Dewey, *The Public and Its Problems* (New York: H. Holt and Company, 1927).

it will *dictate* specific courses of action that are meant to adequately respond to it. Pragmatism, in the form I defend here, is not a philosophical version of opportunism and expediency. It is, on the contrary, an attitude that consists of *listening to what the world that surrounds us (and we are part of) has to tell us*, a world made of humans and other-than-humans (especially ecosystems) that obviously need to be better ventriloquized.

"Dialoguians and disseminators, unite!" as we both need co-construction and dissemination. Dissemination because we need to find better phonation devices to listen to the complexity of our world, co-construction because this is, after all, what assemblies are supposed to achieve. As Bruno Latour points out, we inhabit, in many respects, a shared world (*un monde commun*)—a universe, even if this world is also, citing William James, a *pluriverse* that assemblies are meant to recompose.[13] In other words, there cannot be two worlds—world A and world B—at least in terms of factuality (a world where climate change would not exist vs. a world where it would; a world where the United States presidency has been stolen via election fraud vs. a world where it hasn't).

If we can acknowledge that politicians and citizens (with the help of social media) can sometimes manage to live in a bubble or an echo chamber, we can also acknowledge that bubbles always end up bursting, and that echo chambers are, at the end of the day, just rooms—even if social media has managed to make those rooms very large, indeterminate, and shifting in size. Another important feature of pragmatism, as conceived by Peirce, lies in our capacity to be *surprised* by our experiences—what he called "fallibilism"[14]—which means that our beliefs, as strong as they might be, can end up being contradicted by what the world,

13. Bruno Latour, *Politics of Nature: How to Bring the Sciences into Democracy* (Cambridge, MA: Harvard University Press, 2004); and William James, *A pluralistic Universe: Hibbert Lectures at Manchester College on the Present Situation in Philosophy* (Lincoln, NE: University of Nebraska Press, 1996 [1909]).
14. Charles Sanders Peirce, "The Scientific Attitude and Fallibilism," in *Philosophical Writings of Peirce*, ed. Justus Buchler (New York: Dover, 1955), 42–59.

in its recalcitrance, keeps telling us. Can we organize assemblies in such a way that this recalcitrance is able to fully express itself, to change our course of action, our sympathies, and our allegiances? This requires, for sure, a politics of organizing, but also an organizing of our politics.

Jean Godefroy Bidima

Twelve Theses

on the Palaver

1 Like other processes of gathering and regrouping, assemblies follow varying motives. An assembly such as the palaver is said to be irenic when it shows how a society articulates its relation: to the norm, to its expectations and to its aspirations. But the palaver can also take the form of a battlefield, the conflict then expressing the founding dissensus of the social sphere. This is also shown by its various motives among the Beti of Cameroon. The *tsoo* rite was purifying and the *ésié* restorative, while the *metè* (a word whose root refers to saliva) was a public blessing, and the *ngam* or *mvigi* scanned the future. The fear of nothingness, the preservation or dissolution of power, anger and, more generally, enthusiasm are classic triggers for the gathering of an assembly. The "Assemblies of God" that are spreading across Africa and that are the tropical conversion of American Pentecostalism—messianic movements such as Kimbanguism in the Congo, Celestial Christianity in Côte d'Ivoire, the Aladura Church in Nigeria and the Gbanamè Church in Benin—are all based on enthusiasm.

2 Even when it is not agonistic, the palaver retains an element of competition. An oratorical competition in which *captatio benevolentiae* alternates with simulation, "honest dissimulation"[1] with dishonest dissimulation. In the case of the agonistic or irenic palaver, what is at stake is not so much the object of the discussion—payment of the dowry, transactions regarding widowhood rights, reparation of a dishonour, pacification of an inter-individual or community conflict—as the making sense of this object. The palaver assembly also takes place with the help of invisible actors. The past is summoned along with tribal memory, just as when jurists in the Western world summon case law to better inform their decisions.

1. Torquatto Accetto, *De l'honnête dissimulation*, trans. Mireille Blanc Sanchez (Lagrasse: Verdier, 1990), 42.

3 The right to speak is one of the motives of the assemblies. In the 2000s, in order to challenge the authorities, Ivorians took over one and then several public squares in Abidjan.[2] They transformed them into open-air popular assemblies. Assemblies where the police was not needed to maintain order, assemblies that did not impose an agenda, but where a new agenda unfolded each day as and when participants arrived. One of these squares in Abidjan was named "the Sorbonne." The Abidjan Sorbonne referred historically to the *disputationes* held at the Sorbonne in the Middle Ages. But this colonial reminiscence obliterates another aspect of the Sorbonne *disputatio*: its rhetorical, metaphysical, ethical, and theological rigidity. For the historical Sorbonne, as a faculty of theology, was also where heresies were condemned. The very opposite of this Ivorian Sorbonne, where speech was in flux: uttered, shouted, mocked, played out, and thwarted. At the end of the daily assemblies, no minutes were taken and no oaths had to be respected, but there was a willingness to return the next day to occupy this space for speech and play.

4 The *mise en scène* of the assemblies transforms territories into "spaces" where the imaginary and the real meet. Before and during the colonial period, for the palaver to take place, among the Beti, the Bulu, and the Fang—populations living in the south of Cameroon, in the north of Gabon, and in Equatorial Guinea—the privileged place was the *Aba'a*, a congregational house run by the "fathers" of the group. Here was a "territory" transformed, by the palaver, into a "space" for discussion, for sharing words, food, and criticisms. Regardless of the type of palaver—irenic or agonistic—one could not convene these meetings in a kitchen or on one's veranda. The choice of the *Aba'a* reflected the significance of the patriarchy in these otherwise patrilineal societies. Among the Beti, the "courtyard" was also favoured,

2. Aghi Bahi, "La 'Sorbonne' d'Abidjan, rêve de démocratie ou naissance d'un espace public," *Revue africaine de sociologie* 7, no. 1 (2003): 1–17.

preferably under a tree in the dry season. In this case, the palaver recalled the relation of the subjects to the chthonic forces: the ground was struck to express indignation or approval, figures were drawn on it using a cane or fly swatter, and dust was used to swear an oath or take a pledge. The assizes of the *Ɛmokr* palaver, among the Adjoukrou of Côte d'Ivoire, are held in a space on the border between the territories of the two groups in dispute, or in another village serving as a site of mediation: a place where the assemblies in dispute recognize the possibility of sharing the blame and the benefits of peace. Because it divides and unites at the same time, this particular place exists in the impossibility of closure.

In order to have access to the public space of discussion, no thought was given, even during the Enlightenment, to those who, as in the Greek agora, did not have the opportunity to access the spaces of discussion such as later the literary salons, the Masonic lodges, the theaters: namely, the slaves. For political thinkers like Jürgen Habermas, the question of the space of assemblies was submerged in that of public space. And yet the production of the power to deliberate and discuss also requires a semiotics of space.

5 All assemblies start from a hermeneutic premise: we can understand each other. But when we think we understand, we are simply caught. In an assembly, one discusses, argues and converses, but one is "entangled," as it were, in this conversation. Assemblies set in motion types of conversations that both promise to make sense of the group's history and blur that sense.

The first blurring of meaning is the *misunderstanding*. The philosopher Vladimir Jankélévitch places it in the domain of the absurd. It is not a "mishearing"[3] but a profound dissymmetry in the linguistic exchange. "This asymmetry of a false truth that is right and wrong, wrong to be right

3. Vladimir Jankélévitch, *Le Je-ne-sais-quoi et le Presque rien. 2: La Méconnaissance, le malentendu* (Paris: Le Seuil, 1980), 186.

Marc Abélès, *Ochollo dignitaries speaking in an assembly*, Gemu Gofa, Ethiopia, 1974–75

and right to be wrong, and that reflects so well our average condition, is the principle of the misunderstanding."[4] The palaver of purification and reparation among the Beti of Cameroon often plays on this "misunderstanding." In cases of fratricide, matricide, and parricide, the group, during the palaver, evacuates shock and trauma by unloading the guilt on an abstract entity. In this palaver, the murderer is placed in a position of misunderstanding: "he is both right and wrong and neither right nor wrong." He is often seen as a victim of evil spirits who have taken hold of him and used him to commit murder. Society exculpates itself by offloading guilt onto an abstract third party: the evil spirit whose wrath must be appeased through a purifying and restorative rite, for it could not bear to condemn this murderer who is a product of its educational ambitions without at the same time condemning the organizations that transmitted them. The murderer is at once wrong (he has killed) and not wrong (he has been the plaything of evil spirits).

The second blurring of meaning is a matter of *disagreement*. Jacques Rancière defines it as follows: "By

4. Jankélévitch, *Le Je-ne-sais-quoi*, 185.

disagreement we mean a specific type of speech situation: that in which one of the interlocutors both hears and does not hear what the other says. The disagreement is not the conflict between the one who says white and the one who says black. It is the conflict between the one who says white and the one who says white but does not hear the same thing under the name of whiteness."[5] This disagreement is often caused during the palaver by the use of riddles and apophthegms. It also arises through the continuous creation of new words in the lexicon of the languages used. In the palaver, there is often a tension between the language of the young and that of the old, between the language of the initiated and that of the uninitiated. They use the same words but hear different things.

Let's call the third blurring of meaning the *differend*. For the question of the criteria of judgement inevitably arises when disputes are decided. Jean-François Lyotard introduced the notion to characterize the partiality of the criteria of judgement. "A case of differend between two parties takes place when the regulation of the conflict that opposes them is done in the idiom of one of the parties while the

5. Jacques Rancière, *La Mésentente, politique et philosophie* (Paris: Galilée, 1995), 12.

Marc Abélès, *Arrangement of sitting stones for the assemblies of the Ochollo people*, Gemu Gofa, Ethiopia, 1974–75

wrong suffered by the other is not signified in that idiom."[6] Colonial palaver is a perfect example of what is meant by differend. Here, for example, is how René Graffin, a priest of the Congregation of the Holy Spirit, related palaver sessions that took place in an African village:

> "The palaver must be settled. Some men have two or three wives. Which one is legitimate? Here is a man who once gave his legitimate wife as a gift. Another woman is refused by her husband because he has bought a little girl ... But as she can neither leave the child with her 'husband' nor send her back to her old man ..., what to do with her? ... And a practical solution must be found immediately."[7]

In this case as in others, the anthropological and theological dispute posed by the matrimonial problem is settled in the legal and theological idiom of Western civilization. The impossibility of the palaver arises from the fact that the criterion for judgement is based on a cultural differend. It is impossible for the assembly to put the differend into words because the dispute is settled using the rule of the colonial masters.

6 In both formal and informal assemblies, it is not only a question of words and speech: people shout, cry, laugh. Don't British members of parliament often express agreement collectively (Hear! Hear!)? In the French National Assembly, by contrast, one often hears individual shouts from members of the assembly. In African palaver sessions, approval is sometimes also expressed by cries of "youyou": these cries, which are also cries of laughter punctuated by cries of pain or disapproval, serve to emphazise the playful, sarcastic, or dramatic nature of the situation under discussion. The cries of the assemblies can also be a matter of manipulation and

6. Jean-François Lyotard, *The Differend: Phrases in Dispute*, trans. Georges Van Den Abbeele (Minneapolis: University of Minnesota Press, 1988), 9.
7. René Graffin, "À travers le pays Mvéle," *Annales Apostoliques* (November–December 1927): 181.

of what Wilhelm Reich called the "emotional plague" of the masses disoriented and politicized by fascism. But the cry is not only a "plague"; it can serve to structure, as shown by the place of the child's primal cry in medieval European law, which alone confirmed the viability of the marriage or enabled the transmission of property within the couple.[8]

7 "The *tajmaât* or village assembly or, nowadays, the village committee," writes the ethnologist of Kabylia, Alain Mahé, "is made up of an *amin* (president) assisted by an *ukil* and by as many *tamen* (both representatives and respondents) as the village has lineages. During plenary assemblies, all men are obliged to attend the debates on pain of a fine. Everyone has a formal right to speak, but very few use it."[9] This decision not to speak during a village assembly indicates that, while noise, hubbub, laughter, and shouting maintain the atmosphere of the assemblies, silence also plays an important role. The silence observed during village palavers and assemblies is there, not to impede the meaning of the words that are circulating, but to establish something more fundamental, as during the *ésòk* among the Beti of southern Cameroon and especially during the ordeals. The assembly that speaks, exchanges and gesticulates must also wait, listen, lend an ear, and open wide its eyes to follow the protocols of the ordeals. Nature enters into contact with humankind, another part of itself, in order to supplement its judgement, to refute or approve its own laws. The aim of the ordeal is to show that a continuity exists between human societies and nature, by following a holistic approach of human societies.[10] Among the Kabye of northern Togo, the two parties in conflict had to submit to the boiling oil test, which verified the innocence

8. Robert Jacob, "Le Cri du nouveau-né, la famille et la terre', in *Haro! Noël! Oyé! Pratique du cri au Moyen-Âge*, eds. Didier Lett and Nicolas Offenstadt (Paris: Publications de la Sorbonne, 2003), 45.
9. Alain Mahé, "Les Assemblées villageoises dans la Kabylie contemporaine. Traditionalisme par excès de modernité ou modernisme par excès de traditionalisme?" *Études rurales* (July–December 2000): 181.
10. Raymond Verdier, "Parole du Corps et corps du Monde: l'ordalie archaïque," *Revue du Mauss* 50 (2017): 183–93.

of the person who managed to hold a ring dipped in boiling oil without getting his or her hands burned.[11] The silence of the assembly that participates in the outcome of the ordeal is intended to open itself to the unexpected. This silence is often lacking in political assemblies that are more inclined to deal with what is said and what is to be said than with this "threshold of meaning." So how can it be integrated?

8 To survive, a community needs to know, if only implicitly, that the actors can understand each other and that what is being discussed in the assembly can lead to an understanding. The speaking turn that is both respected and interrupted, the reliance on moving elements through the evocation of the memory of ancestors via apophthegms and proverbs, the summoning of acclamations and shouts that are authorized: all help to forge the self-institution of the society. Acclamations and applause often follow the outcome of the ordeals and represent a kind of breathing space that lends a dash of institutionality to what seems disordered and spontaneous.

9 The "deliberations" of the *Poro* assemblies, a rite of passage to the age of majority among the Senufo of northern Côte d'Ivoire, begin with the *tyogolo*, a seven-year initiation period observed by young adolescents. Then, at the moment of entering the sacred forest, all candidates for initiation and initiates are considered equal. During the deliberations of these assemblies, what is decided is not immutable. The palaver of the *Poro* refers to a restart of the discussion and is therefore not closed.[12] The discussion is adjourned so that speech can be recharged, like a battery. This "adjournment of speech" and the possibility of its resumption are found in the palaver sessions of the Beti. Consensus is then only the

11. Jean Godefroy Bidima, "Justice de/par la Nature: l'ordalie à la lumière de la distinction Nature/Culture à partir de Descola," in *Puissances de la Nature*, ed. Raymond Verdier (Paris: L'Harmattan, 2013), 47–58.
12. Andras Zemplini, "Les Assemblées secrètes du Poro Senoufo," in *Le Genre humain*, no. 40–41, "Qui veut prendre la parole?", ed. Marcel Detienne (Paris: Seuil, 2003): 122.

other side of dissensus: at the end of the deliberation, they say "*Bine kiñ dzia biñgoñ bibè*" (We speak with one unanimous voice, but with different throats). Unanimity is always provisional, as is dissensus. The Beti palaver goes beyond the "binarized" forms of classical deliberation—agreement or disagreement, consensus *vs.* dissensus, misunderstanding *vs.* understanding. It marks speech with the seal of incompleteness. The end of the palaver is not consensus, but a dissensus subject to the norm, a dissensus that accepts its incompleteness, its finitude, and that seems to say: "We'll come back to it." This fundamental incompleteness of speech indicates that the links that the assemblies want to re-found are fragile.

10 The palaver, as an assembly, is the place where the political question is reformulated in African societies. It is also a paradigm for thinking, to a certain extent, about politics and its crisis. "Deliberation" is practised so that speech can be "recharged" with its potential.

11 The assemblies pose several questions to our post-postmodernity. The first concerns the role of communications in the digital age. How do we move from assemblies where concrete subjects interact to virtual "assemblies"? What is lost or gained in this shift? How might the virtual world benefit concrete assemblies like the recent "Arab Spring"? With assemblies like the Ivorian Sorbonne, it is state sovereignty that is called into question. The state no longer has a monopoly on the organization of institutions, and the prevented speech ends up being expressed. Lastly, assemblies pose the problem of the relation between manipulation and the loss of power through speech in the public space and the media. They put orality back in the spotlight and, to a certain extent, give priority to the constitution of this very fragile reality that is "speech." But the study of assemblies warns us against this plurality of voices in assemblies, voices that often stifle the delivery of speech.

12 Deliberative politics must take account of reception and contact. This is what distinguishes “cold assemblies” (where civil society seeks its way through argumentation and other legal claims) from “hot assemblies” (where something more fundamental is at work). Assemblies like the African palaver warn us about the possibility of “losing speech.” And the end of speech, in favour of communication and contacts without flavour or depth, will also be the end of the links that structure and oblige.

An Assembly

raumlabor

Forms of

Floating University, Berlin, Germany, 2018

We like to see the city as a form of assembly—we are inspired by this abundance of cooperation across all scales. The spaces we design advocate new potential protocols for collaborative and consent-driven urban transformation, in touch with the many facets of human and non-human needs and conditions of existence.

The Floating University is situated in Berlin and describes itself as a nature-culture learning site. It inhabits an open-air infrastructure space, a rainwater retention pool. Ephemeral and light architectural interventions allow for ever-changing forms of coming together, working, relaxing, and exchanging. They provide a setting for chance encounters and cross-pollination between programs in the most diverse fields.

Floating is a self-governing entity that can be seen as a commons with members as commoners, caring about the future of the common resource—the Floating. The assemblies, formal and informal, experiment with how to bring together individual artistic drives, collaborative energies, and collective decision-making.

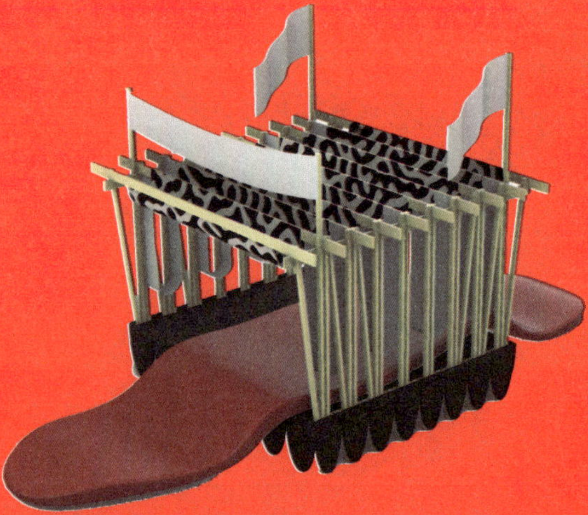

We are interested in open forms which come without a clear protocol of inhabitation and use. Presenting a landscape of possibilities, the gathering space we propose invites living beings to choose and find their place within. It is a versatile space that can be used for lectures, discussions, performances, and movie nights. Or simply to be discovered and relaxed in, to regenerate the energies.

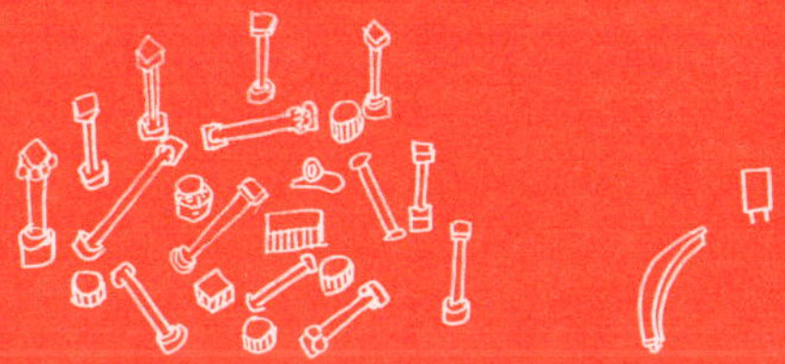

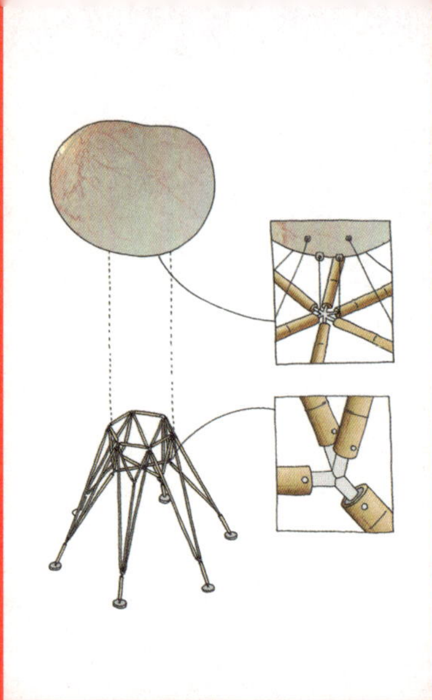

NO PRISONS
NO CAGES
NO PIPELINES

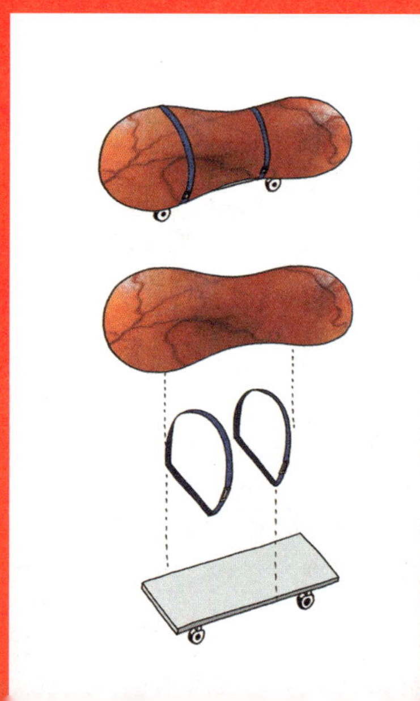

The design presents a flock of objects—a family consisting of four characters. The "Big Bamboo" with long legs and a round membrane head is accompanied by gut-like formations placed on the skateboards. The two "Furry Friends" show many pockets that can offer one or another surprise (such as leaflets). A set of rolling tribunes preserve the traces of posters from earlier events, and flags and banners signal current agendas. Maybe over time, more of them will join the installation and the assembly will become even more joyful, energetic, and changeable.

Forms of Assembly, Centre Pompidou, Paris, May 2022
Co-produced by Centre Pompidou and Evens Foundation, based on the proposal commissioned for this book.

Galerie 2

Any form of assembly in and around these strange objects will include a multiplicity of individual acts of appropriation, choice, bodily placement, sensations, and proximities. Maybe they will induce a feeling of uncertain ground. Why am I here? What are we doing? Should we do this differently? While at the same time, maybe there could be feelings like: this is nice, nice to meet you, this is an interesting discussion, hm, I didn't see it that way, let's get up and do some exercise and then continue. We present objects without a script.

The proposal for this book and the installation at the Centre Pompidou were developed by Markus Bader, Luka Murovec, Louise Nguyen, and Leonie Steudle.

Forms of Assembly, Centre Pompidou, Paris, May 2022
Co-produced by Centre Pompidou and Evens Foundation, based on the proposal commissioned for this book.

IV.

Ayreen Anastas & Rene Gabri

Fragments of Life

as Assembly

1 *Every Thursday a group of women meet to be together. They prepare some food, not a meal per se, but light things; special sweets baked, rolled, stuffed, cared for. Then there will be fruits, cucumbers with salt, seeds, nuts, coffee, tea, lots of anticipation, lots of speech. They will call it "doreh," not assembly, which alludes to a circle and invokes the turn which everyone must take in order to prepare the space of these weekly encounters.*

How do we invite and bring bodies together? How do we become sensitive toward attending to such encounters not simply as spaces of production, but as generative of who we become, as spaces of life-giving and life-bearing? Our thesis, if this short treatise is to have one, is that we are how we assemble. Better formulated, we could say, our becomings are formed through our assemblings. And the accompanying question we will ask is: how do you (as in the plural "you all") assemble?

2 *We arrive in a village that is tucked away inside a mountain gorge. It is picturesque, retreated from the main road; it would be very easy to pass by it without ever knowing of its existence. Here, we learn about an old hammam that is and has been maintained by the villagers for a long long time. No one can tell us exactly how long, but they can tell us how. Each month, one family in the village must take care, must have acquired the wood, the necessary elements and tools—all that will be needed to operate the hammam, to maintain it, and for all the villagers to use it.*

The forms, pretexts, and places of assembly are infinite. They influence not only how bodies come together—in quantity, in character, in tone, in purpose, in potential use or horizon—but also how bodies relate to one another. These spaces are never neutral, and they color or orient the forms we do or undo when we bodies come together. Bodies are always implicated in an idea of assembly. And every space of assembly is also a possibility for the emergence of certain bodies and for asking how those bodies may or may not relate to one another.

Next pages: Ayreen Anastas and Rene Gabri, *Scenes of Assembly 1–8*, 2022

TEHRAN
IRAN
WOMEN

Doreh WEEKLY THURSDAYS
I. Home Living Room

INGREDIENTS: COFFEE
FOOD
COOKING
CAKES

WE ARE HOW WE ASSEMBLE
ASSEMBLING AS A FORCE THAT FORMS OUR BECOMINGS.
GENDERING OF ASSEMBLY
REPRODUCTION
PRODUCTION OF
CONVERSATION

MAGHREB
FAMILIES
WATER
WOOD
LOOFA
TOWELS

Hammam MONTHLY - DAILY
2. Bathhouse in Common

BODIES OF ENDURANCE
CARE
HOW DO WE CARE — HABITS — INSTINCTS
CARE TAKING
CARE GIVING & ASSEMBLY
INSTITUTIONS
COMMONS
CARE
PLACE OF CARE AS PLACE OF ASSEMBLY
BODIES OF ASSEMBLY

EAST VILLAGE
PERFORMERS
BROOM
MOP
CLEANING SPACE BEFORE AND AFTER

Black Box DAILY
3. Rehearsal Space

REHEARSING FORMS OF ASSEMBLY
THEATERS OF ASSEMBLY
ASSEMBLY AS RITUAL — PRACTICE — EVERY PROCESS OF LIFE
PREPARATION
PREPARING OR PICKING UP AFTER ASSEMBLY
RITUALS OF PREPARING
PRE & POST OF ASSEMBLY

LOWER EAST SIDE

Political Family - Urban Commune
4. Kitchen in Common

MILITANTS
RUNAWAYS
MISFITS
ANARCHISTS → COMMUNAL MEALS → LIBERATED FOUND BORROWED INGREDIENTS
FOOD COOKING DINNER AS ASSEMBLY → COMMUNISTS MAOISTS SITUATIONISTS STUDENTS WORKERS COMMUNARDS
FRANCE
AUSTRIA
SWITZERLAND
ASSEMBLIES OF THE QUOTIDIEN
FORM AND ORGANIZATION
HABIT VS. AFFINITY
EVERYDAY LIFE
FORMAL
INFORMAL

Becoming of a Rural Commune
5. Square - Factory - University

→ BARRICADES
BRICKS POSTERS
SLOGANS PAMPHLETS
PROTEST MANIFESTO
PRACTICE
FORM OF LIFE
AUTONOMY
ASSEMBLY AS PRACTICE AND PATH OF EXISTING REALITY TO BE PUT TO QUESTION
ONE INSTANT AS A LINE OF FLIGHT
EVENT OF ASSEMBLY
LASTING A LIFETIME

EVERYONE
PALESTINE
VISIBILITY
INVISIBILITY
RUPTURE
RADICAL
INTERRUPTION
ONCE A YEAR
LAND DAY - MARCH 30

General Strike
6. Stores, Schools, Workshops, Workplaces, Spaces of Production and Reproduction

DETERRITORIALIZING LINE
WHEN ALL THE SPACES OF ASSEMBLY OF LIFE HAVE BEEN OCCUPIED
WITHDRAWAL OF ENERGY
NOTHING STOPPAGE
INOPERATIVE UNDO UNWORK
THE PRESENCE OF AN ABSENCE
INVISIBLE ASSEMBLY
ASSEMBLING AGAINST A MILITARIZED OCCUPIED STATE
CRITIQUE OF VIOLENCE
ASSEMBLING UNDER STATE VIOLENCE

CHINATOWN — DAILY

Museum Independent Study
7. Ex-Industrial Loft Institutional Space

SPACE OF STUDY
LEARNING
ART CULTURAL
BOOKS
TEXTS
READINGS
SCREENINGS
DISCUSSIONS
STUDIOS OF ASSEMBLY
FORECLOSURES
→ VOCATIONAL
ARTISTS
CURATORS
CRITICS
ART HISTORIANS
QUESTION OF AFFECTION
CAN THE ASSEMBLY SCALE BODIES
ASSEMBLY AND INSTITUTIONS
INSTITUTIONAL & AFFECT
THE RISK OF STATE MONOPOLY ON ASSEMBLY

Autonomous Art Politics Thought Discussion
8. Ex-Office Space Extra-Para Stitutional Space

LOWER MANHATTAN
WALL STREET
BEAVER STREET
WEEKLY - MONDAYS
OPEN FROM
FREE
QUESTIONS
PRACTICES
THOUGHT
ACTION
ART
SPACES OF CAPTIVITY
STUDY
BECOMING COMMUNE
REGULARITY
RECURRING
EVERYDAY
HABIT
THE STRUGGLE FOR FREE SPACES OF ASSEMBLY
DE-PROFESSIONALIZATION
ONE
FIND AND
REVOCATIONAL
TRANS-VERSAL
PLANES OF CONSISTENCY
EXITING EXISTING
EVERYONE STRUGGLING AGAINST
SPACES OF ASSEMBLY
CAPITALIST
COLONIAL
IMPERIAL
RACIST
PATRIARCHAL
HETERO
ASSEMBLY OF THE FORCES
COMMONS
ART AND OF ASSEMBLY
PROFESSIONALIZATION OF ASSEMBLY
VS.
ASSEMBLY AS A FORM OF LIFE

HABIT
FREQUENCY
MATERIALS NEEDED
AGENTS
PROTAGONISTS
BODIES
CONTEXT
QUESTIONS
PLACE
FRICTIONS
TENSIONS
SITUATION
CONDITIONS

TRIBECA

Rental Event Space

9. Ex-Industrial Loft

ARTISTS
ACTIVISTS
POLITICAL THEORISTS
PERFORMERS
EVENT
INSTITUTIONAL LIMITS
THE NEED FOR SPACES TO ASSEMBLE
FORCES WHICH FEAR
COMMODIFICATION OF SPACE CAPTURE
ASSEMBLY FOR RENT MONETIZE
DE-POLITICIZE
PRIVATIZATION
CONTROL OF
SPACES FOR ASSEMBLY
CHANNELING
OF ASSEMBLY

SHARJAH

Day-Laborer Congregation Site

10. Square - Park - Meeting Place

EVERY MORNING
DAY WORKERS LABORERS
PRECARIOUS
UNDOCUMENTED
MIGRANTS
GUESTS
TREES
DAWN OF
ASSEMBLY
EVERYDAY COMMUNISM
TO INHABIT SPACE
TO IMPLICITLY CHARGE A SPACE POLITICALLY
TO POSE A THREAT
THE ASSEMBLING AS PERPETUAL
THE ORDER WILL ALWAYS FEAR
PRECARITY PRE-EMPTION
POTENCY
FEAR OF ASSEMBLY
PRE-EMPT ASSEMBLY
POLICING ASSEMBLY

TUNIS

Union of Unemployed

11. Central Street Thoroughfare

KRISIS
KAIROS
UNEMPLOYED
WORKLESS
COMMUNISTS
MILITANTS
ORGANIZERS
REVOLUTIONARIES
POLICE
AND ANTI-
POLICE
TIME FOR
REVOLUTION
UNTIMELY
THE CITY AS FACTORY
AFTER THE FACTORY
THE CHALLENGE OF
ORGANIZING
NO PLACES OF WORK
NO WORK
NO PLACES TO ORGANIZE
UNIONIZE
TO FORM COALITION
POLICING OF SPACE
THREAT OF ASSEMBLY

SYMBOL OF CAPITAL

Wall Street

12. Financial Center - Public Symbol

IN
SOLIDARITY
CONJUNCTION
AND
SITUATION
CONJUNCTURE
CALL
THREAT
RESPONSE
TIME FOR
HOLDING
OLIGARCHS
RESPONSIBLE
CENTER OF INEQUALITY
CONJUNCTION
DISJUNCTION
REIMAGINING SOLIDARITY
TIME BETWEEN A CALL
A RESPONSE

BOWLING GREEN

General Assembly

13. Historic Park - Colonial Center

ONE
CHOSEN
DAY
THE BEGINNING
ARTISTS
AGITATORS
ANARCHISTS
HORIZONTAL
ASSEMBLERS
MILITANTS
TO OCCUPY
OR NOT TO
OCCUPY
PROTEST VS. ASSEMBLY
ADDRESSING ABSTRACTIONS
" SINGULAR BEINGS
BECOMINGS

TOMKINS SQUARE PARK

Preparing for Occupation

14. City Park - Square - Site of Riot Revolt

SPEAKING TO AN
OUTSIDE VS. ONE
ANOTHER
WEEKLY
MILITANTS
REVOLUTIONARIES
'OCCUPIERS'
ANARCHISTS
ANTI-CAPITALISTS
HOW DO WE
ESTABLISH A
MODE
A MANNER OF ASSEMBLING
FINDING A COMMON
QUESTION OF LANGUAGE
VIOLENCE – NON VIOLENCE
HOW DO WE MAKE PLACE
OUT OF SPACE

THE CALLING

Molecular Modular Gathering

15. a Call - Calling Assembly - Common Place

THOSE WHO RESPOND
NINE DAYS
EXPANDING COMMONING
COMMUNAL COMMUNIZING
METRO TIME
PARIS FOR EXAMPLE
ANY PLACE WHATEVER
DILATED
INTENSIFIED
TIME
CRISIS OF
EVERYTHING
WELCOME TO AS
THE NEW
PARADIGM
THE LANGUAGE
WHICH CALLS
SITUATES
IMAGINES THE
ASSEMBLY
TO COME
ASSEMBLY AND
THE CALL
→ AS A CALLING FOR / FORTH
AN OUTSIDE / WITHIN
INTIMATE / EXTIMATE
ALWAS A
COMMUNITY THAT – IS COMING

16. Whatever Metro - Whatever City Whatever Day

SINGULARITIES
MULTITUDES
EVERY
MOMENT
IMMANENT
VIRTUAL
CONCRETE
REAL
ASSEMBLY AS / A SOCIAL
INFRASTRUCTURE FOR
COMMUNAL OR
EXISTENCE
WHATEVER AS INDIFFERENCE
RANDOMNESS
AS BEING SUCH
COMING TOGETHER
PRECISELY SUCH
AS IT IS
THE IMMANENT
ASSEMBLY
NEVER
CLOSED
ON THIS
OCCASSION
IN THIS
ENCOUNTER
THIS COULD
HAPPEN
ONLY THIS CAN
HAPPEN
ASSEMBLY
AND THOSE
MISSING
PRE-DETERMINED
HOW TO INHABIT
THE EXISTING
INFRASTRUCTURE
USE THEM TOWARD
OUR OWN FORMS
NEEDS FOR ASSEMBLY
WHAT THE
INFRASTRUCTURES
TRY TO ERASE
COVER OVER

These spaces can remind us or make us forget that we are bodies, and that these bodies are fragile, with different needs and vulnerabilities. They exist in habitats full of other bodies, which require our care and attention. Thus a sweat lodge, a sauna, an eternal spring, or hammam are no less spaces of assembly and no less political than anything that could consider itself to be a house of assembly. One could speculate that such spaces are originary sites where a sensibility for the inseparability of the care for bodies, including the social body and the body of earth, and the care for worlds, or politics, has been practiced and cultivated.

Just as every form of assembling needs a place to assemble, every place of assembly needs its caretakers and caregivers. The circulation and sharing of this care for assembling is the assembly's lifeblood. Moreover, just as this space is not simply physical nor necessarily fixed or permanent, the forms of care it encompasses are never reducible to a particular idea of care. But this attention to the care and its communization, whatever forms it may take, will be the marker for nourishment and its ability to nourish the bodies which come together.

3 *Hidden just off Broadway in the village is a cavernous black box. It is not a theater, though the space has all the elements of theatricality. It is large enough for many bodies to come together; the floor is a large wooden platform, gentle enough to fall, to crawl, to play, dance, sing. It has very high ceilings, drawing your eyes to various forms of lighting, which can produce different effects. If you speak in such a space your voice carries further than usual, as it is largely empty. A group of mostly young searchers gather five days a week, in the evenings for four hours, sharing with someone named Richard, who experienced and was a part of the explosion of intensities in the 1960s and 1970s, including intimately knowing their reverberations in the spheres and understandings of theater and performance. He will guide them for the next four or five weeks through extensive exercises, rituals, breathing, panting, chanting, stretching, spanning, but before all or any of that, two people are in*

charge each day to clean the floor and to arrange the space from the previous day's use. To enter these rehearsals of assembly, all are also asked to change their clothes not simply for the purpose of being dressed in something more comfortable, but also as a part of the same action, the ritual of clearing and preparing their space of assembly.

Such rituals of preparation and reflection are how moments of assembling begin to weave themselves into the fabric of life. The assembly can itself be a ritual, or it can be preceded by and followed with rituals. These rituals are not the "life-world" simply of the assembly, they are the "life-world" itself. In other words, both what precedes and what comes after the assembly belong to the assembly, and equally what belongs to life is assembly. Life as a constant care before and after our modes of assembly.

It is as though we are always within processes, whether we know it or not, conscious or unconscious, of preparing for the assembly to come. Or picking up from the traces of the ones which preceded us.

4 *In the same city, in those same streets, in those very years of heat and intensification referred to as the 1960s, a bit further east and south, in a large expanse of the island, before the "property envelopers" discovered the money to be made branding neighborhoods then summarily called the Lower East Side, a group of artists, poets, political misfits and militants, anarchists, meet up in the evenings for dinner. They refer to themselves as "the family" but are sometimes called "the motherfuckers" after signing an action using that name in allusion to the concluding words of a poem by Amiri Baraka, back when he was still called LeRoi Jones, "up against the wall motherfucker," a phrase often uttered by cops before handcuffing and apprehending "suspects." Our friend B. tells us these dinners were their only protocol and form of assembly. All elective affinities, actions, notices, coordinations, if ever needed, were developed and communicated there. Some "liberated" the ingredients, some by turns tended to the cooking, others to the cleaning. B., in his turn, took to cooking Soba noodles, which*

he had discovered while searching for foods to heal his liver, through a dancer named Irma at the Oshawa Foundation on Second Avenue. This is where the sharing of a meal became a basic infrastructure not only for sharing life and friendship, but also as the basic element of a political becoming.

The assembly is a space and time for a collective political becoming. This political character is attained neither by simply deliberating over decisions, nor by making determinations of power, understood as a possession or as the capacity for domination, control, or the exertion of hierarchical force. Rather, the politics of assembly are immanent to the ways the bodies come together. How can that space-time be taken care of? Who is able to give or be given care? The power of the assembly is generated in and through each act of care, all the while enhancing the potencies of each caregiver and caretaker. That giving and taking of care is how the forces of the assembly infinitely proliferate rather than centralize. Every assembling is political, as it exhibits, exposes, or performs a mode of—and an implicit reflection on—existing in common, and the forms of care this requires. That daily habit of assembling together for a meal is the form this care took for B. and the family.

This is how we come together. This is how we care for our worlds. This is how we consider things. This is how we question things. This is how we hear things, listen, smell, cook, clean, taste, feel things and view them, touch them or are touched by them. This is how we commune, this is how we live. This is how we want to live.

This political character of the assembly can only be avowed or disavowed but it cannot be abolished.

5 *In the months of June, July, August, September, or any month thereafter in 1968, a group of young students move in refuge, assembling after confrontations with Austrian neo-Nazis. They move and assemble with other groups in Switzerland to conduct militant actions against armies, dictators, churches and in favor of refugees and workers' struggle, in particular to support workers who want to take over and manage their*

CIRCLE
FLOW
TEA
FOOD
COFFEE
SWEETS
PLACE
HOME
BODIES
CONVERSATIONS
STORIES
MOVEMENT
THURSDAYS
WEEKLY
TURN
REVOLUTION
CIRCLES OF FRIENDSHIP
TRANSFORMATION MACHINE
SOAP
LOOFAH
BODIES
WATER
STEAM
WOOD
FIRE
ROOM
COMMUNAL CARE
CARING FOR THE COMMON
THE COMMUNAL
BODY + ENCOUNTER WITH ENHANCEMENT ELEMENTS
PRE-PARE
ASSEMBLE
POST-CARE
PICKUP AFTER
MOP
BROOM
WATER
DUSTBIN
WIPE
OPEN
CLEAR
MAKE
SPACE
WAY
REHEARSE
REPEAT
PART
CLOSE
RECOVER
PREPARING REHEARSING MULTIPLYING
THE THEATERS
FORMS OF
ASSEMBLY

own factory. In the early 1970s, those same young militants decide to get together and experiment a life-in-common in a rural area in the Southeast of France. In their coming together, the gesture of many other commoners is repeated. A life of subsistence and solidarity is established, nourished, and practiced. Every Sunday evening after dinner, an assembly is held, to think together, introduce, decide together, various projects, presentations, composing of groups, affinities, actions, and plans to keep the ship sailing.

May 1968, an assembly of a multiplicity of assemblies with all their different modes and durations. A radiating force field which gathers all the assemblies past and yet to come. An assembly as a generator of further spaces and processes of communization. An assembly as a sailing ship in the hostile seas of societies composed of coerced work and forms of immiseration masked as voluntary professions. An assembly as an abolitionist practice against salaries, private property, hierarchies, and every form of containment and imprisonment. An assembly as assemblage, of earth, a sunflower seed, a sheep, an olive tree, a children's radio signal, a long kitchen table, some medicinal plants, almonds, and laughters. An assembly as the form which can turn an instant in time into an enduring practice and experience of autonomy.

6 *On the 30th of March, 1976, 1977, 1978, 1979, 1980, or 1981, a child in Palestine does not go to school, does not assemble in the everyday manner of the morning bell gathering of sheep, of schoolchildren entering the classroom to sit continuously for six hours with some break in between, on the same chair, same desk. No, the child that day does not go to school. The day is named after the land, assembling to dis-activate all other normal and normalized assembling, to assemble in the manner of a protest, or assemble in an invisible mode—that is, a mode only visible by its effects—which entails the withdrawal of all activities, absence, refusal, to politics of dispossession by the occupier colonial state, effects manifesting in soldiers running through the old streets of the city of Bethlehem breaking locks*

of closed stores, or spraying over to erase the emergent insurgent graffiti on the walls.

A general strike to refuse the continued expropriation of land and to refuse the measures taken to hinder these refusals. A strike against the confiscation of the lands that host the forms of life, which in their being how they are, in their uses and habits, threaten any colonial regime.

A withdrawing assembly exposing the dissembling of regimes of legalisms, with their laws of "Barren Lands," their rights "to confiscate," preventing access, entry—long enough to overwrite the existential territories of communities, and sever them from their habits of assembling with the colonial implants, impositions, orders, laws. A strike against "the colonial knows best what to do with the land ..."

Some forms of assembly can be thought of as invisible. An invisible assembly appears in its dis-appearing: it assembles in dis-assembling all the parts which are required to assemble even further parts. The first assemblies of a strike or a general strike could take place long before the strike, and surely there will be further assemblies after the strike commences, but its definitive moment is in this assembly as disassembly—this ghostly assembly where the multitudes can be imagined in their collective act of refusal and negation. In this sense, it can also be imagined as a form of negative assembly, but precisely in this capacity to negate all the forced forms of assembly that are required to make the existing order of things, with its concomitant divisions and partitions possible, operative. At the heart of any assembly which does not emerge out of coercion, there has and will always be this blinding and explosive act of dis-appearance of a collective body which emerges in its withdrawal from the pre-arranged arrangements of bodies, the pre-figured spaces of figuration.

But this invisible assembly does not emerge out of the blue or out of thin air. It emerges exactly in the blue and in the thin air which can color any life at any particular time with an unbearable sadness depriving breath from life. But the blues of this invisible form of assembling are invariably driven and converted toward new arrangements, which turn the blue note of sadness into the promissory blue of the sea and the vast blue of the sky.

7 *Returning to our street named Broadway, just below Canal in Chinatown, a group of artists and writers meet several times a week, they read texts and discuss them, they invite guests, mostly thinkers, art historians, and artists who share a certain hatred of capitalism. The space is a typical nineteenth-century light industrial space converted into a common place for discussions and a dozen or so artist studios. They are part of an independent study program and most who apply to take part every year share some horizon of art and its potencies to question our worlds. All the elements of a collective political becoming are there—when they assemble together discussions are intense, committed, but the call which has brought them together is bound by vocation; how will they survive as artists, critics, curators? And these are questions that for most are placed at the level of individuals and careers. All the questions that should be asked concerning the common fate of our existence are asked amongst one another in the designated times of assembling, or in the informal ones late at night within smaller circles; but this professional over-coding is difficult to break out of, as everything that enters and leaves the space is valued and circumnavigated by its underlying survivability within the delimited field of study, in this case art.*

Are we assembling when we study together? Are we assembling when we go to the cinema or to a concert or the theater? Are we assembling in a talk at a museum or an art space? Are we assembling in the classrooms of schools and universities? It would seem that assembly is woven within the fabric of these forms and yet something is missing. If assembly is at the heart of how we share existence and think about things, chew on, break down, renew, reclaim, circulate our words and worlds, then it also opens the processes and spaces where professions and their associated productivity can be called to halt or even revoked.

What convenes an assembly and animates its life is not a professional end; one does not assemble for a job, nor to determine a suitable career, one does not assemble to make contacts, nor to learn something useful to apply to the potential spaces of work. One also does not assemble to be entertained. The assembly, as much as it may be directed to a doing, undoing, an action or inaction, is always of a collective nature. And however it may have a particular end implied, it is the indeterminate character that keeps it alive. It is how we live and it is one of the means which gives form to life.

Its political character is not only in what is shared but also how that sharing affects the bodies which are present. An assembly's political "charters" are grounded in and by affection; thus in the abilities to open to forms of common feeling, sensing, understanding, undergoing.

If it is a site of assembly, then it is a site, *the* site, which can be acted upon, whereby not only *things* can be made or unmade, but *we* can be made or unmade. It is the site in which what is shared is the common condition of being and existing.

Thus, a place of study, a cinema or performance hall, a dance studio, a kitchen or a sauna, a forest marked for destruction or the path of a planned pipeline, can all be sites of assembly. But what makes them such is not the nature of the site itself. A site can be designated or designed as a house of assembly, but the nomination or architectural program does not an assembly make. It is neither the specific vocation or activity designated by such a site, nor the fact of bodies coming together in that site, which will an assembly make. Rather, it is this process capable of transforming any given site or assembling of bodies into something else, not simply toward a new use but a use that can alter the site itself and or the bodies themselves, usually both.

8 *Further down Broadway we arrive to Bowling Green park and the old Customs House where the writer Herman Melville must have seen, in addition to the multitudes arriving from Ellis Island, a thousand scriveners and potential Bartlebys working*

STUDY
RISKS OF ENCLOSURE
RISKS OF FORECLOSURE
RISKS OF DEVICES OF
GENERAL STRIKE
RECIPES FOR THE REVOLUTION
OF EVERYDAY LIFE
ASSEMBLING THE COMMUNE
SOCIAL STRIKE
STRIKE OF A LIFETIME
HABITS
MEANS
CAPACITIES OF ORGANIZING
RECLAIMING
ASSEMBLY OF ASSEMBLIES
OF FORMS
OF LIFE
OF COMMONS
OUR
OF AUTONOMY
OF COMMUNALITY

in the nascent financial district centered around Wall Street, whose origins include not only the trade of shares and bonds, but also the "sale" and "rental" of captured and enslaved peoples from Africa.

The Customs House was built on the grounds of a fort which was the settler colonial origins of this company town. It was also purportedly the site of "the first popular assembly," convened in the city on the 28th day of August, 1641. Of course, historians making such a claim could never imagine that assembly could be understood as those practices which had woven together the lives of the area's original inhabitants long before the presence of colonists. Not ironically, this aforementioned assembly had been called to determine and begin what would result in an escalating course of violence directed against the region's original inhabitants.

Broadway is the main artery that circumnavigates Mannahatta from north to south and breaks with the gridded planning, moving on a north-south axis like the big avenues but unlike them swaying from west to east, until of course it reaches the southern shores of the island. Wecquaesgeek Trail was its original name, a more organic path following the contours of the island and leading to the territories of the Wecquaesgeek who were one of the Lenape tribes comprising the area's original inhabitants.

Just off of Broadway and below Wall Street, circa 1999, a group of artists will find a disused floor of an office building located at Beaver Street. Beaver was one of the main streets which the Dutch colonists had built leading out from the central square just outside the initial fort. They named it after one of the main and lucrative peltries, otter furs being another, that the West India Company first exploited trade in from the region.

The artists are not all aware of this entire history in the moment they choose to sign a lease in order to create this space for encounter, learning and ongoing assembly. What they know is that every formal space designated for art or study which they have inhabited up until this point of their lives has always demanded that such activity be done within a more or less rigid call to order. In the university, they gather to learn, often accruing debt and subsequently being forced to search for a profession to get them out of debt. In the spaces for art, they will always be asked to ensconce and make sense of what they search for or "research" in the histories and forms that art has produced, rather than the histories and forms their lives and their communities' lives have taken. In time, they may arrive to a deeper answer that the call to order has been none other than those of the colony.

For our purposes here, assembly in these "calls to order" will not be seen for what it is: each calling, a chance to build and at the same time elaborate the communal.

The artists are searching for another kind of situation for being together and know enough to fight the processes of institutionalization since it is largely institutions which have "prepared" them to be so inadequate and incapable for what they perceive to be grounding their searching.

Maybe in that moment, they see it as something closer to a mortal struggle to upend the stranglehold that capitalist life and reality impose over them. Many of them are displaced or exiled, sharing histories of impositions of violence, even colonial processes. They do not yet know that capitalism is merely one facet of a colonial matrix of power (e.g. control of economy, authority, gender/sexuality, subjectivity/knowledge), but they know enough to ask what is required to reimagine and construct community at the birth of a new century. They know no other means to attend to this question than to establish an open space for thinking together. They assemble weekly, for the first four years almost every Monday, reading texts, sharing works, watching films, hosting comrades in struggle, beginning to find the words and terms and questions which can animate their search, intensify their practices of autonomy and recover the premises for a life-in-common.

For all that is assembled, including bodies, there are also histories which inform them, whether foreclosing them from or opening them to an outside. Moreover, these histories have embedded within them agencies and exigencies, ghostly matters, which require tending to. When these matters can be taken into common hands, felt, considered within processes of assembly, they can begin to inform the course life can take. They can become the sources for any possibility or understanding of "a future." In this way, the life of any assembly is always informed by the site upon which it takes hold. And this relation to that site cannot be an oblivious one. The site itself is an agent of the assembly. And these "matters" compose also the forms and practices of assembly which each of the assemblers brings with them. For this, those professionals and professional sites of assembly are the most dangerous, because they often serve to cut everyone off from the embedded experiences of assembly retained in the places and the bodies of those who assemble, forcing them, instead, into readymade forms with pre-scripted ends and extreme limitations in scope. Assembly is not an object nor can it ever have its experts. At its core, there is an anarchic principle which undoes any authority over the assembly. And for this, assembly is less a means of self-governance and closer to a practice of remaining ungovernable, and there is its true political force.

Assembly is something we all have experienced at the core of living together: we are all experts in it or *it* is not. However, in its institutionalized forms, stages, and professionalized guises, it slips into yet another instrument of the exertion of control, influence, or power as possession or force of coercion. But assembly can never be a means to an end. It is rather a means through which life is experienced, inhabited, and reflected communally.

We could say that what distinguishes it from any gathering of bodies whatsoever is not the place or specificity of the form it takes, but the capacity, intention, or openness to put this moment, this place, this condition, these relations of and to life into question and discussion together. It could be said that life is incessantly interrupted and suspended, resuming only in those moments of assembly, those which are freely composed and which tend to the questions its partakers have determined requires care, requires responding to.

And we can say that these questions themselves also have a history and an orientation, an implied seeking. But this seeking of the assembly that we are attempting to think and conjure can never be mistaken for those who assemble in the name of states or a colony, those who assemble as instruments or see assembly as instrument, which is more akin to a police operation, a seeking with a particular end in mind, for instance, securing the colony's expansion and imposing its authority, its dominion.

The assembly that this text and such friends who have assembled in common places like Beaver Street incarnate can be none other than a search for an ethics, *for*, and at the same time *as*, a form of life. And if it can be said that the only sense in any form is in its forming, then it must also be said that this sense and its forming always emerges in common, in assemblages, in milieus, in packs. Assembly could be the name for those infinite processes of forming and reforming together the form of life as always and already an experience of a sharing of life.

Manolo Callahan

Conviviality Rooted in Struggle:

Learning from the Zapatistas

Without a doubt, assemblies have captured the imagination of an emergent anti-capitalist resurgence, and have been the site of experimentation and invention in a range of political struggles operating at different scales across the globe. Renewed enthusiasm for assembly and for the possibilities generated through assembling has continued to gain in momentum, in part due to the success of large gatherings, beginning in 1996 with the series of Zapatista *encuentros*, followed by the 1999 Seattle WTO protests, and continuing with the wave of anti-globalization moments initially activated by People's Global Action, along with the World Social Forum, the Arab Spring, the Indignados, and Occupy, and, as recently mobilized under the banner of Black Lives Matter, the strikes against feminicides and violence against migrants.[1] Everywhere groups are relearning and reclaiming the habits of assembly. It seems people want to "find each other and assemble."[2]

The many efforts toward assembly reveal a good deal about the political stakes of the moment—what many have come to understand and define as a *catastrophic* stage of racial patriarchal capitalism—though assembly promises a path out of the current system.[3] In the pursuit of assembly some have been quick to execute specific forms or practices—insisting for example on identifying and imposing certain protocols, such as those claimed by a propertied, rights-bearing subject, more common to Western representative Democracies.[4] At the other end of the spectrum, some groups have been quick to celebrate the political potential

1. I am following Rosa-Linda Fregoso and Cynthia Bejarno among others in my use of feminicide. For an explanation of this approach, see for example, Rosa-Linda Fregoso and Cynthia Bejarno, eds., "Introduction: A Cartography of Feminicide in the Américas," in *Terrorizing Women: Feminicide in the Américas* (Durham, NC: Duke University Press, 2010), 1–44.
2. Michael Hardt and Antonio Negri, *Assembly*, (Oxford: Oxford University Press, 2017), xxii.
3. Arturo Escobar suggests "that we might feasibly construe the current conjuncture in terms of a civilizational crisis." Arturo Escobar, *Pluriversal Politics: The Real and the Possible* (Durham, NC: Duke University Press, 2020), xxxii.
4. I am capitalizing Democracy to make a distinction between Democracy, a formal bureaucratic system and essential technology of modernity, and democracy, as the shared impulse towards collective decision-making that Miguel Abensour

Bruno Serralongue, *Arrivée du Sous-commandant Marcos et sa garde* (The arrival of sub-commander Marcos and his guard), 1996, Encuentro series, inkjet on Baryta paper mounted on Dibond, 127 × 156 cm

of almost any gathering and to declare these formations assemblies. This gesture has sought to elevate spaces from salons, bar seminars, or protest spaces to the status of assembly. In the din of exalting assembly either as a regulated decision-making body composed of sovereign, reasoning individuals, or, as a more or less intentional, amiable gathering, what gets lost is another possibility for assembly—namely that assembly can be an exercise of conviviality rooted in struggle. Conviviality, we suggest, is a praxis animated by a dynamic, collective energy of interdependent community regeneration, advanced through collectively generated convivial tools otherwise uninhibited by capitalist command or discipline.[5]

names as "insurgent" democracy. Miguel Abesnour, *Democracy Against the State: Marx and the Machiavellian Moment* (Cambridge: Polity Press, 2011).

5. See: Ivan Illich, *Tools for Conviviality* (London: Marion Boyars, 1973); *Toward a History of Needs* (Berkeley: Heyday Books, 1977); and Manuel Callahan, "In Defense of Conviviality and the Collective Subject," *Polis* 33 (2012).

Bruno Serralongue, *Départ des participants*, Oventic (Departure of the participants, Oventic), 1996, Encuentro series,Ilfochrome print on aluminum, 127.5 × 158.5 cm

While we resist any gross generalizations, in most instances assembly is understood in instrumental terms, as suggested by Michael Hardt and Antonio Negri, in order to "grasp the power of coming together and acting politically in concert."[6] "Let us assume that no one assembly can rightly become the basis for a generalization about all assemblies," cautions Judith Butler. "The efforts," they continue, "to associate a particular uprising or mobilization with democracy itself is a temptation as thrilling as it is erroneous—it cuts short the conflictual process through which the idea of the people is articulated and negotiated." In "We the People—Thoughts on Freedom of Assembly," Butler addresses how we claim public space, and relatedly, asks: "how would we understand public assembly as a political enactment that is distinct from speech?" Emerging in the maw of Occupy, Butler's query attempts to discern the source of the political energy of assembling of late. However,

6. Hardt and Negri, *Assembly*, p. xxi.

Bruno Serralongue, *Les Tribunes de l'Aguascalientes d'Oventic* (Tribunes of the Oventic Aguascalientes), 1996, Encuentro series, inkjet on Baryta paper mounted on Dibond, 127 × 156 cm

the Western modernist subject expects to assemble, as Butler insists, through a speech act, both constituting and constitutive of "we the people."[7]

Unfortunately, assembly seems to bear the weight of layers of abstraction integral to a Western "free market liberal Democracy."[8] Most often these epistemological boundaries restrict assembly to a deliberative decision-making, or to the "performative enactment" of an emergent rights-bearing subject and group. Underlying Butler's inquiry in this instance (as well as Hardt and Negri's) are resounding "abstract universalisms" that communicate the West's principal conceit about its exclusive claims on what constitutes the political. It is a frame that could when applied, as Achille Mbembe has cautioned, result in a "normative reading of the politics of sovereignty." According to Mbembe "the ultimate expression of sovereignty is the production of

7. Judith Butler, *Notes Toward a Performative Theory of Assembly* (Cambridge, MA: Harvard University Press, 2015), 155.
8. Ronald A. T. Judy, "Democracy or Ideology," *Boundary 2* 33, no. 3 (2006): 35–59.

Bruno Serralongue, *Assemblée plénière à La Realidad* (Plenary assembly in La Realidad), 1996, Encuentro series, Ilfochrome print on aluminum, 127.5 × 158.5 cm

general norms by a body (the *demos*) made up of free and equal men and women. These men and women are posited as full subjects capable of self-understanding, self-consciousness, and self-representation. Politics, therefore, is defined as twofold: a project of autonomy and the achieving of agreement among a collectivity through communication and recognition. This, we are told, is what differentiates it from war."[9]

Following Mbembe's call to transcend the epistemological divide, we might ask what assembly can reveal to us as an analytic, that is as a catalyst that exposes the limits of Western ways of knowing, yet also introduces the possibilities of assembly as a convivial tool—one that can be refashioned for interdependent community regeneration across a multiplicity of local struggles. How might we imagine assembly as something other than a very specific, exclusive political form and practice—as either an efficient or inefficient

9. Achille Mbembe, "Necropolitics," *Public Culture* 15, no. 1 (2003): 13–14.

means of political participation in a political institution that enacts an idealized moment of Western Democracy, or as a collectively determined, interdependent device for shared decision-making and action? It is not our intention to construct the assembly as a battleground between two discrete, competing cosmovisions. However, we are less interested in assembly framed exclusively as a decision-making body or one over determined by representation, that, by definition, embodies "we the people"—one of the principal abstractions that have in the past undermined active, horizontal, and consistent participation. While deliberation is a critical dimension of assembly, engagement with assembly should not be limited to a conceptualization of assembly as a strategy and practice of intervention, or one that necessarily produces measurable results during each iteration. Assembly rooted in place is more likely animated by obligations as opposed to rights—how do we collectively determine the obligations we have to one another, to the physical space we occupy, and the other creatures that also claim it when we assemble? What are the mechanisms that other communities of struggle deploy in naming and managing the obligations of place, and how/why does this question remain difficult to pose for those of us who have been systematically uprooted and denied place?

Here we might also consider one vital alternative to the affirmative potential of framing assembly as a Western liberal free market right, or indeed as convivial tool, and conceive of it as something of a threshold, "as a spatial pattern that gives form to in-between spaces of encounter, exchange, and mutual recognition." "Those spaces, once performed," according to Stavros Stavrides, "offer an alternative to a culture of barriers, a culture that defines the city as an agglomeration of identity enclaves."[10] Thus, threshold can also be a site of decontamination, a de-compression chamber where we might relinquish the arrogance of

10. Stavros Stravides, *City of Thresholds* (New York: Common Notions, 2021), 200–208.

coloniality and rediscover the benefit of place.[11] Assembly as threshold also suggests, as Gerald Raunig and Kike España explain that "in every new composition, there is an act of instituting and there is a duration of instituting, a persistent chain of interventions into a territory, a sociality, an ecology, against the project form, against the non-situated practice of many artists, but also of activists as professional revolutionaries." However, the conspiracies and complicities weaving projects, spaces, and institutions together are not without their challenges, "playing in a terrain of high-risk of institutional capture and, at the same time, a climate of instituent power preserving and caring for undercommons social life."[12] Assembly as threshold might then simply be an opportunity to provoke its members into choosing between remaining dependent on industrial tools and systems, or turning to embrace vernacular knowledges and practices that can enable multiple autonomous alternatives.

And while more normative views of assembly unfold within particular geographies, there are other acts of assembly that are less overdetermined by the modalities of abstraction that provide an alibi for the Global North; especially those industrially forged in service of an imagined community, either through print, visual, and later digital media.[13] The act of assembly can be more immediate and less abstract, grounded in the complicities and conspiracies of place. But, more importantly, assembly can be the opportunity for a radically different social relation not mediated by racial patriarchal capitalism as a social form.[14] In this

11. Anibal Quijano, "Coloniality of Power, Eurocentrism, and Latin America," *Nepantla* 1, no. 3 (2000): 533–80.
12. Gerald Raunig and Kike España, "Monstrous Complicities," New Alphabet School HKW. See also: Fred Moten and Stefano Harney, *The Undercommons. Fugitive Planning and Black* Study (New York: Minor Compositions, 2013).
13. See: Brenna Bhandar and Alberto Toscano, "Race, Real Estate and Real Abstraction," *Radical Philosophy* 194 (November–December 2015): 8–17; and Benedict Anderson, *Imagined Community* (London: Verso, 1991).
14. Moishe Postone argues Karl Marx's mature critical theory engages capitalism as "a unique form of social mediation that structures modernity itself as a historically specific form of social life." Moishe Postone, "The Task of Critical Theory Today: Rethinking the Critique of Capitalism and Its Futures," *Current Perspectives in Social Theory* 33 (2015): 5.

Bruno Serralongue, *Aguascalientes F. Gomez I*, 1996, Encuentro series, inkjet on Baryta paper mounted on Dibond, 127 × 156 cm

sense, assembly can be that moment when we must choose between a convivial tool against a commodified industrial tool or system, and one that is overdetermined by some bureaucratic, ideological, or institutional force no longer under the control of "the community." By contrast, as a political space claimed by "societies in movement," assembly has been the site to refuse "political paternities" and reclaim historical knowledge of struggle rooted in specific locales.[15]

The Zapatistas and the National Indigenous Congress (CNI) provide useful points of reference for assembly as a convivial tool. The Zapatistas, like other Indigenous communities throughout Mexico, have grappled with the question of the survival of their communities by reclaiming

15. See: Raúl Zibechi, "Subterranean Echos: Resistance and Politics '*desde el Sótano*'" *Socialism and Democracy* 19 no. 3 (November 2005): 13–39; Raquel Gutiérrez, "The Rhythms of the Pachakuti: Brief Reflections Regarding How We Have Come to Know Emancipatory Struggles and the Significance of the Term Social Emancipation" *South Atlantic Quarterly* 111, no. 1 (Winter 2012): 51–64; and Ana Esther Ceceña, "The Subversion of Historical Knowledge of the Struggle: Zapatistas in the 21st Century," *Antipode* 36, no. 3 (June 2004): 361–70.

Bruno Serralongue, *Aguascalientes F. Gomez II*, 1996, Encuentro series, inkjet on Baryta paper mounted on Dibond, 127 × 156 cm

a *sistema de asamblea*, alongside a *sistema de cargo*, *sistema de tequio*, and *sistema de fiesta*, to name just a few convivial tools.[16] Included here would be the emergence of the seven principles of *mandar obedeciendo* as a convivial tool.[17] These interdependent convivial technologies have been the focus of Indigenous communities reviving cultural practices, vernacular knowledges, and political forms often corrupted by state and market forces, but reclaimed through struggle. While there is not enough space here to fully examine

16. By *cargo* we mean collective, community-determined, entrusted obligation for community renewal. A *tequio*, on the other hand, refers to a community-defined work project. Jaime Martínez Luna, "The Fourth Principle" in *New World of Indigenous Resistance* (San Francisco: City Lights Books, 2012).
17. The seven principles of *mandar obedeciendo* are: 1. to lead by obeying (*obedecer y no mandar*); 2. to represent, not replace (*representar y no suplantar*); 3. to work from below and not seek to rise (*bajar y no subir*); 4. to serve, not self-serve (*servir y no servirse*); 5. to convince, not conquer (*convencer y no vencer*); 6. to construct, not destroy (*construir y no destruir*); 7. to propose, not impose (*proponer y no imponer*). For a discussion of *mandar obedeciendo* in practice, see: Mariana Mora, "Mandar Obedeciendo; or, Pedagogy and the Art of Governing" in *Kuxlejal politics: Indigenous Autonomy, Race, and Decolonizing Research in Zapatista Communities* (Austin, TX: University of Texas Press, 2017).

assembly in the Zapatista or broader Indigenous context in Mexico, even a cursory review of how the Zapatistas have made use of a politics of encounter confirms how they have claimed assembly as a convivial tool and put it to strategic uses.[18] Moreover, they have advanced encounters by adding *escuelitas*, *seminarios*, and *conversatorios*; new spaces formed in order to share radical insights regarding the critical elements of what supports a community—including the organized relation to land, work, and labor—managed through a locally rooted assembly, a political tool not overwhelmed by, for example, competing vanguards or contaminated by abstractions. Thus, the Zapatista commitment to a politics of encounter not only convened a space in which it is possible "to go beyond solidarity"; these spaces of encounter also incorporated key moments of research, learning, documenting, and performing, to advance a politics of assembly, as we are currently witnessing with the Zapatista Journey for Life across Europe beginning in July 2021.[19]

An example of an urban Zapatismo attempting to relearn the habits of assembly through a politics of encounter is Universidad de la Tierra, Califas (UT Califas), a network of autonomous spaces of learning convened in a geography (Northern California) that has lost the habits of assembly, the obligations of *cargo*, and the determined efforts of *tequio*. It is, for the most part, a project in a zone overdetermined by what Ivan Illich named the "modernization of poverty," in which "the community" no longer claims the tools required for its autonomous regeneration. It is a socially mediated community overdetermined by commodity and the professionalization that insures a dependence on commodity-driven needs.[20] In response, UT Califas activates a networked pedagogy through a web of temporary

18. Manuel Callahan, "'Why Not Share a Dream?' Zapatismo as Political and Cultural Practice," *Humboldt Journal of Social Relations* 29, no. 1 (2005): 6–37.
19. Manuel Callahan, "Zapatista Civic Pedagogy in a Time of War," in *When the Roots Start Moving. To Navigate Backwards / Resonating with Zapatismo*, eds. Alessandra Pomarico and Nikolay Oleinikov (Chto Delat & Free Home University, Archive Books, 2021).
20. Illich, *Toward a History of Needs* (Berkeley: Heyday Books, 1977).

autonomous zones of knowledge production (TAZKP), a constellation of autonomous learning spaces that make it possible to reclaim and re-construct a social infrastructure of community, in order to explore how to disrupt the "modernization of poverty," refuse the "technological imperative," and abandon the professionalization that unravels the social fabric and social infrastructure of community.

Reclaimed cultural practices/spaces, such as *tertulia*, *mitote*, and *tianguis,* as well as other ritualized spaces of gathering that are constructed as part of a more deliberate intervention, including *ateneos* and *coyunturas*, comprise UT Califas' learning infrastructure.[21] More recently, UT Califas has advanced efforts to relearn the habits of assembly through *tsikbal*. A Mayan term that translates to "shred the word," *tsikbal* refers to the multifaceted, everyday, informal side conversations that take place between community members in order to address concerns, diffuse tensions, and minimize confusion before assembling in the larger gathering. In other words, as a convivial tool, *tsikbal* insures the participation and contribution of each member of the community in such a way that the larger, community-wide assembly need not be confined to or overwhelmed by one authorizing moment established through the performative speech act, the "performative enactments," that declare an attachment to an abstraction, e.g., "we the people." UT Califas has "appropriated" this particular technology first by establishing an autonomous learning space, titled Tsikbal, that meets monthly, and also by deploying Tsikbal as a site to weave together other networks of learning while nurturing *tequios de investigación*. Much like other sites of fugitivity, Tskibal focuses less on the concept of assembly as claimed by the Global North, and more on explorations of how assembly has been claimed as part of a profound intersection of convivial commitments and practices more common to the

21. Manolo Callahan, "Insurgent Learning and Convivial Research: Universidad de la Tierra, Califas," *artseverywhere*, https://www.artseverywhere.ca/insurgent-learning-convivial-research-universidad-de-la-tierra-califas.

Global South. Thus, as a convivial tool, *tsikbal* points to our obligation to the collectivity we constitute.

While we engage with assembly as a site of struggle, we have been trying to weave together here several ideas that engage the question of what we mean by assembly and how to move beyond the democratic despotic assembly form.[22] As a convivial tool, assembly can be a critical element in the social infrastructure of community, a community that has completely re-imagined political participation. Like all convivial tools, assembly embodies core elements unique to convivial devices. Specifically, it enables interdependence as reproduced through mutually agreed practices for the purpose of the community's regeneration as an exercise of a collective imaginary, and does so in alliance with a particular valence, determined by a locally rooted history. Thus, assembly can be claimed not so much as a reified, one dimensional abstraction, but rather engaged with as something more flexible, composed of key components that we can observe, reproduce, and circulate for the purposes of a broad inclusive collective praxis. As such, assemblies are as varied as the communities that claim them, and exhibit the peculiarities of the specific contexts from which they emerge, as well as the struggles that they advance. Thus, assembly becomes an embodied space that begins to constitute the social infrastructure of autonomy we have been in search of, without realizing we have been holding that space all along. Assembly as technology transfer—that is as a space where other convivial tools can be shared, rather than the execution of a tool designed to "take hold of the common"—is a space for the "production of subjectivity necessary to create lasting social relations."[23] "We have to

22. I am using W.E.B. Du Bois's term, "democratic despotism," to bring into focus the limits of Western free market liberal Democracy by what Du Bois identified as the American paradox: "this paradox which allows in America the most rapid advance of democracy to go hand in hand in its very centers with increased aristocracy and hatred toward darker races, and which excuses and defends an inhumanity that does not shrink from the public burning of human beings." W.E.B. Du Bois, "The African Roots of War," *Atlantic Monthly* 115, no. 5 (May 1915): 709.
23. Hardt and Negri, *Assembly*, xx; xiv.

fight the job," according to Stefano Harney and Fred Moten. "We have to fight the terms and conditions, the exclusions and separations, that subordinate our work to their job. Theory must be our weapon in that struggle and it must be given in our practice, in how we gather, along our way."[24, 25]

24. Stefano Harney and Fred Moten, *All Incomplete*, (New York: Minor Compositions, 2021), 153.

25. The author would like to thank the comrades from the Center for Convivial Research and Autonomy and their work in hosting Universidad de la Tierra, Califas and Tsikbal.

Sandra Benites &
Ana Terra Yawalapiti

On Assemblies

In conversation
with Pablo Lafuente

at the Xingu
and Among
the Guarani

Within the Brazilian territory, there are around 300 Indigenous peoples, many of them with their own language, and each of them with their own living traditions. Their ways of gathering and organizing life in common, following ancestral ways and braiding these with new approaches when appropriate, are always shaped by an attempt to defend Indigenous territory and life. This text is the result of a series of conversations that took place from October to December 2021 with Ana Terra Yawalapiti and Sandra Benites (Guarani Nhandewa), two Indigenous women from two different peoples, both acting as leaders among their own and as mediators with non-Indigenous contexts. In the fragments collected here, they present some of the ways in which their peoples make collective decisions about matters that concern them.

Next page: An assembly at the Women's House of East / Upper Xingu, Brazil, 2021

1. Assemblies Among the Yawalapiti and Other Peoples from the Xingu, and the Story of the Women's House by Ana Terra Yawalapiti

The Indigenous territory of Xingu is inhabited by sixteen different Indigenous peoples.[1] They are peoples who share certain traditions, such as those related to food. Languages vary, and we each have our way of organizing ourselves, which is passed from generation to generation. There is also a shared organizational structure: the Xingu Governance, a term non-Indigenous people may understand. Through this structure, all the Indigenous peoples from the Xingu make collective decisions. For example, if I wanted to organize a project in the name of the whole of the Xingu, I wouldn't be able to decide on my own, I'd need to bring this project to the General Assembly of the Xingu Governance. There it would be discussed and eventually either approved or denied by the Xingu as a whole. Within each community, for example within the Yawalapiti, things function similarly. The Yawalapiti are the *tucum* people:[2] we were baptized with this name because our ancestors lived in a territory which included many of those palm trees. We Yawalapiti are part of the jaguar clan, and our people nearly became extinct.

1. The Xingu Indigenous Territory was created in 1961 in the state of Mato Grosso do Sul, in the Center West region of Brazil. Its 2.642.003 ha, which include Amazonian rainforest and cerrado, or drier semi-deciduous forests, are divided into four regions (Upper Xingu, Middle Xingu, Lower Xingu, and East Xingu) where the following Indigenous peoples live: Aweti, Ikpeng, Kaiabi, Kalapalo, Kamaiurá, Kisêdjê, Kuikuro, Matipu, Mehinako, Nahukuá, Naruvotu, Tapayuna, Trumai, Wauja, Yudja, and Yawalapiti. Its legal status combines a nature reserve and a demarcated Indigenous land, therefore its official name: "Xingu Indigenous Park." Such denomination is rejected by the Indigenous communities who live in the region, who refer to it as an Indigenous Territory. Hence the name of the Indigenous association that represents all the people from the Xingu, the Associação Terra Indígena Xingu (Xingu Indigenous Territory Association, or ATIX). See: https://pib.socioambiental.org/pt/Povo:Xingu.
2. *Tucum* refers to a palm tree of the Astrocaryum family, and also to a spiny palm (Bactris setosa), both of which yield a long, strong fiber.

Today we have a small assembly and an association, which regularly changes its directors.

The Yawalapiti *cacique*, or chief, cannot be changed. The process to appoint the cacique is different from what happens among the non-Indigenous, where votes are cast and representatives come and go. Once the cacique is chosen, they occupy that position forever, until they pass away. The cacique is traditionally chosen through birth rights, so there is a wait until they reach their teenage years at which point they begin to prepare and go through the ritual. The grandfather or father may make this claim, and bring it to the center of the village. Or, alternatively, in situations of crisis, the whole community gathers at the center and chooses together. In our case, we suddenly lost our leader to COVID-19, and that is what happened: the community, including women, gathered and, in a rush, chose a person to lead us. That's the way it works.

For some decision processes, we adopt assembly forms from the non-Indigenous, and organize meetings to choose the directors of the Yalawapiti association. It's the same in the Xingu General Assembly, where the election process is similar to the process of electing the President of Brazil: all of the sixteen peoples gather to vote in one of the *polos*, or regional centers—each region has one *polo*. In the assembly it's decided where the next meeting will take place, as each year it is held in a different region in order to allow for exchanges with other peoples and cultures.

As the number of people who may participate is limited, each village names representatives and the selection is made on the basis of the profile of the people. Until recently I was the adjunct directory of the Upper Xingu region. Within the association there are four regional directors and four adjunct directors, and we have the responsibility of bringing information to the base. Our role is to inform all the peoples from the Xingu. Participants are also decided upon in a similar way: we inform everyone that there will be a meeting, and ask for volunteers, according to a certain profile. For example, my participation was in part due to the fact that only a few women are used to speaking Portuguese in public or participating in such events. The participation of women is today a requirement, brought forward by us women.

During these interethnic assemblies, we share information that affects our territories, our rights, and the good things that might benefit us. Not everyone is able to read, so when a document arrives we need to group each of the peoples together in order to translate into their respective languages. In this moment the peoples come apart, and each group debates, decides, and upon returning a representative, shares what that particular group have decided. But generally, in order to avoid a conflict, we consult with the others on what they thought beforehand. For example, my people will ask other people what they thought—whether they think a certain issue or topic would be a good thing for us—and we enter into an agreement outside of the meeting, because we don't want to have different opinions, and we try to avoid misunderstandings. In the general meeting only the final decisions of each people can be spoken: a representative of each group contributes the opinion of the collective, and says "we think this way, and that's it."

When a disagreement between peoples emerges, one of the sides must concede, in order to avoid actual conflict. For example, if my region doesn't agree with what another region is saying, we talk so as not to fight, and so that nobody leaves the conversation disappointed. We always reach a shared understanding.

***

In choosing who participates in the Acampamento Terra Livre (Free Land Camp),[3] we try to select people who are familiar with politics and with debating, so that they can understand what's happening, and contribute to the event

3. The Acampamento Terra Livre is a gathering of Indigenous peoples that has taken place yearly in Brasília since 2004. Its first edition coincided with the foundation of the Articulação dos Povos Indígenas do Brasil (Articulation of the Indigenous Peoples of Brazil, or APIB). See: https://apiboficial.org/.

together with the other relatives.[4] Once I witnessed a very critical debate there, because some of the participants wanted to confront the police and to fight, and others didn't. Eventually those who didn't want to fight convinced everyone else this was the best choice, because if we did so we'd confirm what the non-Indigenous always say about us. We understood each other and came to an agreement. We try hard not to enter into conflict with other Indigenous peoples. Even when relatives do things that are wrong, we try to talk with them. We never confront them; it's very hard for us to do so. It's easier to confront or disagree with government officials or non-Indigenous policemen than our own relatives.

If the Indigenous peoples come together in agreement and support then the results are always better, because you can't get far through offending others. My grandfather Paru Kanato Yawalapiti was an Indigenous diplomat. When there were problems within another Indigenous community, he went to the village by foot or canoe to try to solve those problems. He helped resolve things, even if there were relatives more accustomed to fighting. Both ways of being have existed since the old times. But when the threat of the non-Indigenous arrived, we came together. Us, who are not warring people, came together with those who practiced war, in order to fight for our territory and bring our people together.

***

At the time of my grandparents, things were different: the peoples from Xingu didn't speak Portuguese, and didn't share the same language, but there were always translations from one people's language to another. One or two people decided, and the others accompanied: whatever the cacique decided, everyone followed. This was the way until two years ago. We haven't had a general or regional assembly

4. The word *parente*, or relative, is used by Indigenous persons in Brazil to refer to other Indigenous persons, independently of the peoples they are part of.

Ana Terra and Indigenous leaders during the first meeting of the Xingu women, Aldeia Ilha Grande, Brazil, May 2019

for the last two years, since we lost our leaders. My uncle Aritana Yawalapiti was considered the general cacique in my region. Despite being Yawalapiti, he and my father Pirakumã Yawalapiti were prepared by the Kamaiurá, their mother's people, to be cacique. After my uncle became the leader of the Yawalapiti, my father gained the role of mediator between the village and the city. He became a spokesman, a leader of both worlds. The first General Assembly without them took place in December 2021, the first time since the COVID-19 pandemic.

***

Traditionally, in Upper Xingu, like in the other regions of the territory, there was no Women's House.[5] The spaces for us women were in our own houses. We had our meetings and developed our movement in our own homes, there was

5. Villages in the Upper Xingu consist of communal houses located along the perimeter of an oval clearing. At the center of the oval sits the Men's House, a gathering space for men where the sacred flutes are kept. Women are not allowed to see these flutes, which are played inside the Men's House or at night, when the women have gone to rest.

never a space where we could make decisions together, for the whole of the community. Decisions were taken by men in the Men's House: while we were in our homes, men gathered and decided things in relation to the community. Everything began with things we did in my own house, my parents' house. Our *ocas* are big, so many things may happen within them: living, cooking, having meetings.[6] Each time we made some craftwork, for example a hammock, women gathered to organize a *mutirão*, and a meeting took place.[7] I cooked for everyone, and we talked, exchanged ideas. From those situations emerged the idea of having a space for the Yawalapiti women. I suggested we could create a space for women to talk, to do our things, make our decisions, and the women agreed. We forgot about it, and after some time we realized we needed a space to store our things. We made things collectively, but the tools were kept in each of our homes.

In order for this to happen, we needed the authorization of our cacique. I had the courage to talk to the Yawalapiti elders. They always had morning meetings with my father, who often traveled and had a lot of information to share. I took advantage of this, sat by their side, and presented the idea. They asked me why, and what it was for, and I had to explain in detail. They approved.

As soon as we had the authorization, we organized several meetings. But the conversation moved slowly, and didn't progress. I talked to my sister Watatakalu, who had contacts that could mobilize support, and perhaps raise money to buy materials, petrol or food for the *mutirão*. All the women began to participate, it was a beautiful thing to see.

We hadn't talked about it publicly until then. The first time we went to the forest I took a picture of some women carrying wood. It's a unique image, which shows the women

6. An *oca* is an Indigenous home, which in the Xingu takes the form of a large oval construction with a thatched roof where, traditionally, a group of male brothers and their families live, together with cousins and others.
7. A *mutirão* is a collective mobilization without remuneration with the goal of completing a specific task that benefits the community.

carrying a large, heavy log. When we returned, I posted the photograph on social media, and everyone saw that it was a serious thing. We slowly gathered some donations, nails, food, fuel. We had some losses, too. After some time, we were offered R$ 10.000,00[8] but when we asked for the men's support, some didn't allow us to use the association's bank account, so we lost the donation. Afterwards we received another, smaller offer. We gathered together and decided we couldn't miss that chance, so the women agreed that we should receive it in my personal account. They sent me to the city to buy the materials, and so the project continued. At the time we were thinking on a small scale, just for the Yawalapiti women. We didn't want a big space to become known, we just wanted a space.

Like in any other place, there are people who create obstacles, and the house didn't go ahead. When I lost my father, I lost the will to do things, to mobilize others. We decided on new coordinators, but things didn't move. The construction stopped, and the house was demolished.

However, it seems the universe had different plans. After some time, during the pandemic, one of the organizations who supported us offered financial resources specifically to the Xingu women, and asked our coordinators which projects we wanted to realize. We didn't think twice. We wanted what we had always wanted: spaces for women. So instead of creating a single Women's House in the Yawalapiti village, we proposed two houses in two Xingu regions. The first house was recently inaugurated in the Kisêdjê people's region, in East Xingu. They call it the Women's Cohabitation House. And in December, on the occasion of the second General Assembly of the Xingu Women, we inaugurated the second house, in the *polo* Leonardo in Upper Xingu. Instead of attending to one specific people, the house will be available for the nine peoples of Upper Xingu. Something that was small became big.

8. Approximately €1,500 today.

Our movement is always collective, both for men and women. We conquered the women's space in order to explore whether we can think about things that can contribute to the struggle men are engaging in, to the organization of our traditions, to our culture and to our politics. The Women's Assembly, which in 2021 had its second edition, intends to be a space for women to understand each other, and hear ideas from one another. In this assembly there is also space for men, because we want to hear their opinions in relation to our work and our movement. We don't want to do things in the wrong way, and we don't want to upset men. There's always room for them to contribute their views on our work.

2. Assemblies as Encounter Among the Guarani by Sandra Benites

For us Guarani an assembly is an encounter, *nhemboapé*. *Nhemboaté* are those who gather. Be it for a ceremony or a ritual, or for a community council, an encounter is also an educational process, passing knowledge from one generation to another. What the *juruá*[9] call an assembly, for us is an encounter.

Indigenous assemblies are not places to argue or fight, or to talk like *juruá* politicians do. For the *juruá*, an assembly is an occasion for arguments, convened when something needs to be discussed. This practice didn't use to exist among the Guarani, but it happens a lot today. When we

Guarani women assembly at the Aldeia Guarani, Manciambu, Brazil, 2021

9. *Juruá* refers, in Guarani, to the non-Indigenous.

fight against a specific legislation that harms the rights of Indigenous people, we gather or visit other villages to organize ourselves and, for example, to block roads. They are often assemblies addressing questions related to territory, in order to confront the *juruá*, to go to Brasília to protest or have meetings with the federal administration, or to gather money to make that trip possible.

***

But assemblies have always existed within our communities, with another format, in an Indigenous manner. For us, organizing that isn't collective doesn't make a difference. Collectivity comes through the assembly because that is where people gather and organize themselves.

The type of conversation determines the *nhemboaterá*; the place where we gather or meet. For example, the *Casa de Reza* (Prayer House) is the place where advice is given, where teaching takes place and where the conversation is sacred. The baptism of children and plants also takes place within the Prayer House. These things happen there because they are about wisdom, about ways of transmitting serenity. But if the community is experiencing tensions or disagreements, or something complex is affecting it, a more rigid conversation is necessary—and this happens in the *Casa de Reuniões* (Meeting House). Every village has a house where all gather to talk about matters relating to the community and the issues that require conversation. If there are problems to be solved, that's also the place for us to go. Sometimes, when a difficult matter that requires the intervention of the leaders emerges, it is discussed in the cacique's house, in a more focused environment. In fact, this conversation may happen in several places, but never in the Prayer House.

In the Prayer House the encounter is led by the elder men and elder women (*Xeramoi* and *Xejaryi*), *pajés*[10] who

10. *Pajé* is a word of Tupi-Guarani origin that identifies the person responsible for the rituals.

have knowledge to pass to others. They act as mediators for these conversations. Those who participate in the encounter in the Prayer House can't leave on their own and sleep in their homes; they must sleep there, and only leave after waking up the next morning. That is a rule. That is also the reason why the Prayer House is large, because everyone will have to sleep there: adults, children, parents—everyone together. In the Meeting House it is not the spiritual leaders, but the community leaders such as the cacique who mediate—the leaders who contribute to the community in general.

***

We Guarani organize a large-scale encounter, which we call *nhemboaty guaçu*, to discuss things that relate to the whole community, and to talk about the future. The assembly discusses both the past and the future: we understand the past as our ancestral knowledge and memory, and we discuss it in order to make paths for the future. The assembly and the discussion itself are sacred.

For the Guarani, the assembly happens as a ritual. It shapes collective thought, by discussing differences and diversity. Because within the community there are different *tekós*, or ways of being: the women's *tekó*, the men's *tekó*, the children's *tekó*, and they are shaped over time, with our education, so that the wellbeing of all, the *tekó porã rã*, takes form. This construction moves from the individual to the collective, and from the collective to the individual, as though it were a crossing.

The process of listening to the different *tekó* requires a lot of conversation. The *juruá* talk about dialogue, but I don't think that word is appropriate for the Guarani. What happens is an encounter. For us Guarani the act of listening, or *rendu*, is not just done through our ears, it is also done through our skin, our flesh, our feelings. In order to understand, to create a balance through the respect for difference,

the encounter needs to happen. And so we give shape to our *tekó porã rã*, in order to continue ahead.

***

As with the *juruá*, assemblies also respond to demands, but in our case they are internal. They are demands that result from a new, different element, which affects the successive generations, the children, ourselves. Assemblies happen when life requires them, when we need to think about how we will carry ahead with our things, how we can build a path in relation to the demands that emerge. *Juruá* law, written on paper, leads to misunderstandings, because what is on paper might be important, but it is never fully settled. Laws must emerge from demands. Assemblies are a way of dodging problems, of moving from one place to another. The process cannot be rigid, because if you are too stiff, you can't move from one position to another.

My grandmother used to say that when you register something on paper, it stops moving, it no longer accompanies the *tekó*. It is paralyzed, like the *juruá* do with their laws. The law says that what is written must be respected, but that it has already happened—the path of our people has continued, and the space and elements that surround us have changed. Things can be written, but it is not advisable to be trapped in a specific formulation—things must be renewed and discussed constantly. It is important to ask whether the law continues to apply to the current situation. Are we still living in the same situation?

That's why the assembly is important to build new paths—to discuss and create new norms and rights. And when a norm is created within the community, it is in oral form, because it is lived, built from experience. It emerges from experiences that are diverse, and therefore it is necessary to create collective norms that serve all, in their diversity, not just a few.

Previous page: First meeting of the Xingu women, Aldeia Ilha Grande, Brazil, May 2019

***

An instance of resolution of a problem by the cacique is Júlio's story, who decided he was no longer Júlio. Even though I was a small child, I remember it was a difficult thing for the community. At the Prayer House, after the ritual finishes, boys sleep on one side, and the girls on the other. Júlio didn't want to sleep with the boys, he wanted to sleep with the girls. The girls' fathers questioned the fact that a boy was sleeping with the girls, they thought he was there to take advantage of them. When the questioning happened, the community was convened, together with Júlio, to clarify the situation. Women in the village, who were aware of what was happening, encouraged them to speak freely. As the community is small, everyone knows each other. Júlio said they were no longer Júlio, and said that if anyone thought they were taking advantage, it wasn't true, as their cousins and parents could give testimony. The cacique always avoids hurting any of the sides, and tries to show to both the need to have respect for one another. And so he asked Júlio to leave, and continued talking to the girls' fathers, because, as he said, it was them who created the problem, because of their lack of understanding. The problem wasn't Júlio, or their transition, but the fathers' prejudice. The fathers weren't understanding, but they later began to understand. Once the cacique gave an answer to the question, they couldn't continue to do so, because it had become a rule.

***

The general assembly discusses the future, how to pass on knowledge, and how to teach. It gathers children, men, women, elders—and every one of them is traditionally respected in their *tekó,* has their time and voice, and presents their dance. That is why the general assembly lasts for three or four days. It is an encounter in which the elders may share their wisdom with the younger generations.

We Guarani continue to make visits to our relatives, in other villages, and discuss things we share, in order to carry forward with the things that matter to our people. There are differences in each village, and each village discusses their reality. Yet, we have many things in common, such as agriculture, food, territory, health, respect, how to deal with the different *tekó* without excluding anyone ... Everyone has their time to speak. There are sacred singing, and also moments of joy, of sharing food.

When the assembly weakens, the Guarani lose direction, as is happening today in the state of Mato Grosso do Sul, where under the new, younger leadership, meetings are no longer taking place, some families are being privileged, and references are getting lost. The Guarani Mbya in the south and southeast of Brazil keep their strength, because they continue to participate yearly in the general assembly, and also have encounters with other villages, and with their neighbors. They gather to play football, but when they do so they are not just playing football, they also engage in other activities, they go to the Prayer House, they have meetings; that is, they organize an assembly in the form of an encounter.

Andrés Jaque/Office for Political Innovation

Escaravox

In the early years of the twentieth century, the Madrid City Council constructed the Legazpi Municipal Slaughterhouse on the bank of the Manzanares River. Known today as "Matadero Madrid" and covering an area of twelve hectares, the complex of forty-eight Neo-Mudéjar buildings closed in 1996 and fell into neglect for several years, before it was eventually converted into a municipal cultural center in 2007, like so many other former industrial installations in

NAVE
16

Europe. But despite this ferment of activity, the vast size of the complex and its many bare courtyards with no shade made evident the lack both of public attendance, and of commitment from the City Hall with regards to its maintenance. Paradoxically, the Legazpi neighborhood has a large proportion of elderly residents needing social interaction, as well as many families from Latin American and North African countries who would readily make intensive use of the inside spaces.

The aim of our project is to endow Matadero Madrid with the necessary material devices and protocols for allowing local residents to take over the spaces as they see fit, and to attract the many small music and theater groups or poetry associations of Madrid, evenly scattered throughout the capital's extensive territory—which, although they individually stimulate the local contexts in which their activities develop, together constitute the biggest cultural infrastructure in the city.

To achieve this, the scheme proposes equipping the open spaces of the old abattoir with varied types of 40-meter-span shading devices with sound-amplifying systems, stage lighting, and audiovisual projection systems, so that in combination with sliding stands, they may serve as auxiliary structures for public performances. The infrastructures are designed to be made available for people to use, without being invited or curated, through a simple process following the conventions of the local municipal tennis courts, which are booked by the hour.

The devices have been given different names in accordance with their use. "Escaravox Lux" and "Escaravox Sonum" are large tents fitted with large pneumatic wheels which make it possible to change their position and orientation. The "Ofimóvil" is a tent designed for joint projects and has storage spaces, tables for meetings and work, and internet connection, and is powered by photovoltaic plaques. The "Siestero," a tent designed for resting, offers protection from sun and rain, and places to stretch out where children can have a nap and elderly or convalescent people can relax.

The structure's materials are based on the idea of an odd assemblage of inexpensive elements. Costing approximately €100,000, they were made from recycled industrial products including structures from rural irrigation systems, supermarket trolleys, synthetic crop covers, rubble sacks, and plastic chairs from bars and restaurants—all of them low-cost and easy to maintain. A composite of readymades, using existing technologies in ways different from their original intent. It is a technological reappropriation process, which the office relates to the possibility of queer uses of available systems.

Shadow Architecture and

Aleksandra Wasilkowska

the Parliament of Bazaaristan

Here the ambassador, the deputy, the poet, and the thief equally make their way through the crowd, and the price is the same for everyone as part of anonymous negotiation. This egalitarianism gives also a sense of freedom to the bazaar crowd which is liberated, from the moment of entering, from the everyday constraints of social status.

Jacek Kurczewski, Mariusz Cichomski, Krzysztof Wiliński, *The Great Warsaw Bazaars*

Bazaars are more than just a space where goods and services are bought and sold. They are a locus where the paths of different social classes and ethnic groups converge and crisscross. Social status matters less here than wit, the ability to negotiate, and the specific kind of fervor that is inspired by material and immaterial exchange.

There is no doubt that the informal economy of bazaars as well as alternative economies that often emerge in times of crisis such as time banks, cash-free exchange, or alternative currencies, will have an even greater impact on the organization of future cities. According to OECD estimates, some 1.8 billion people, nearly half the global labor force, are now working in the shadow economy.

4–5–6 LIPCA
BAZAR NA PTASIEJ
BAZARISTAN
Drink & FLY

Bazaaristan, Wroclaw, Poland, 2013
In the old marketplace of Wroclaw, between the fruit and vegetable stalls, a performative exhibition of contemporary art along with debates, performances, and workshops was held for three days. Curated by Aleksandra Wasilkowska, including the participation of merchants, artists, architects, and officials.

The *Parliament of Bazaaristan* pavilion is an architectural doppelgänger, an assemblage of the elitist architecture of power and the inclusive architecture of bazaars standing in its shadow. The structure is capable of evolving from monumental and rigid plan similar to parliaments or churches (ill. 1) to more decentralized and open structures like stalls and bazaars (ill. 2, 3, 4, 5). The form of the pavilion consists of small and replicable modules that can be easily reconfigured, folded, stored, or transported (ill. 6, 7) depending on the community needs.

This hybrid typology is meant to produce a clash of two different social bubbles: artists and vendors, furnishing a space of constructive conflict in order to expand the imagination and foster empathy towards the other. The double-identity pavilion will simultaneously serve intellectual exchange and the exchange of goods and services. It may be located at the heart of the bazaar, or in any other space. Inscribed in a fifteen meter-diameter circle, the quasi-rotunda with symmetrical side aisles, a colonnade, and multiple speaking tribunes alludes to classical and monumental buildings, such as the utopian *Museum* Étienne-Louis Boulée designed in 1789.

At the same time, the proportions of the pavilion's different components in the form of stalls and displays reference the architecture of bazaars and open-air markets. The measuring unit is the module of the standard box for carrying produce (vegetables, fruit, bottles, etc.): 600 mm wide, 400 mm deep, 250 mm high. The box module is compatible with the dimensions of the seat, which is twice as large, and allows for the participants to be comfortably seated. All elements of the pavilion are self-supporting, screwed-together, reusable, and transportable. The stalls and tribunes have been designed with durable materials (steel, aluminum, or wood) so that after the event the pavilion may either be used whole, or the individual stalls may be distributed among the vendors.

Within a single space and a single budget, a double-function structure is accomplished in which different functions, economies, and agendas can freely mix. What remains once the assembly event has been completed is therefore not waste material, but valuable components of everyday life: street stalls. The pavilion is a prototype for an inclusive model of building cultural institutions in the future. Informal architecture, such as stalls or bazaars, can complement public institutions such as museums or parliaments. Let us imagine a prime minister who has to make her way through a labyrinth of stalls and a crowd of vendors in order to reach the rostrum and deliver her speech, or an artist who, on her way to the temple of art, confronts her practice with the fervor of the bazaar. Or, conversely, let us imagine vendors displaying their goods on parliament seats, or artists' sculptures. *Parliament of Bazaaristan* is a utopian project of a hybrid, continuous-use space, where both overarching relations of power and the distinctions between the center and the periphery are constantly renegotiated.

ill. 1

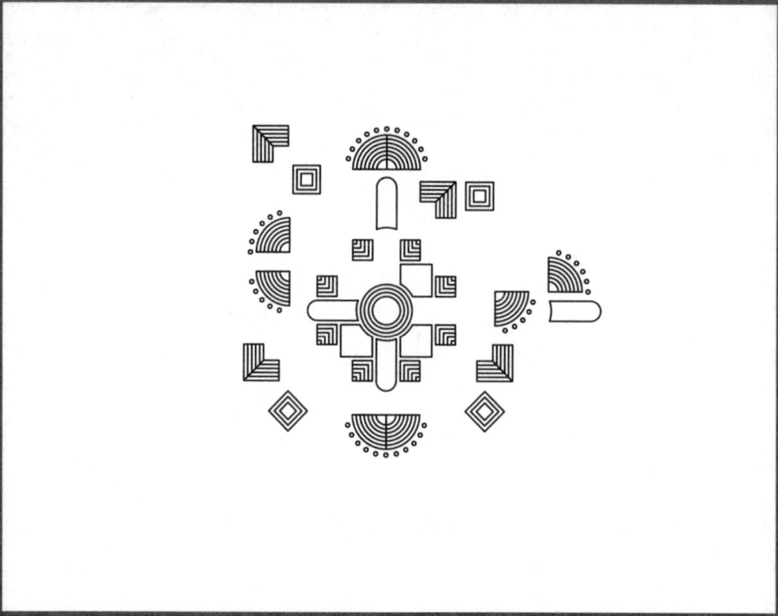

ill. 2

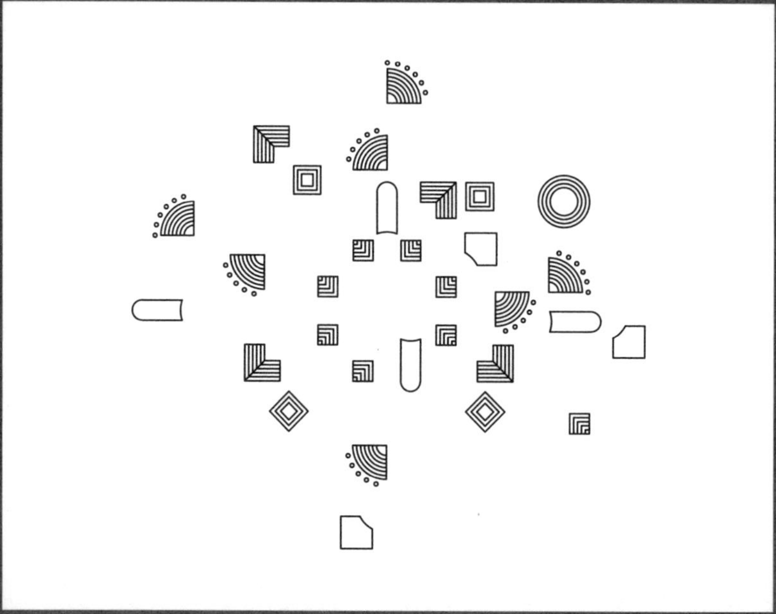

ill. 3

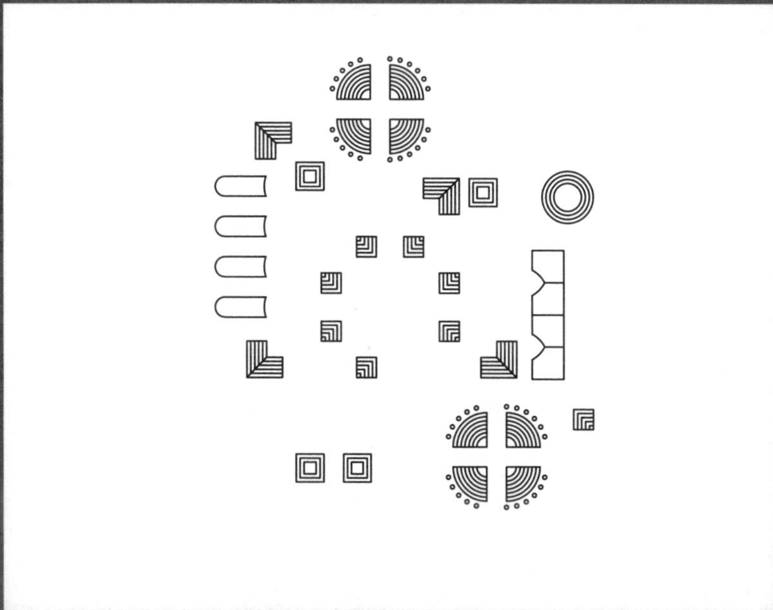

ill. 4

ill. 5

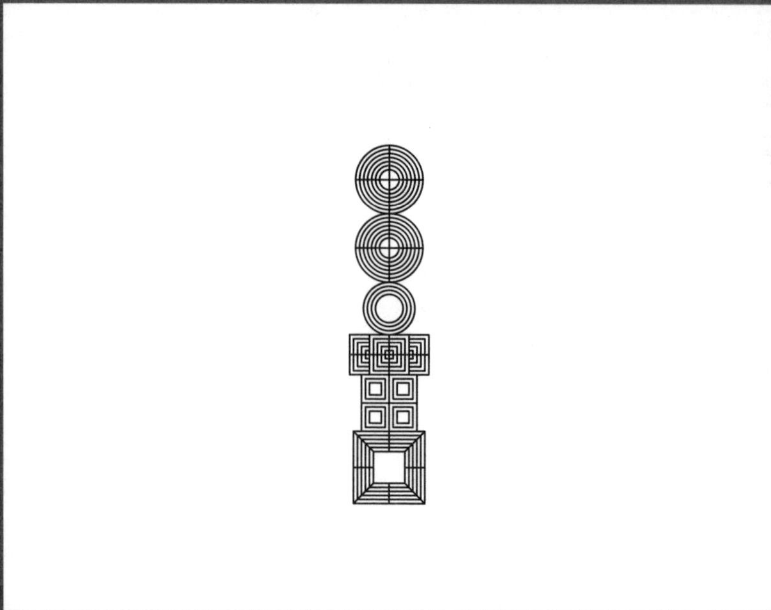

ill. 6

ill. 7

Aleksandra Wasilkowska and Michal Piasecki, *Assemblage in Public*, Chelsea College of Art and Design, London, United Kingdom, 2010
Commissioned by the artistic collective Critical Practice for their event "Parade," the pavilion was built on site by the artists, in collaboration with students of Chelsea College of Art and Design. The open, repeatable, and interchangeable structure of the pavilion was composed of 4,000 borrowed crates, which were returned to stores scattered throughout London when the event drew to a close.

Catherine Malabou

The Non Governable

In conversation
with Laurent Jeanpierre

Laurent Jeanpierre: In *Au voleur! Anarchisme et philosophie* (Thief! Anarchism and Philosophy), you propose to consider anew, through the lens of anarchist political thought, some of the thinkers in contemporary critical theory—Giorgio Agamben, Jacques Derrida, Michel Foucault, Emmanuel Levinas, Jacques Rancière, or Reiner Schürmann—who fall under the category of what you call "philosophical anarchism."[1] You intend to question, as you write, "the anarchist failure of the political concepts of anarchy." One of the starting points of your inquiry is situational: you affirm that "horizontality is currently in crisis. Dissociated, split, torn apart due to its own uniformity."[2] The statement is puzzling, as it's more common to evoke, in contemporary politics, the crisis of verticality, of legitimacy, of representation; and then to call for the horizontalization of power relations in particular for political action. This is not your initial diagnostic. Could you explain your point of entry into the time period and into the problems of contemporary anarchism?

Catherine Malabou: I don't deny there is a crisis of verticality, but I think it's a consequence of the crisis of horizontality. We live today in the era of what I have called the "unlimited uberization of life." What that means, is that the version of capitalism that had already begun its morphological mutuation in the 1990s, by going from a pyramidal structure to a neuronal structure in networks, has entered another phase of transformation since the financial crisis of 2008. This new phase marks a libertarian, or right-wing anarchist transformation, within which each individual neuron has the apparent freedom to develop its own networks, without depending on the others, and without any concern for the central unit of which it is

1. Catherine Malabou, *Au voleur! Anarchisme et philosophie* (Paris: Presses Universitaires de France, 2022).
2. *Au voleur*, 14

a part. As such, each point in the network has come, today, to manage itself, meaning it can freely, or almost freely, rent out his or her apartment, complete transactions and exchanges, and take advantage of or provide services without going through centralized monitoring procedures. On the macro-economic level, that implies, in particular, the proliferation of crypto-currencies and of all the selling processes that bypass traditional banking and notarial authorities. Not to mention calling into question systems of taxation. We must not forget that Friedrich Hayek, the ultra-liberal economist whose ideas, some say, are close to libertarianism, assimilates taxes to a form of servitude. Obviously, this type of idea provokes a crisis of verticality as well. We are currently witnessing a reinforcement, which is sometimes extreme, of state-governmental power (as in Russia) that does not in fact concern only authoritarian or dictatorial States. Rarely have the police at home and the desire for hegemony abroad been so powerful. But these oligarchic and imperialist tendencies are precisely merely the protective shell of a horizontalist laissez-faire. Paradoxically, today, the more powerful the State is, the less help it provides. The stronger its control apparatus, the less it intervenes in the redistribution of social justice. Take, for example, the downfall of public services in France.

Laurent Jeanpierre: In this same analysis of the last two decades, you oppose "dawning anarchism" (*anarchisme d'éveil*) to "de facto anarchism" (*anarchisme de fait*) which has accelerated along with the neoliberal mode of capitalist economy. The new political anarchism is emerging around the world by way of "the rise in collective initiatives and experimentation in alternative political coherences" such as during occupations, *Zones à Défendre* (zones to defend, or ZADs), or social movements independent of the traditional organs of representation, and in the "organization" of "modes of decision-making relying on collective and self-governed management of a struggle, an environment, a terrain, or a structure."[3] Can we, and should we, distinguish between the self-governing and deliberative horizon of a significant part of the former and current anarchist political tradition and what you call, alongside Pierre-Joseph Proudhon, "governmental prejudice," against which anarchist thought has attempted to rise up?[4] How can anarchist autonomy or anarchist self-organization distinguish itself from the government of self (and others), and from self-government?

Catherine Malabou: Indeed, the crisis of horizontality also stems from the fact that the new faces of social movements have emerged as new modalities of anarchist expression, without necessarily identifying as such. The Yellow Vests come to mind right away, of course. The refusal to be affiliated with unions or parties, the great diversity of the members of its groups, as well as the cohesion generated around anti-government sentiment on the whole has led us to believe that the battle fields have changed. The difficulty of labeling them has often led their critics to conclude that they were populists or even fascists. Such judgments obviously have nothing to do with reality, which in fact troubles traditional political or corporatist categorizations. There appear to be two competing types of anarchism today, de facto anarchism, mentioned earlier, and dawning anarchism, which consists of resistance to subordination and exploitation. The difficulty today lies in managing to articulate the difference between the two as the rhetoric of traditional anarchism lags with respect to present-day issues. The last great expressions of anarchism have been during the anti-globalization movement of

3. Malabou, *Au Voleur*, 15–16.
4. Pierre-Joseph Proudhon, *Idée générale de la révolution au XIXe siècle. Choix d'études sur la pratique révolutionnaire et industrielle* (Paris: Hachette-BNF, 2013 [1851]), 41.

the 1990s, in Seattle for example. They remain valid but have to be redesigned.

The government is the real target of criticism put forth by all anarchist tendencies. The governmental prejudice denounced by Proudhon is the idea that societies, individuals, and peoples cannot survive without a division between those who obey and those who give orders, and not without dissymmetry between these groups. Different rhetoric, seeming to express the contrary, consists in highlighting the opposition between governmental prejudice and self-governance, which guarantees freedom and autonomy. But as long as the division between obeying and giving orders, even with respect to those who are self-governed, is preserved, the logic of control is maintained. Autonomy is therefore not the government of self, but a way of cultivating the ungovernable within oneself. Until recently, philosophers like Foucault or Agamben have called this a "form of life"—inventing a form of life and substituting the government of self for the use of oneself, as in the relational mode between instrumentalist and instrument. This seems to be a good starting point to me.

Laurent Jeanpierre: How do direct democracy and the popular or citizen assemblies associated with it fit into the arsenal of political anarchism and of the action-oriented criticism of the governmental paradigm? Are they part of the means of political anarchism, as certain thinkers affirm, on the same level, for example, as mutual aid (which seems to have grasped your attention)?

Catherine Malabou: Obviously, assemblies are essential to the anarchist expression process. They are actually not foreign to mutual aid. When we read Pierre Kropotkine, we see that mutual aid, a natural tendency that has been irrevocably lost over time and through evolution, can only be reborn in the form of social entities.[5] Such entities, precisely like assemblies, tend not to lead back to some lost origin of democracy, but rather, to develop, precisely, the political meaning of mutuality, which remains entirely to be invented. Participative democracy and citizen-based initiatives are obviously the levers of it. Now, I see two problems here. The first is that assemblies are often infiltrated at some point by traditional parties. This is what happened to the Yellow Vest Assemblies of Assemblies and what ruined the process. The second problem: I indicate in my book that we should gather inspiration from the Taiwanese model of government, which declares itself openly anarchist and "totally transparent," in that citizens can participate directly in governmental initiatives through platforms that give them access to the open-source codes of the institutions. Audrey Tang, the wonderful Taiwanese Minister of Information defines herself as an anarchist and civic hacker. ZADs and assemblies are good, but it's also necessary to take into account the technological and cybernetic possibilities provided by dawning anarchism. In any case, it is important to think very seriously about them. The stagnation of Nuit debout points to the need to re-elaborate our strategies of resistance.

Laurent Jeanpierre: You write, "I think that anarchists themselves, though they have described possible alternatives to government (short terms, federations, communes, self-governance, consensus or decision-making platforms), have not sufficiently explored the space opened by the transgression of the division between ordering and obeying."[6] Could you explain this statement? What has political anarchism lacked in its ability to think not about the ungovernable, but about what you call the "non governable"? The question seems ever more pressing since, as you

5. Pierre Kropotkine, *Mutual Aid: A Factor of Evolution* (London: Freedom Press, 2009 [1902]).
6. Malabou, *Au Voleur*, 51.

say, "the recent spontaneous popular protest movements have made it difficult to mark any clear division between what, in these movements, belongs to the ungovernable and what belongs to the non governable."[7]

Catherine Malabou: Theorists known as "post-anarchists" (Todd May, Saul Newman, Lewis Call), since about the 1990s, have called for the deconstruction of traditional anarchism due to the obsolete nature of some of its values: benevolence toward human nature, the call to reason, the belief in centralism ("the enemy is the State"), blindness toward the fragmented nature of power, etc. No matter what we think of these statements, they have the merit of having highlighted the absence of rigorous philosophical reflection associated with a form of anarchism that has essentially not changed its catchwords since the end of the nineteenth century. This situation is linked to the fact that in traditional anarchism there is a refusal to consider it as a philosophy. This is something that has been very detrimental. If we take for example the quite important subject of the critique of the government: what exactly is criticized? What, for anarchists, represents this part of consciousness, of the psyche and of bodies that does not allow itself to be governed? And what should it be called? "Ungovernable"? The word seems too weak to me, still too open to negotiation. I have suggested "non governable" to insist on a feeling of indifference, the fact that one is foreign to the paradigm of ordering-obeying; and I have tried to describe this indifference and this foreignness. Of course, it is initially the responsibility of philosophy to take on such a task. Without philosophy, anarchism is doomed to repeat itself in the celebration of its own past. I have also dedicated the entire conclusion of my book to the question of the meaning

7. Malabou, *Au Voleur*, 53.

of the expression "being an anarchist." This question must be asked at some point, and it obviously calls for significant ontological consideration.

Laurent Jeanpierre: At the end of your meditation on the work of Rancière, you conclude that anarchist political experiences of life without government are doomed to be obliterated or repressed: their actual potential "lacks proof despite historical factual occurrences." It appears as if they have been hit by a kind of collective "denial" "for a reason that we may never know."[8] We can witness anarchist forms of living, you suggest, but they cannot be presented, and represented even less, except perhaps in the sublimated form of a pointillist painting by Paul Signac or Georges Seurat, two anarchist painters. Why this repression, this forgetting, this anarchist trauma? What effects can we expect to emerge from such a psychic configuration?

Catherine Malabou: I am not entirely capable of explaining why the idea of the absence of government and of an origin of politics, other than the generally accepted notion of a people asking for protection from a State, is so difficult to accept and to believe in. Straight away come to mind disorder, the absence of laws, and in the worst representations of anarchism, cruelty, sadism and the unleashing of the instincts of destruction and death. I have tried to provide my version of this fact: Sigmund Freud raised the question in *Beyond the Pleasure Principle*. What happens when the psyche is no longer regulated by the pleasure principle, in other words by the government of energy that keeps it at the lowest level and prevents it from making the system explode? What happens, he asks, when the dykes are broken under the effect of trauma (accidents, wars) that breaks open the protective envelope and the "protective shield" of the psyche? Freud

8. Malabou, *Au Voleur*, 374.

lets the reader come up with the answer. It's either generalized chaos or another form of organization that appears (the principle of Nirvana).[9] But yet, we see that the absence of government always implies something traumatic as it contains the idea of total loneliness and abandonment. No one is there to protect us, we sense. But maybe it's from that point on that the consideration of new political orders can take shape. And that autonomy becomes pertinent. However, as I was saying, no philosopher has ever analyzed this or taken it seriously. That's a fact. We are constantly having to vouch for anarchism. Its demonstration does not suffice. Pointillist painting was an extraordinary attempt to depict anarchism. I am sure that other attempts of this kind exist and will continue to exist. After all, it's not a bad fate ...

9. The "principle of Nirvana" is a concept created by Barbara Low in *A Brief Account of the Freudian Theory* (New York: Harcourt, Brace & Howe, 1920), then used by Freud to designate the tendency of psychism to lower the level of all excitement, of any amount of energy, to zero, or to the lowest level possible. At first sight, it resembles the pleasure principle, but it is in fact associated with the death drive—death being understood as the absolute reduction in tension. See: Sigmund Freud, *Beyond the Pleasure Principle & Other Writings* (London: Penguin, 2009).

Contributors

ANDREAS ANGELIDAKIS lives and works in Athens. Trained as an architect (Sci-ARC bArch, Columbia MSAAD), Angelidakis maintains a practice centered on research and exhibition, often examined through the lens of the internet. Angelidakis has consistently challenged the end-product of architectural practice by reversing the representation-to-realization sequence of the production of buildings. He often starts with an existing building, producing models, films, ruins, installations, or alternative histories, blurring fact and fiction, smoothing out the borders between the real and the virtual. Recent exhibitions include *The State of the Art of Architecture 1st Chicago Architecture Biennial*, *12th Baltic Triennial* at CAC Vilnius 2015, *Supersuperstudio*, PAC Milano 2015, documenta 14 Athens and Kassel.

AYREEN ANASTAS is a wanderer and a friend of Zarathustra. She is currently wandering with Roland in the magic mountain and in the labyrinth called *comment vivre ensemble*. The question she retains: How to dis-activate the seeping of power in every aspect of life and language whilst maintaining and nourishing the desire to live together? Her surname, like any other, calls for the separation of life from its form of existence and for relegating it alphabetically to the bureaucracy of the state and the spectacle. To renounce one's name in order to protect one's life, and its form from becoming an entry in a dictionary.

FRÉDÉRIQUE AÏT-TOUATI is a theater director and scholar, working at the intersections of the history of science and literature. She is a Research Fellow at the French National Center for Scientific Research (CNRS) in Paris and the author of several books, including *Fictions of the Cosmos: Science and Literature in the Seventeenth Century* (Chicago: Chicago University Press, 2011), and the collaborative book *Terra Forma* (Cambridge, MA: MIT Press, 2022). Aït-Touati directs the Experimental School of Political Arts (SPEAP) created by Bruno Latour, which is dedicated to questions of representation of public affairs and controversies. She has been staging plays together with Latour and her company (zonecritiquecie.org) for over ten years, works which have been recently presented in Paris, New York, the Taipei Biennale, and the Berliner Festspiele.

HANS ASENBAUM is a Postdoctoral Research Fellow at the Center for Deliberative Democracy and Global Governance at the University of Canberra. He holds a PhD from the Center for the Study of Democracy at the University of Westminster in London, and is a co-convener of the Participatory and Deliberative Democracy specialist group of the Political Studies Association (PSA). His research interests include identity and inclusion in new participatory spaces, digital politics, and theories of radical democracy. Hans' work has been published in the *American Political Science Review*, *Political Studies*, *New Media & Society*, and *Politics & Gender*.

RICHARD BANÉGAS is a Professor of Political science at Sciences Po Center for International Studies, and former chief editor of *Politique africaine*. He dedicated most of his research to West African politics and the African Great Lakes region. From 2015–21, he coordinated a collective research on identification and citizenship in Africa, which led to the publication of an edited volume *Identification and Citizenship in Africa: Biometrics, the Documentary State and Bureaucratic Writings of the Self*, (London: Routledge, 2021). Another *book, ID Wars in Côte d'Ivoire*, is forthcoming with Oxford University Press. With Columbia University, he led another program on street politics and street parliaments in Africa. His research focused on Côte d'Ivoire where he explored issues of citizenship, violence, and youth mobilization.

SANDRA BENITES is a Guarani Nhandewa educator and curator. She is researching for a PhD in Social Anthropology at the Museu Nacional – Universidade Federal do Rio de Janeiro (UFRJ). She has curated *Dja Guata Porã: Rio de Janeiro Indígena,* MAR, Rio de Janeiro, 2017–18, and *Sawé: Liderança Indígena e a Defesa do Território,* Sesc Ipiranga, São Paulo, in process. From 2020–22 she was Adjunct Curator for Brazilian Art at the Museu de Arte de São Paulo (MASP), and currently works as a curator at the Museu da Cultura Indígena in São Paulo.

JEAN GODEFROY BIDIMA is the former Program Director at the Collège International de Philosophie in Paris, and, since 2004, has been a tenured Full Professor and Yvonne Arnoult Chairholder in French and Francophone Studies at Tulane University (New Orleans, USA). His research interests include medical ethics from a cross-cultural perspective, critical theory, African philosophies, and aesthetics. He is the author of *Théorie critique et modernité négro-africaine: De l'École de Francfort à la Docta spes africana* (Paris: Les Éditions de la Sorbonne,1993); *La Palabre: Une juridiction de la parole* (Paris: Éditions Michalon, 1997), and recently co-edited with Laura Hengehold *African Philosophies in the 21st Century* (Lantham, MD: Rowman and Littlefield International, 2021).

PATRICK BOUCHERON is Professor at the Collège de France and has held the chair "History of Powers in Western Europe, 13th–16th century" since 2015. While his work focuses primarily on the urban history of medieval Italy and on the monumental expression of princely power, since his election to the Collège de France he has been attempting to reconfigure a history of powers since the Middle Ages, in particular based on the concepts of fictions and political experiences. In January 2021, he began a new cycle of courses on the Black Death. His books translated into English include *The Power of Images: Sienna, 1338,* (London: Polity, 2018); *France in the World: A New Global History*, (New York: Other Press, 2019); *Machiavelli: the art of Teaching People What to Fear*, (New York: Other Press, 2019); *Trace and Aura: The Recurring Lives of St. Ambrose of Milan*, (New York: Other Press, 2019).

FLORENCE BRISSET-FOUCAULT is a Lecturer in political science at the University Paris 1 Panthéon-Sorbonne, and a Researcher at the Institut des Mondes Africains (IMAF). She is a Junior Fellow at the Institut Universitaire de France (2019–24) and co-edits the *Journal of Eastern African Studies*. Her research interests lie in the history and sociology of political thought; the modalities of critique and the imagination of citizenship in East Africa which she has explored through the study of print and broadcast media, electoral and street politics; and the social history of identity papers in Uganda. Her first book, *Talkative Polity: Radio, Domination and Citizenship in Uganda* (Athens, OH: Ohio University Press, 2019) is based on the ethnography of Uganda's People's Parliaments.

MANUEL CALLAHAN is an insurgent learner and convivial researcher for the Center for Convivial Research and Autonomy. His work explores three interwoven areas: the US/Mexico border and Greater Borderlands historically and in the present; Indigenous struggles across the Americas including Zapatismo and Zapatista struggles emerging from Chiapas; and convivial research, a community-based research approach that engages autonomous struggles throughout Greater Mexico. This research includes engaging conviviality as a praxis, especially as a site of convivial tools to confront what W.E.B. Du Bois named as "democratic despotism." He also participates in the Universidad de la Tierra, Califas, and remains an active member of Acción Zapatista.

FRANÇOIS COOREN holds a PhD from the Université de Montréal (1996), where he is now a Professor and Chair of the Department of Communication. His research focuses on organizational communication, language and social interaction, and communication theory. He is past president of the International Communication Association (ICA, 2010–11), an ICA Fellow, a Distinguished Scholar of the NCA (National communication Association), a past president of the International Association for Dialogue Analysis (IADA, 2012–21) and a former editor-in-chief of *Communication Theory* (2005–8).

ARMANDO CUTOLO teaches Anthropology and Ethnology at the Department of Social, Political and Cognitive Sciences of the University of Siena. After carrying out research on relations of personal dependence and on the politics of memory in an Akan society of Côte d'Ivoire, he has worked on the *Jeunes Patriotes* nationalist movement, focusing on its network of permanent assemblies, and on the "patriotic orators" animating them. He has published extensively on these topics, and has edited two special issues of the journal *Politique Africaine* (no. 112, "Enjeux de l'autochtonie," with Peter Geschiere; and no. 127, "Parlements de la rue," with R. Banégas and F. Brisset-Foucault). He is currently preparing a book on Ivorian nationalism and political oratory to be published by Karthala, and another with R. Banégas on identification in Côte d'Ivoire titled *ID Wars in Côte d'Ivoire*, forthcoming with Oxford University Press.

ANNE DAVIDIAN is a curator and editor working at the intersections of arts and social sciences. She has been involved in the conception of two experimental art spaces: Chalet Society (2012–15; Co-Director), and Kassandras, Athens, a laboratory for artists, designers, and social practitioners (2016–18; Co-Founder). Davidian is responsible for the French branch of the Evens Foundation, for which she develops research and experimentation projects with a particular interest in political imaginaries. In 2018, she initiated a cross-disciplinary inquiry *Assemblies: Modern Rituals*. In 2021, she conceived with LE BAL "En Presence des Images," a series of literary commissions for the French daily *Libération*.

PASCALE DUFOUR is a full Professor in the Department of Political Science at the Université de Montréal. She works on social movements and collective action in comparative perspective (Canada, Europe). She is the Director of the Collectif de recherche Action Politique et Démocratie (CAPED). Her current projects focus on the institutional foundations of contestation in the cases of housing and education struggles (France, Spain, Quebec); informal practices of engagement through urban gardening, and food recovery. With Francis Dupuis-Déri she recently co-published *Profilages policiers* (QC: PUM, Les presses de l'Université de Montréal, 2022) and *Cross-Border Solidarities in Twenty-First Century Contexts: Feminist Perspectives and Activist* Practices, eds. Janet M. Conway, Pascale Dufour, and Dominique Masson, (Lantham, MD: Rowman and Lillefield International, 2021).

BEN EERSELS is the coordinator of G1000, the Belgium platform for democratic innovation. Originally, the G1000 was a citizen initiative that organized a large-scale citizen assembly, during which hundreds of Belgian citizens discussed the most important political issues of that time. Today, G1000 is an independent non-profit organization that develops, supports, and promotes new forms of deliberation that support democracy from the local to the national level, such as the famous Ostbelgien Model. Before joining G1000, Ben Eersels worked as participation expert in the healthcare sector and for local governments, and he completed a PhD dissertation on political participation in the late medieval towns in the Low Countries.

TALLULAH FRAPPIER is a PhD candidate working at the intersections of design, political science, and human-computer interaction. After graduating in digital graphic design, she did a one-year residency program at the living lab of the Cité des Sciences et de l'Industrie in Paris, working on gesture museography. She then joined the department of Design at the École Normale Supérieur Paris-Saclay to study design research. In 2020, she started her thesis on the design of deliberative platforms at Université Paris 1 Panthéon-Sorbonne.

DELPHINE GARDEY is a historian and sociologist, Professor at the Geneva School of Social Sciences, University of Geneva. Ex Fellow at the Max Planck Institute for the History of Science and at The Wissenschaftskolleg zu Berlin, and at the Institute for Advanced Studies in Paris, she published on social and gender history in *La Dactylographe et l'expéditionnaire*, (Paris: Editions Bellin, 2001); on feminist theory in *Politics of Coalition*, (Zürich, SEISMO, 2016); on gender and biomedicine *Histoire politique du clitoris*, (Paris: Textuel, 2021); on the history of information society in *Schreiben, Rechnen, Ablegen,* (Baden-Württemberg: Konstanz University Press, 2018); on parliamentary history and anthropology in *Le Linge du Palais-Bourbon,* (Lormont: Le Bord de l'eau, 2015); and the essay "Gender and Parliaments," in *Handbook of Parliamentary Studies*, (Cheltenham: Edward Elgar Publishing, 2020).

RENE GABRI. April 1, 2022. On this day this person with this name wrote these exact words. In a book, the idea will be that they will remain forever imprinted. But what if the words could alter with the life they purport to describe or ascribe characteristics to. Then on each reading, the words would assemble and reassemble around ever-growing urgencies facing the life they act in the name of. Sometimes these words would veer toward what is called poetry, losing the necessity to define themselves, they would reassemble sense itself. On other occasions, they may seek other words, lost or recovered, helping them to find their sense of meaning again. Rather than affix themselves and risk edification, they would prefer to be in a constant movement between resisting capture and affirming other possibilities for the life of words, for the life of worlds. To be anything called artist would, like being called a word, a name, always implicate a chase between that calling and that perpetual fugitivity that escapes whatever, wherever and whenever it finds itself fixed, framed, figured, as in figured out.

ALANA GERECKE, PhD, is a settler scholar and artist of mixed European descent based in Vancouver, Canada, on the unceded and ancestral territories of the Squamish, Musqueam, and Tsleil-Waututh nations. Her research on urban choreographies is currently supported by a Jack and Doris Shadbolt Fellowship in the Humanities (Urban Studies, Simon Fraser University) and an artist residency at Vancouver's Dance Center. Her book project, *Moving Publics* (under contract with McGill-Queen's University Press), examines the social and spatial politics of site-based dance along the Canadian west coast. Recent publications include contributions to *Performance Matters Journal*, *Canadian Theater Research*, and *The Futures of Dance Studies* anthology (2020).

ANDRÉS JAQUE is an architect, researcher, and curator, whose work explores architecture as the entanglement of bodies, technologies, and environments. He is the founder of the New York and Madrid-based architectural agency Office for Political Innovation; the Dean of the Columbia University Graduate School of Architecture, Planning and Preservation (GSAPP); Director of Columbia University's Advanced Architectural Design Program; and the Chief Curator of the 13th Shanghai Biennale, *Bodies of Water*. His books include *Superpowers of Scale* (Columbia, MO: Columbia Books, 2020), *More-Than-Human,* eds. Andrés Jacque, Lucia Pietroiusti, and Marina Otero, (London: Idea Books, 2021), *Transmaterial* (Santiago de Chile: ARQ, 2017), among others, and his work is part of the collections of the Museum of Modern Art, MoMA, and of the Art Institute of Chicago.

LAURENT JEANPIERRE is a sociologist and political scientist, and Professor in the Department of Political Science at the University of Paris 1 Panthéon-Sorbonne. His research focuses on political change and social mutations. He has worked on revolutionary situations and unexpected social mobilizations such as that of the Yellow Vests in France in 2019, in *In Girum: Les leçons politiques des ronds-points,* (Paris: La Découverte,

2019). He is currently working on prefigurative politics and real utopias in ecology. His last published work is *La perspective du possible*, eds. Haud Guéguen and Laurent Jeanpierre, (Paris: La Découverte, 2022).

PABLO LAFUENTE is a curator, educator and writer living in Rio de Janeiro. He worked as Curator for the Office for Contemporary Art Norway (OCA, 2005–13) and Editor at Afterall and Afterall Books in London (2001–13). He was also part of the curatorial team of the 31st Bienal de São Paulo (2014) and has curated, among others, *A Singular Form,* Secession, Vienna, 2014, and *Dja Guata Porã: Rio de Janeiro Indígena,* MAR, Rio de Janeiro, 2017–18. He is currently co-Artistic Director of the Museu de Arte Moderna do Rio de Janeiro (MAM Rio).

LAURA LEVIN is Associate Dean, Research in York University's School of the Arts, Media, Performance and Design. She is author of *Performing Ground: Space, Camouflage, and the Art of Blending In* (Ann Saddlemyer Prize) and Co-Editor of *Performance Studies in Canada*, with M. Schweitzer (Patrick O'Neill Award). Levin has led and collaborated on several artistic projects at the intersection of political performance, site-specificity, archives, and digital media. Recently she served as dramaturg on *Jess Dobkin's Wetrospective* (AGYU, 2021) and SpiderWebShow's VR play, *You Should Have Stayed Home* (2022). She is Director of the SSHRC project, Hemispheric Encounters: Developing Transnational Research-Creation Practices.

STACEY LIOU is Assistant Professor of Political Science at the University of Florida. She is a political theorist whose research focuses on popular action and performativity, with additional interests in rhetoric and the politics of language. Her current book project examines the public generation of shared meanings about popular assemblies such as protests and riots, analyzing public interpretations of two landmark assemblies in 1990s Los Angeles. Stacey's work has been published in outlets including *Political Theory, European Journal of Political Theory*, and *Space & Polity.*

CATHERINE MALABOU is a Professor of Philosophy at the Center for Research in Modern European Philosophy at Kingston University, UK, and in the department of Comparative Literature and European Languages and Studies at UC Irvine. Her last books include *Before Tomorrow: Epigenesis and Rationality*, trans. Carolyn Shread (Cambridge, MA: Polity Press, 2016) *Morphing Intelligence, From IQ to IA* trans. Carolyn Shread (New York: Columbia University Press, 2018), *Le Plaisir effacé: Clitoris et pensée* (Paris: Rivages, 2020), to be published in English by Polity Press in June 2022, and *Au Voleur! Anarchisme et philosophie* (Paris: Presses Universitaires de France, 2022).

CHARLOTTE MALTERRE-BARTHES is an architect, urban designer, and Assistant Professor of Architectural and Urban Design at the Swiss Federal Institute of Technology Lausanne (EPFL) leading the research laboratory RIOT (Research and Intervention on architecture and territory). Most recently Assistant Professor at the Harvard Graduate School of Design, Malterre-Barthes' interests are related to urgent aspects of contemporary urbanization, material extraction and climate emergency, and how struggling communities can gain greater access to resources, better governance, and ecological/social justice. In 2021, she started the initiative 'A Global Moratorium on New Construction' interrogating current protocols of development. While directing the MAS Urban Design at the Chair of Marc Angélil, Malterre-Barthes has earned her doctoral degree from the Swiss Federal Institute of Technology in Zurich on the political economy of commodities on the built environment. She is the coauthor of prize-winning books *Migrant Marseille: Architectures of Social Segregation and Urban Inclusivity* (Berlin: Ruby Press, 2020), *Some Haunted Spaces in Singapore* (Zürich: Edition Patrick Frey, 2018), and *Housing Cairo: The Informal Response* (Berlin: Ruby Press, 2016), amongst others. Malterre-Barthes is a founding member of the Parity Group and of the Parity Front, activist networks dedicated to improving gender equality and diversity in architecture.

FLORIAN MALZACHER is an independent performing arts curator, dramaturge and writer. He was artistic director of Impulse Theater Festival in Cologne, Dusseldorf and Mulheim/Ruhr, and co-curator of steirischer herbst festival in Graz/Austria. Currently he is working on projects like *Training for the Future* (together with Jonas Staal) and *The Art of Assembly*. Among his publications are *Truth Is Concrete: A Handbook for Artistic Strategies in Real Politics*, eds. Steirischer Herbst and Florian Malzacher (Berlin: Sternberg Press, 2014), *Not Just a Mirror: Looking for the Political Theater of Today* (Berlin: Alexander Verlag Berlin, 2015), *Empty Stages, Crowded Flats: Performativity as Curatorial* Strategy, eds. Florian Malzacher and Joanna Warsza (Berlin: Alexander Verlag Berlin, 2017), and *Gesellschaftsspiele: Politisches Theater heute* (Berlin: Alexander Verlag Berlin, 2020).

MARKUS MIESSEN is an architect (www.studiomiessen.com), writer, Director of Studio Miessen, and Professor of Urban Regeneration at the University of Luxembourg (www.masterarchitecture.lu), where he holds the chair of the City of Esch (www.cultures ofassembly.org). He received his PhD from the Centre for Research Architecture at Goldsmiths, London, supervised by Eyal Weizman.
His work revolves around questions of critical spatial practice, institution building, and spatial politics. Miessen has previously taught at the Architectural Association (London), and has been a Harvard Fellow. Most recently, he has held a Stiftungsprofessur for Critical Spatial Practice at the Städelschule (Frankfurt), and was Distinguished Professor of Practice at the University of Southern California (Los Angeles). Amongst many other books and writings, Miessen is the author of *The Nightmare of Participation and Crossbenching: Towards Participation as Critical Spatial Practice*, (Berlin: Sternberg Press, 2016).

RAUMLABOR is a collective of nine members. Architects, artists, performers, inventors, and curators, the group developed in 1999 from a common interest in an expanded understanding of architecture, which has since been established as urban practice. raumlabor's working method is situational and action-oriented, with a focus on the collaborative production of space as an open and unbiased process. In 2021, raumlabor was awarded the Golden Lion as the Best Participant at the Biennale Architettura in Venice, for their installation featuring the *Floating University*.

ANA TERRA YAWALAPITI is a leader and activist from the Xingu Indigenous Territory, an artisan, and a mother. She conceived the idea for the *Casas das Mulheres* (Women's Houses) that have recently been created in Xingu, and is part of the *Movimento das Mulheres do Território Indígena do Xingu* (Xingu Indigenous Territory Women's Movement – MMTIX).

PHILIPPE URFALINO is Senior Researcher at the French National Center for Scientific Research (CNRS), and Professor at the Institute for Advanced Studies in Social Sciences (EHESS) in Paris. He has published books on French cultural policies and on pharmaceutical drug agencies, and co-edited the collective work *Iceland's Financial Crisis: The Politics of Blame, Protest, and Reconstruction, 2008–2015* (London: Routledge, 2018). In his most recent book, *Deciding Together: The Making of Collective Obligation* (Paris: Éditions du Seuil, 2021), he proposes a theoretical framework for collective decision-making. He is currently writing a book on political bodies titled *Trouble in General Will*, forthcoming with Gallimard.

ALEKSANDRA WASILKOWSKA is an architect whose practice is situated at the intersection of architecture, urban planning, stage design, and art. She is the author and editor of the publishing series *Shadow Architecture* (Warsaw: The Other Space Foundation, 2013), and *City Is the City*, (Warsaw: Instytut Teatralny, 2020), in which she explores spaces functioning at the fringes of architecture, such as bazaars, stalls, or toilets, based on self-organization and collectivity. She is the curator of the exhibitions *Bazaaristan and Claw* held within the space of existing Polish bazaars. At the same time, she runs an architectural practice in Warsaw, specializing in the revitalization of bazaars, urban planning, and the design of public buildings.

YELLOW VESTS (collective). For this book, some of the co-initiators of the Yellow Vests' Assembly of Assemblies in Commercy and Saint Nazaire decided to write, three years later, a critical review of their experience. The article was mainly written by one person, then read and amended by three others. It represents a specific position, which does not necessarily reflect the different positions of those who led and participated in this unprecedented experience in France.

Credits

Images

p. 11 © Foro Social de Segovia / p. 12 © Kristin Bauman / p. 17 CC BY-SA 4.0 Subodhkiran / p. 18, 22, 27 © Bruno Serralongue. Courtesy of the artist and Air de Paris, Romainville / p. 21 © Åse M. P. Pulk / p. 30–31 Photo © Anne Davidian / p. 42–48 © Mario Fernando Vazquez. Courtesy of Cristina Vazquez / p. 56–57, 63, 66–67 © Yves Monteil / p. 62 © Théophile Trossat / p. 94 Photo © Daan / p. 102–3 Photo © Lidia Rossner. Produced by HAU Hebbel am Ufer / p. 107 © raumlabor / p. 110–11 Photo © Martin Argyroglo / p. 116 Photo © Lidia Rossner. Produced by 7th Berlin Biennale / p.117 Photo © Ruben Hamelink. Produced by Fondazione Sandretto Re Rebaudeng, Turin / p. 118–19 Photo © Nieuwe Beelden Makers. Produced by BAK, basis voor actuele kunst / p. 129 © Bayerische Staatsbibliothek, Munich / p. 132–33 © Palazzo Pubblico, Siena / p. 137 © Christian Boiseaux / p. 144–45, 156–57 © Florence Brisset-Foucault / p. 150–52 © Richard Banégas / p. 167, 174–75, 183 CC0 Paris Musées, Musée Carnavalet – Histoire de Paris / p. 185 © Joseph Grima and Markus Miessen. Filmography © Elian Stefa / p. 187 CC BY-SA 3.0 Adrian Sulc / p. 196 (left), 197 Photo © JongOh Kimp / p. 196–97 Photo © Pablo Ferao / p. 201–3 © Studio Miessen / p. 212 Photo © Paris Musées, Musée Carnavalet, Dist. RMN–Grand Palais, image Ville de Paris / p. 214 © Archives de l'Assemblée nationale, Paris, gift of Jules-Louis Breton / p. 215 © Archives de l'Assemblée nationale, Paris / p. 216-17 Photo © RMN–Grand Palais, Château de Versailles, image Gérard Blot / p. 222-23 Ville de Paris, Bibliothèque historique, CPA-0725-(01) / p. 240–47 Photo © Stathis Mamalakis / p. 292–93 © Marc Abélès / p. 302–07 © raumlabor / p. 302 Photo © Alexander Stumm / p. 303 Photo © Pierre Adenis / p. 305 Photo © Zita Oberwalder, Courtesy of MAEID / p. 308–9 Photo © Hervé Veronese / p. 316–26 © Ayreen Anastas and René Gabri. Courtesy of the artists and Parks Luksemburg / p. 334–41 © Bruno Serralongue. Courtesy the artist and Air de Paris, Romainville / p. 350–51 © Kuiaitsi Bob Kuikuro / p. 356, 362–63 © Maria Fernanda Ribeiro and Nádia Pontes / p. 359 © Elisa Mbya / p. 368–73 Photo © Miguel de Guzmán / p. 377–79 Photo © postNoviki / p. 382–84 © Aleksandra Wasilkowska / p. 385 Courtesy of Critical Pratice

Texts

p. 316–30, *Fragments of Life as Assembly*, © Ayreen Anastas and Rene Gabri

Every effort has been made to contact the rightful owners with regards to copyrights and permissions. We apologize for any inadvertent errors or omissions.

Acknowledgements

Before becoming a book, this project was thought of as a live, public forum for bringing together different fields of knowledge that address the question of political forms, in particular the form of the assembly. What is now a book was intented to sum up a series of cross-disciplinary conversations with anthropologists, historians, philosophers, political scientists, artists, architects, and activists, embracing both theoretical and practical considerations. The pandemic put our real-life encounters on hold, and so the book emerged as a possible place to open a conversation that we hope will continue in other forms and in other spaces.

The Evens Foundation would like to thank David Farrell, Hélène Landemore, Richard Sennett, and Yves Sintomer for their scientific advice which informed the first exploratory phase of our research. Our thanks extend to many others with whom we discussed the possible forms the project could take, notably the Centre Pompidou and Jean-Max Colard, with whom we imagined a partnership for the experimental phase: together we commissioned and produced the proposal designed for this book by architects collective raumlabor as an assembly space for the Centre Pompidou in Paris. Our thanks go to the Economic, Social, and Environmental Council (CESE) and Jean-Michel Fourniau for offering us the opportunity to join the group of researchers who closely observed the first major national experiment in deliberative democracy in France—the Citizens' Convention for Climate (2019–20), to Gregory Castera and Sandra Terdjman (Council) for their initial proposal for the assembly forum, as well as to Binna Choi (Casco Art Institute), Sandi Hilal (DAAR), and Matteo Lucchetti (Visible Project) for inspiring conversations.

The editors and the Evens Foundation would like to express their gratitude to the authors of the book, whose contributions offer a rich array of possible ways of thinking and practicing an assembly, as well as to the architects who took on the challenge of imagining new gathering spaces. Our warmest thanks go to Lucas Roussel for his insights into the content, iconography, and the overall shape of the book, to Katrina Black for her committed and enlightening work on the texts, and to Patrick Lennon and Amanda Murphy for their precise and thoughtful translations. We would like to acknowledge the excellent work of Laure Giletti and Gregory Dapra who imagined the perfect form for the book. And special thanks to Caroline Schneider, Stuart Berlotti-Bailey, and the team at Sternberg Press whose guidance and insights have been essential.

We are grateful to Filipa Ramos for her artistic ideas that enriched the book, to Maria Ines Rodriguez for pointing out a number of inspiring examples of assemblies, and to Thomas Boutoux for his continuous advice and intellectual generosity.

We would also like to thank Alexandre Devals for his advice and all those who helped and facilitated the gathering of the iconography: Marc Abélès, Pablo Lafuente, Omar Foglio, the Foro Social de Segovia, Aude Jagut, Kuiaitsi Bob Kuikuro, Pilar Marrero, Elisa Mbya, Nadia Pontes, Bruno Serralongue, and Cristina Vasquez.

Colophon

What Makes an Assembly?
Stories, Experiments, and Inquiries

EDITORS
Anne Davidian & Laurent Jeanpierre

EDITORIAL COORDINATOR
Lucas Roussel

LINE EDITING & PROOFREADING
Katrina Black

TRANSLATION
Pablo Lafuente
(p. 347–67)
Patrick Lennon
(p. 9–34, 83–93, 125–41, 143–62, 287–98)
Amanda Murphy
(p. 53–72, 163–77, 387–96)

DESIGN
Laure Giletti & Gregory Dapra

PRINTING
Die Keure, Bruges, Belgium

ISBN 978 3 95679 645 6

PUBLISHED BY
Evens Foundation
Frankrijklei 37 bus 12
2000 Antwerp, Belgium
www.evensfoundation.be

Sternberg Press
71–75 Shelton Street
London WC2H 9JQ, UK
www.sternberg-press.com

DISTRIBUTED BY
The MIT Press, Art Data, Les presses du réel, and Idea Books

This publication is part of *Assemblies: Modern Rituals*, a cross-disciplinary inquiry initiated by the Evens Foundation and curated by Anne Davidian.